Architect's Pocket Book

This book is dedicated to the memory of
Charlotte Baden-Powell, for all her work, energy and
enthusiasm for creating this invaluable source for Architects.

Architect's Pocket Book

Fourth edition

Charlotte Baden-Powell

Fourth edition updated by Jonathan Hetreed and Ann Ross

AMSTERDAM • BOSTON • HEIDELBERG • LONDON • NEW YORK • OXFORD
PARIS • SAN DIEGO • SAN FRANCISCO • SINGAPORE • SYDNEY • TOKYO
Architectural Press is an imprint of Elsevier

ELSEVIER

Architectural
Press

Architectural Press is an imprint of Elsevier
The Boulevard, Langford Lane, Kidlington, Oxford, OX5 1GB
30 Corporate Drive, Suite 400, Burlington, MA 01803, USA

First published 1997
Reprinted 1998, 1999
Second edition 2001
Reprinted with amendments 2002, 2003
Reprinted 2004, 2005, 2006
Third edition 2008
Fourth edition 2011

British Library Cataloguing in Publication Data
A catalogue record for this book is available from the British Library

Library of Congress Number: 2010940380

ISBN: 978-0-08-096959-6

For information on all Architectural Press publications
visit our website at www.elsevierdirect.com

Printed and bound in the UK

10 11 12 13   12 11 10 9 8 7 6 5 4 3 2 1

Working together to grow
libraries in developing countries

www.elsevier.com | www.bookaid.org | www.sabre.org

ELSEVIER   BOOK AID
International   Sabre Foundation

Contents

Preface to the Fourth Edition

In the four years since we started working on the third edition, technical changes in architecture have continued apace alongside the world's economic dramas. Environmental and sustainability issues have continued to develop in importance both in our own practice and in the design and construction field overall.

We believe this edition stays true to the spirit of Charlotte Baden-Powell's original in scale, purpose and orientation; we have updated and slimmed some of the technical information on lighting and other services, and revised sections on structures, building elements and materials. Elsevier carried out some research with readers and we are grateful to them for their candid and helpful responses.

Chapter 2 has been renamed 'Planning, Policy and Guidance', better reflecting its broad scope. Every chapter has been revised and we have continued to learn throughout the process. We have been ably assisted by new contributors, acknowledged elsewhere.

We welcome readers' comments and suggestions on this edition and on the electronic format.

Jonathan Hetreed and Ann Ross

Preface to the Third Edition

I first met Charlotte Baden-Powell to discuss the possibility of editing this edition in 2006, after an introduction from Peter Clegg. This remarkable book was clearly a very personal work for her and once I had enlisted Ann Ross's help, the three of us discussed how the spirit and modest simplicity of the book should be maintained while its contemporary coverage was enhanced. It was important to Charlotte that the book stayed small and retained its immediacy, and that we worked in a similar field of smaller scale architecture to her own.

As we have updated and revised sections, we have enlarged some and reduced others and thereby achieved the goal of a similar size; we hope in doing so that the really useful information in the book has been retained and supplemented while the losses have been only in depth or detail, for which more specific technical source material can be consulted.

The only instances in which we have included sections absent from the previous edition were those giving the briefest outlines of costs, law, insulation and computer-aided design for architects – all four subject to frequent detailed changes but we thought worth describing in general terms.

Just as Charlotte did, we welcome readers' responses, so that the book can continue to be improved.

Jonathan Hetreed

Preface to the Second Edition

'I *know* it's somewhere – but where?' . . .
. . . any architect, any time

The inspiration for this pocket book was the front section of the *Building Technician's Diaries* which were published in the 1960s and 70s. These small airmail paper pages were densely packed with useful information for the architect, surveyor and builder. Obviously concise, often rule-of-thumb but nevertheless marvellously useful. These diaries are no longer available and are of course wildly out of date. So it seemed to me that there is a need for a new small and more complete compendium which can sit beside the drawing board/computer and also be carried easily to site.

It is aimed primarily at the smaller practice and is particularly suitable for small works. The subjects range from general arithmetic and geometric data through building regulation requirements, the sizes of furniture, fittings, joists, materials, U-values, lighting data and much more.

The choice of what to include is necessarily subjective and is the result of running my own practice for 38 years. The subjects have been gleaned either from much more comprehensive works or the more imaginative and useful aspects of manufacturers' literature. I have deliberately not included anything about costs or legal matters as these change too frequently for the book to be of any lasting value. The choice of contents is inevitably subjective and I would be interested to hear from readers of any items which they would have liked to be included. The blank pages at the end of the book are provided for personal additions.

Every effort has been made to ensure that the information given is accurate at the time of publication. When compiling the book I found many things were incomplete, out-of-date or plainly wrong. The user should be aware that the information is concise, in order to suit the small size of a pocket book. Also that legislation is frequently changing and that the British Standards and Building Regulations are being constantly superseded. If in doubt, or further more detailed explanation is required, consult the source given at the bottom of the page, with the addresses and telephone numbers at the back of the book. Where no reference is given, this is because I have compiled the information from several sources.

This book is not a construction manual, it contains no typical detail drawings, but is instead a collection of information needed before such drawings are prepared.

The second edition contains 30 new pages of subjects ranging from Party Wall Awards and green issues to industrial processes. The new drawings include information about setting-up perspectives, wheelchairs, traditional doors and windows, colour spectrum, etc. Additions have also been made to the original text. Names and addresses have been updated and email and websites added.

The aim of the book is to include information from a wide range of sources. Facts which one knows are somewhere – but where? I like to think that this is the book I should have had to hand, both as a student and while running my private practice. I hope you do too.

Charlotte Baden-Powell

Acknowledgements to the Fourth Edition

We would like to thank the following for their help in checking our additions, revisions and updates:

Richard Dellar	Richard Dellar Consulting Ltd for his help with Costs and law
Nick Burgess	BSc, CEng, MIStructE, Associate and Senior Structural Engineer at Rexon Day Consulting for his revision of Structures
Jonathan Reeves	BA(Hons) M.Arch Dip.Arch RIBA, at jr architecture for his additions to Computer-Aided Design
Dr James Allen	BEng CEng MICE E&M West Consulting Engineers for his section on SUDS
Mike Andrews	Energy Saving Experts, Energy Consultants, for his revisions to Conservation of fuel and power and Sustainability, energy saving and green issues
Robert Peeters	Lighting consultant for his revisions to Lighting and Electrical installation

We would also like to thank:

Henry Fisher	Architectural Assistant for his help with revising and adding drawings
Liz Burton	at Elsevier for her help in preparing the new edition
Tom Ross	for his diligence in updating the addresses

All those who by their constructive comments on the third edition have helped us to make the fourth edition worth doing.

Jonathan Hetreed
Ann Ross

Acknowledgements to the Third Edition

We would like to thank the following for their help in checking our additions, revisions and updates:

Richard Dellar — Dellar Gregory Associates Construction & Claims Consultants for his help with costs and law

Peter Clegg — Architect for his help with sustainability environmental design

Nick Burgess — BSc, CEng, MIStructE, Associate and Senior Structural Engineer at Rexon Day Consulting for his complete revision of Structures

Jonathan Reeves — Architect for his help with Computer-Aided Design

Brian Murphy — Environmental Consultant for his help with insulation

We would also like to thank:

Henry Fisher — Architectural Assistant for his help with revising and adding drawings

Jodi Cusack — at Architectural Press for her help in preparing the new edition.

All those who by their constructive comments on the second edition have helped us to make the third edition worth doing.

Jonathan Hetreed
Ann Ross

Acknowledgements to the Second Edition

I am greatly indebted to the following people for their help and advice:

Choice of contents	John Winter (architect)
	Bill Ungless (architect)
Geometric data	Francis Baden-Powell (architect)
Structural data	Howard Hufford (structural engineer)
	David Cook (geotechnical engineer)
Water byelaws	Graham Mays (Water Research Centre secretary)
Electrical wiring	Brian Fisher (electrical contractor)
Lighting	Martin Wilkinson (lighting consultant)
Joinery	James Toner (building contractor)
General reference data	Peter Gunning (quantity surveyor)
Typography	Peter Brawne (graphic designer)

I should also like to thank the many helpful technical representatives of the manufacturers listed at the back of the book.

My thanks are also due to:

Mari Owen, my secretary, for so patiently struggling with typing, re-typing and endlessly correcting a difficult text;

Neil Warnock-Smith, my publisher, for his support and enthusiasm for the original idea for the book;

Michael Brawne, Professor of Architecture and my husband, for his wise words, help and encouragement throughout.

Charlotte Baden-Powell

1
General Information

Climate maps

Wind – basic wind speeds in metres per second (m/s) and prevailing wind directions →

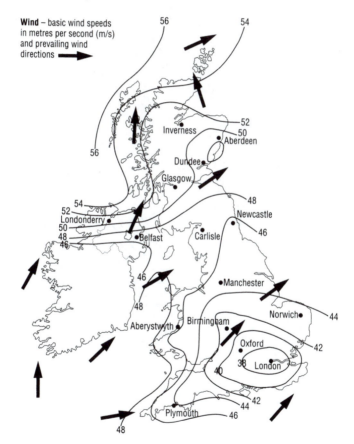

The figures show maximum gust speed likely to be exceeded on average only once in 50 years at 10 m above the ground in open country. To convert metres per second to miles per hour multiply by 2.24.

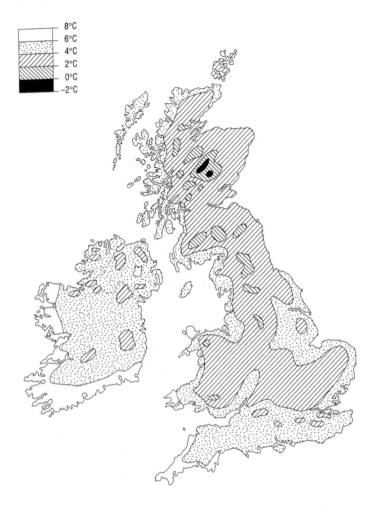

Temperature – average for January

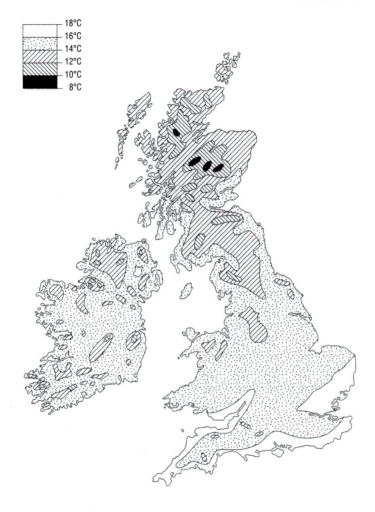

	18°C
	16°C
	14°C
	12°C
	10°C
	8°C

Temperature – average for July

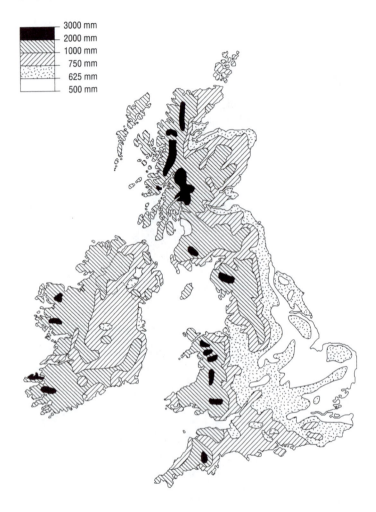

■	3000 mm
	2000 mm
	1000 mm
	750 mm
	625 mm
	500 mm

Rain – annual average

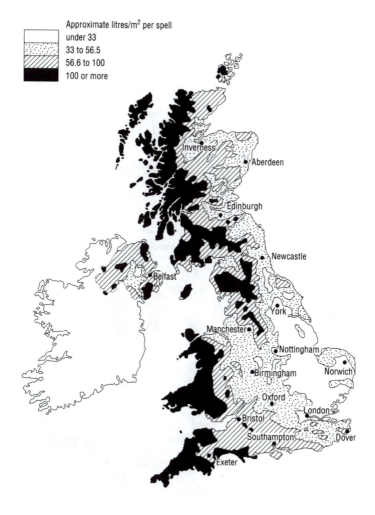

Approximate litres/m² per spell
- under 33
- 33 to 56.5
- 56.6 to 100
- 100 or more

Rain – wind driven

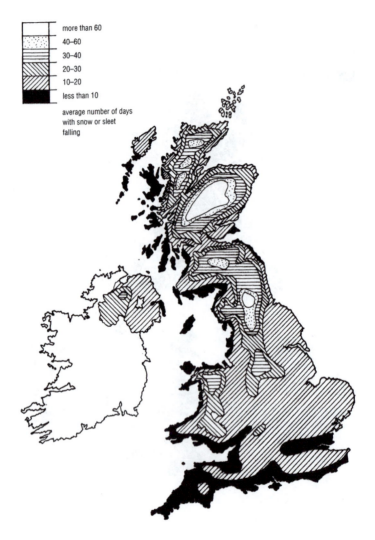

more than 60
40–60
30–40
20–30
10–20
less than 10

average number of days
with snow or sleet
falling

Snow

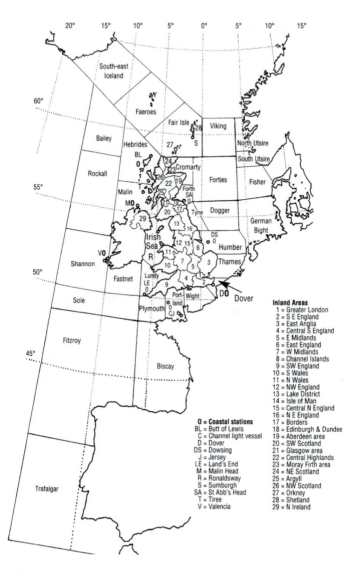

Inland Areas
1 = Greater London
2 = S E England
3 = East Anglia
4 = Central S England
5 = E Midlands
6 = East England
7 = W Midlands
8 = Channel Islands
9 = SW England
10 = S Wales
11 = N Wales
12 = NW England
13 = Lake District
14 = Isle of Man
15 = Central N England
16 = N E England
17 = Borders
18 = Edinburgh & Dundee
19 = Aberdeen area
20 = SW Scotland
21 = Glasgow area
22 = Central Highlands
23 = Moray Firth area
24 = NE Scotland
25 = Argyll
26 = NW Scotland
27 = Orkney
28 = Shetland
29 = N Ireland

O = Coastal stations
BL = Butt of Lewis
C = Channel light vessel
D = Dover
DS = Dowsing
J = Jersey
LE = Land's End
M = Malin Head
R = Ronaldsway
S = Sumburgh
SA = St Abb's Head
T = Tiree
V = Valencia

Sea areas, inland areas and coastal stations
used in weather forecasts by the Meteorological Office

Metric system

The **Système International d'Unités (SI)**, adopted in 1960, is an international and coherent system devised to meet all known needs for measurement in science and technology. It consists of seven base units and the derived units formed as products or quotients of various powers of the base units.

Note that base and derived units, when written as words, are always written with a lower case first letter, even if the word is derived from the name of a person.

SI Base units

metre	**m**	length
kilogram	**kg**	mass
second	**s**	time
ampere	**A**	electric current
kelvin	**K**	thermodynamic temperature
candela	**cd**	luminous intensity
mole	**mol**	amount of substance

SI Prefixes (showing the nine most common)

mega	**M**	× 1 000 000
kilo	**k**	× 1000
hecto	**h**	× 100
deca	**da**	× 10
deci	**d**	÷ 10
centi	**c**	÷ 100
milli	**m**	÷ 1000
micro	**μ**	÷ 1 000 000
nano	**n**	÷ 1 000 000 000

SI Derived units

celsius	**°C**	=	K	temperature
coulomb	**C**	=	As	electric charge
farad	**F**	=	C/V	electric capacitance
henry	**H**	=	W/A	inductance
hertz	**Hz**	=	c/s	frequency
joule	**J**	=	Ws	energy
lumen	**lm**	=	cd.sr	luminous flux
lux	**lx**	=	lm/m^2	illuminance
newton	**N**	=	$kg/m/s^2$	force
ohm	**Ω**	=	V/A	electric resistance
pascal	**Pa**	=	N/m^2	pressure
siemens	**S**	=	1/Ω	electric conductance
tesla	**T**	=	Wb/m^2	magnetic flux density
volt	**V**	=	W/A	electric potential
watt	**W**	=	J/s	power
weber	**Wb**	=	Vs	magnetic flux

SI Supplementary units

radian	**rad**	=	unit of plane angle equal to an angle at the centre of a circle, the arc of which is equal in length to the radius
steradian	**sr**	=	unit of solid angle equal to an angle at the centre of a sphere subtended by a part of the surface equal in area to the square of the radius

Metric units

Length

kilometre	**km**	=	1000 metres
metre	**m**	=	length of path travelled by light in vacuum during a time interval of 1/299 792 458 of a second
decimetre	**dm**	=	1/10 metre
centimetre	**cm**	=	1/100 metre
millimetre	**mm**	=	1/1000 metre
micron	μ	=	1/100 000 metre

Area

hectare	**ha**	=	$10 000 \, m^2$
are	**a**	=	$100 \, m^2$

Volume

cubic metre	$\mathbf{m^3}$	=	$m \times m \times m$
cubic millimetre	$\mathbf{mm^3}$	=	$1/1 000 000 000 \, m^3$

Capacity

hectolitre	**hl**	=	100 litres
litre	**l**	=	cubic decimetre
decilitre	**dl**	=	1/10 litre
centilitre	**cl**	=	1/100 litre
millilitre	**ml**	=	1/1000 litre

Mass or weight

tonne	**t**	=	1000 kilograms
kilogram	**kg**	=	1000 gram
gram	**g**	=	1/1000 kilogram
milligram	**mg**	=	1/1000 gram

Temperature

Kelvin (K)   The kelvin belongs to a group of seven SI base units used as a quantitive unit of thermodynamic temperature. It is named after Lord William Thompson Kelvin, a Scottish physicist (1824–1907). In 1848 he suggested a scale of temperature, now called *kelvin*, in which the zero point is *absolute zero* – the temperature at which the motions of particles cease and their energies become zero. The units of kelvin and degree celsius temperature intervals are identical (thus 1°C = 1 K), but the point of absolute zero in celsius is minus 273.15 K, thus 0°C = 273.15 K.

It is now customary for temperature and temperature intervals to be described in degrees celsius (°C) although colour temperature of light sources is measured in degrees kelvin (K).

Celsius (°C)   The Celsius scale is a scale of temperature on which water freezes at 0° and boils at 100° under standard conditions. It was devised by Anders Celsius, a Swedish astronomer (1701–44). He originally designated zero as the boiling point of water and 100° as freezing point. The scale was later reversed.

Centigrade   A temperature scale using the freezing point of water as zero and the boiling point of water as 100°. The scale is now officially called *celsius* (see above) to avoid confusion in Europe where the word can mean a measure of plane angle and equals 1/10 000 part of a right angle.

Fahrenheit (°F)   A scale of temperature still used in the USA which gives the freezing point of water as 32° and boiling point as 212°. Named after Gabriel Daniel Fahrenheit, a Prussian physicist (1686–1736) who invented the mercurial barometer. The Fahrenheit scale is related to the Celsius scale by the following relationships:

temperature °F = (temperature °C × 1.8) + 32
temperature °C = (temperature °F − 32) ÷ 1.8

Imperial units

Length

mile	=	1760 yards
furlong	=	220 yards
chain	=	22 yards
yard (yd)	=	3 feet
foot (ft)	=	12 inches
inch (in)	=	1/12 foot

Area

square mile	=	640 acres
acre	=	4840 square yards
rood	=	1210 square yards
square yard (sq yd)	=	9 square feet
square foot (sq ft)	=	144 square inches
square inch (sq in)	=	1/144 square foot

Volume

cubic yard	=	27 cubic feet
cubic foot	=	1/27 cubic yard
cubic inch	=	1/1728 cubic foot

Weight

ton	=	2240 pounds
hundredweight (cwt)	=	112 pounds
cental	=	100 pounds
quarter	=	28 pounds
stone	=	14 pounds
pound (lb)	=	16 ounces
ounce (oz)	=	1/16 pound
dram (dr)	=	1/16 ounce
grain (gr)	=	1/7000 pound
pennyweight (dwt)	=	24 grains

Conversion factors

	Imperial to SI		SI to Imperial		
Length	1.609	mile	kilometre	km	0.6215
	0.9144	yard	metre	m	1.094
	0.3048	foot	metre	m	3.281
	25.4	inch	millimetre	mm	0.0394
Area	2.590	sq mile	sq kilometre	km^2	0.3861
	0.4047	acre	hectare	ha	2.471
	0.8361	sq yard	sq metre	m^2	1.196
	0.0929	sq foot	sq metre	m^2	10.7639
	645.16	sq inch	sq millimetre	mm^2	0.00155
Volume	0.7646	cubic yard	cubic metre	m^3	1.3079
	0.02832	cubic foot	cubic metre	m^3	35.31
	16.39	cubic inch	cubic millimetre	mm^3	0.000061
Capacity	28.32	cubic foot	litre	l	0.03531
	0.01639	cubic inch	litre	l	61.0128
	16.39	cubic inch	millilitre	ml	0.06102
	4.546	UK gallon	litre	l	0.21998
	28.4125	fluid ounce	millilitre	ml	0.0352
Mass	1.016	ton	tonne	t	0.98425
	0.4536	pound	kilogram	kg	2.20458
	453.6	pound	gram	g	0.002205
	28.35	ounce	gram	g	0.03527
Density	16.0185	$pound/ft^3$	$kilogram/m^3$	kg/m^3	0.06243
Force	4.4482	pound force	newton	N	0.22481
	14.59	pound f/foot	newton/metre	N/m	0.06854
Pressure, stress					
	4.882	$pound/ft^2$	$kilogram/m^2$	kg/m^2	0.2048
	107.252	$ton\ f/ft^2$	$kilonewton/m^2$	kN/m^2	0.009324
	47.8803	$pound\ f/ft^2$	$newton/m^2$	N/m^2	0.02088
	6894.76	$pound\ f/in^2$	$newton/m^2$	N/m^2	0.000145

	Imperial to SI			SI to Imperial	
Energy	3.6	kilowatt hour	megajoule	MJ	0.27777
Heat	1055.0	Btu	joule	J	0.000948
Heat flow	0.000293	Btu/h	kilowatt	kW	3415.0
Heat transfer	5.67826	Btu/ft²h °F	watt/m² °C	W/m² °C	0.17611
Thermal conductivity	0.144228	Btu in/ft²h °F	watt/m °C	W/m °C	6.93347
Cost	0.0929	£/sq foot	£/sq metre	£/m²	10.7639

Approximate metric/Imperial equivalents

Length

1.5 mm	=	$^1/_{16}''$
3 mm	=	$^1/_8''$
6 mm	=	$^1/_4''$
12.5 mm	=	$^1/_2''$
19 mm	=	$^3/_4''$
25 mm	=	1″
100 mm	=	4″
600 mm	=	2′0″
2000 mm	=	6′8″
3000 mm	=	10′0″

Temperature

°C		°F	
100	=	212	boiling
37	=	98.6	blood heat
21	=	70	living room
19	=	66	bedroom
10	=	50	
0	=	32	freezing
−17.7	=	0	

Heat transfer

1 Btu/ft^{2}h °F =   10 watt/m^2 °C

Lighting

10 lux	=	1 lumen/ft^2

Area

1 hectare	= 2½ acres
0.4 hectare	= 1 acre

Weight

1 kilogram	= 2¼ lbs
28 grams	= 1 ounce
100 grams	= 3½ ounces
454 grams	= 1 lb

Capacity

1 litre	= 1¾ pints
9 litres	= 2 gallons

Pressure

1.5 kN/m^2	= 30 lbs/ft^2
2.5 kN/m^2	= 50 lbs/ft^2
3.5 kN/m^2	= 70 bs/ft^2
5.0 kN/m^2	= 100 lbs/ft^2

Glass thickness

2 mm	= 18 oz
3 mm	= 24 oz
4 mm	= 32 oz
6 mm	= ¼″

Greek alphabet

Capital	Lower case	Name	English transliteration
A	α	alpha	a
B	β	beta	b
Γ	γ	gamma	g
Δ	δ	delta	d
E	ε	epsilon	e
Z	ζ	zeta	z
H	η	eta	ē
Θ	θ	theta	th
I	ι	iota	i
K	κ	kappa	k
Λ	λ	lambda	l
M	μ	mu	m
N	ν	nu	n
Ξ	χ	xi	x
O	o	omicron	o
Π	π	pi	p
P	ρ	rho	r
Σ	σ (ς)*	sigma	s
T	τ	tau	t
γ	υ	upsilon	u
Φ	φ	phi	ph
X	χ	chi	ch, kh
Ψ	ψ	psi	ps
Ω	ω	omega	ō

*ς at end of word

Roman numerals

I = one
V = five
X = ten
L = fifty

C = one hundred
D = five hundred
M = one thousand

Geometric data

Measurement of plane and solid figures

π (pi) $= 3.1416$

Circumference
circle $= \pi \times$ diameter
cone $= \pi \times \frac{1}{2}$ major axis $+ \frac{1}{2}$ minor axis

Surface area
circle $= \pi \times$ radius^2, or $0.7854 \times$ diameter^2
cone $= \frac{1}{2}$ circumference $\times$ slant height
                    $+$ area of base
cylinder $=$ circumference $\times$ length
                    $+$ area of two ends
ellipse $=$ product of axes $\times$ 0.7854 (approx)
parabola $=$ base $\times \frac{2}{3}$ height
parallelogram $=$ base $\times$ height
pyramid $= \frac{1}{2}$ sum of base perimeters $\times$ slant height
                    $+$ area of base
sector of circle $= (\pi \times$ degrees arc $\times$ radius$^2) \div 360$
segment of circle $=$ area of sector minus triangle
sphere $= \pi \times$ diameter^2
triangle $= \frac{1}{2}$ base $\times$ perpendicular height
triangle
(equilateral) $=$ (side)$^2 \times 0.433$

Volume
cone $=$ area of base $\times \frac{1}{3}$ perpendicular height
cylinder $= \pi \times$ radius$^2 \times$ height
pyramid $=$ area of base $\times \frac{1}{3}$ height
sphere $=$ diameter$^3 \times 0.5236$
wedge $=$ area of base $\times \frac{1}{2}$ perpendicular height

Nine regular solids

Various types of polyhedra have exercised the minds of mathematicians throughout the ages, including Euclid, whose great work *The Elements* was intended not so much as a geometry text book but as an introduction to the five regular solids known to the ancient world. This work starts with the equilateral triangle and ends with the construction of the icosahedron.

The five so-called *Platonic* solids form the first and simplest group of polyhedra. They have regular faces, all of which touch one another, and the lines which make up any of the vertices form a regular polygon.

Further variations of the regular polyhedra, unknown in ancient times, are the *Kepler-Poinsot* star polyhedra. In all four cases the vertex figures spring from pentagrams. These polyhedra can be formed from the regular dodecahedron and icosahedron.

Kepler (1571–1630) found the two stellated dodecahedra, and Poinsot (1777–1859) discovered the great dodecahedra and the great icosahedron.

Five platonic solids

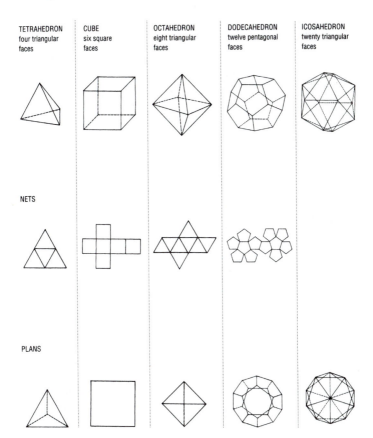

TETRAHEDRON
four triangular
faces

CUBE
six square
faces

OCTAHEDRON
eight triangular
faces

DODECAHEDRON
twelve pentagonal
faces

ICOSAHEDRON
twenty triangular
faces

NETS

PLANS

The Kepler–Poinsot star polyhedra

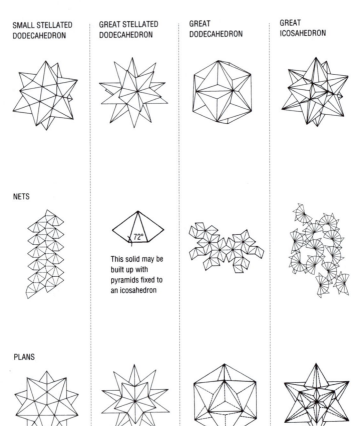

SMALL STELLATED DODECAHEDRON

GREAT STELLATED DODECAHEDRON

GREAT DODECAHEDRON

GREAT ICOSAHEDRON

NETS

72°

This solid may be built up with pyramids fixed to an icosahedron

PLANS

Source: *Mathematical Models*

Golden section

The **golden section** or **golden mean** is an irrational proportion probably known to the ancient Greeks and thought to be divine by Renaissance theorists. It is defined as a line cut in such a way that the smaller section is to the greater as the greater is to the whole, thus:

AC : CB = CB : AB

The ratio of the two lengths is called *phi* Φ.

$$\Phi = \frac{\sqrt{5} + 1}{2} = 1.61803 \ldots$$

For approximate purposes it is 1 : 1.6 or 5 : 8. Φ is the ratio of line lengths in any pentagram.

The **golden rectangle** is one in which Φ is the ratio of one side to the other.

This is implicated in the mathematics of growth as demonstrated in the **Fibonacci series** 0, 1, 1, 2, 3, 5, 8, 13, 21, 34... where each number is the sum of the preceding two. This ratio of successive numbers increasingly approaches that of the golden rectangle.

The **Fibonacci spiral** is a curve that increases constantly in size without changing its basic shape. This is demonstrated by using squares increasing in the Fibonacci scale, i.e. 1, 2, 3, 5, from the diagram of which can be seen three nearly golden rectangles.

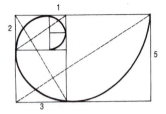

Leonardo Fibonacci (c.1170–1230) was an Italian mathematician who introduced arabic numerals to Christian Europe. He travelled extensively, particularly in North Africa where he learnt the decimal system and the use of zero. He published this system in Europe but mathematicians were slow to adopt it.

Le Corbusier used the Fibonacci series in his system of proportion 'Le Modulor'.

To draw a golden rectangle:

Draw a square ABCD.
Halve the base line at E.
From this point draw a line to corner C and with radius EC drop an arc to find point F.

The golden rectangle is AFGD as also is BFGC.

The angle between the diagonal and the long side of a golden rectangle is approximately 31.45°.

Paper sizes

International paper sizes

The basis of the international series is a rectangle having an area of one square metre (A0), the sides of which are in the proportion of $1:\sqrt{2}$. This is the proportion of the side and diagonal of any square. All the **A** series are of this proportion, enabling them to be doubled or halved and remain in the same proportion, which is useful for photographic enlargement or reduction. A0 is twice A1 which is twice A2 and so on. Where larger sizes than A0 are needed the A is preceded by a figure, thus 4A is four times A0.

The **B** series are sizes intermediate between any two A sizes. This series is used mostly for posters and charts. The **C** series are envelopes to suit the A sizes.

DL or long sizes are obtained by dividing the A and B series into three, four or eight equal parts parallel to the shorter side so that the proportion of $1:\sqrt{2}$ is not maintained. In practice, the long sizes should be produced from the A series only.

The dimensions of these series are of the *trimmed* or *finished* size.

	mm	inches		mm	inches
A0	841 × 1189	$33^{1}/_{8} \times 46\frac{3}{4}$	B0	1000 × 1414	$39^{3}/_{8} \times 55^{5}/_{8}$
A1	594 × 841	$23^{3}/_{8} \times 33^{1}/_{8}$	B1	707 × 1000	$27^{7}/_{8} \times 39^{3}/_{8}$
A2	420 × 594	$16\frac{1}{2} \times 23^{3}/_{8}$	B2	500 × 707	$19^{5}/_{8} \times 27^{7}/_{8}$
A3	297 × 420	$11\frac{3}{4} \times 16\frac{1}{2}$	B3	353 × 500	$13^{7}/_{8} \times 19^{5}/_{8}$
A4	210 × 297	$8\frac{1}{4} \times 11\frac{3}{4}$	B4	250 × 353	$9^{7}/_{8} \times 13^{7}/_{8}$
A5	148 × 210	$5^{7}/_{8} \times 8\frac{1}{4}$	B5	176 × 250	$6^{15}/_{16} \times 9^{7}/_{8}$
A6	105 × 148	$4^{1}/_{8} \times 5^{7}/_{8}$	B6	125 × 176	$4^{15}/_{16} \times 6^{15}/_{16}$
A7	74 × 105	$2^{7}/_{8} \times 4^{1}/_{8}$	B7	88 × 125	$3\frac{1}{2} \times 4^{15}/_{16}$
A8	52 × 74	$2^{1}/_{16} \times 2^{7}/_{8}$	B8	62 × 88	$2^{7}/_{16} \times 3\frac{1}{2}$
A9	37 × 52	$1^{7}/_{16} \times 2^{1}/_{16}$	B9	44 × 62	$1\frac{3}{4} \times 2^{7}/_{16}$
A10	26 × 37	$1^{1}/_{16} \times 1^{7}/_{16}$	B10	31 × 44	$1\frac{1}{4} \times 1\frac{3}{4}$

	mm	inches
C0	917 × 1297	$36^{1}/_{8}$ × $50^{3}/_{8}$
C1	648 × 917	$25½$ × $36^{1}/_{8}$
C2	458 × 648	18 × $25½$
C3	324 × 458	$12¾$ × 18
C4	229 × 324	9 × $12¾$
C5	162 × 229	$6^{3}/_{8}$ × 9
C6	114 × 162	$4½$ × $6^{3}/_{8}$
C7	81 × 114	$3^{3}/_{16}$ × $4½$
DL	110 × 220	$4^{3}/_{8}$ × $8^{5}/_{8}$

Source: *Whitaker's Almanack*

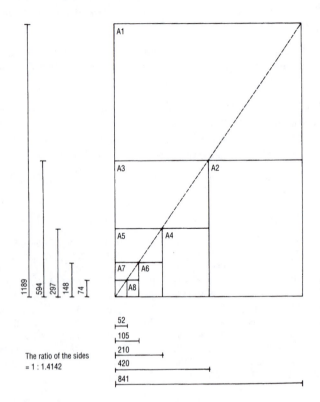

The ratio of the sides = 1 : 1.4142

Paper sizes – **A** series

CAD

Most drawings are now produced on computers enabling instant transfer of information between architects, clients and consultants. There are many computer-aided design (CAD) systems available and the most commonly used programs are AutoCAD, AutoCAD LT, Microstation and Vectorworks, depending on the scale and complexity of projects. Drawings should be constructed in layers organizing the project into different building elements, locations or materials.

Most architectural CAD software can also be used for 3D modelling, which can be useful in terms of design development and communication of ideas. These functions are often complemented by external applications such as Sketch Up, Cinema 4D, 3DS Studio Max and Artlantis, with further graphic enhancement provided by using image editing software like Photoshop.

Standard protocols apply for drawing methods and notation and many manufacturers now supply technical information in CAD format for downloading as DWG, DXF or PDF.

Building Information Modelling (BIM) is also rapidly becoming an essential part of the architectural design process. BIM involves constructing an accurate 3D computer model of the proposed building, which allows elevations, sections and 3D visuals to be extracted from the model rather than drawn, allowing options to be explored more accurately. These systems use parametric objects such as walls, floors, roofs, doors and windows to represent the building design. They also allow information such as quantities, costs or 'u' values to be assigned, allowing the user to interrogate different design options more efficiently.

CAD drawings in this book have been drawn using Vectorworks 2009.

Drawing conventions

Demolition

removal of part

infilling opening

removal of area

making good after forming opening

Steps, ramps, slopes

stair or ramp
(direction of rise)

natural drainage
(direction of fall)

slope
(direction of fall)

flow
(direction of watercourse)

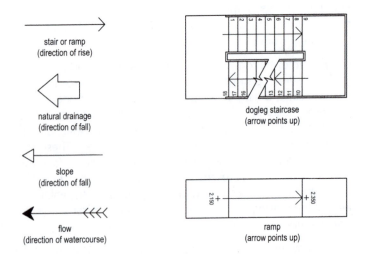

dogleg staircase
(arrow points up)

ramp
(arrow points up)

Drawing conventions – continued

Landscape

contour – existing

contour – proposed

line of no cut/no fill

cut volume (in section)

fall of ground
(arrow points down)

bank
(arrows point down)

cutting
(arrows point down)

grass

planting bed

gate

fence

hedge – existing

hedge – proposed

tree – existing

tree – proposed

tree – protection
(of existing)

Drawing conventions – continued

Masonry

brickwork

blockwork

lightweight block

stonework

engineering brick

brickwork
running bond

stonework
running bond

stonework
random rubble

Timber

rough sawn (any type)

blocking (any type)

softwood
machined all round

hardwood
machined all round

Site-formed materials

concrete

plaster / render
screed

granular fill

asphalt macadam

mulch

topsoil

subsoil

hard fill

Manufactured materials

membrane
board layer
sheet – small scale

sheet – large scale

plywood

glass sheet

blockboard

veneered blockboard

insulation quilt

insulation board

Drawing conventions – continued

Doors

 hinged leaf

 hinged leaf
(alternative)

 hinged leaf
normally closed
(reverse if normally open)

 hinged leaf
opening 180°

 hinged leaf
opening both ways

 bi-parting
pair of hinged leaves

 sliding leaf

 revolving leaves

 sliding/folding leaves
end hung

sliding/folding leaves
centre hung

Windows

 fixed light

 side hung
(arrow points to hinge)

 top hung

 bottom hung

 horizontal pivot

 vertical pivot

 vertical pivot
reversible

 horizontal hinge
projecting out (H window)

 horizontal sliding

 vertical sliding

slide and tilt

tilt and turn

Source: BS 1192 : − 5 : 1998 *Construction drawing practice. Guide for structuring and exchange of CAD data*

Perspective drawing – method of setting up

1 Draw the plan to a scale and set it at the angle at which it is to be viewed.

2 Establish the position of the *Observer* on plan, preferably so that the building falls within a 30° cone. Any wider angled cone will produce a distorted perspective. The centreline of this cone is the *line of sight*.

3 Draw a horizontal line through the plan. This is called the *picture plane*, which is set at 90° to the line of sight. The further the picture plane is from the Observer, the larger the drawing will be.

4 Draw two lines parallel to the visible sides of the building – from the Observer to the picture plane – to determine the *vanishing points* (VP). As this building is orthogonal, these lines are at right angles to one another.

5 Draw the *horizon* where the perspective drawing will be. Draw vertical lines from the picture plane VPs to establish the VPs on the horizon.

6 Draw lines from the Observer to the three lower corners of the plan, cutting the picture plane.

7 Where these lines cut the picture plane at A, B and C, draw vertical lines up to find the three visible corners of the building.

8 Draw a vertical line from one of the two points where the picture plane cuts the plan to establish a *vertical scale line*. Mark this line to the same scale as the plan to determine the bottom and top edges of the building relative to the horizon. The horizon should be at about 1.6 m for normal eye level.

9 Connect these marks to the appropriate vanishing points to complete the outline of the building.

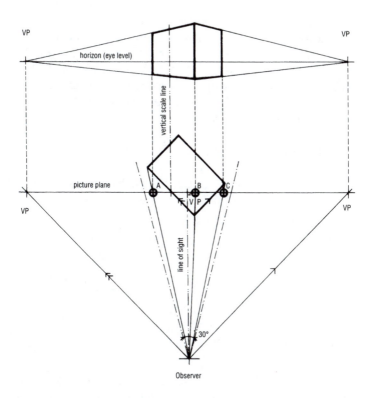

VP

horizon (eye level)

VP

vertical scale line

picture plane

VP

A   B   C

V P

VP

line of sight

30°

Observer

Perspective drawing – method of setting up

The classifications

- CI/SfB is the classification system most widely used by architectural specifiers. The system has been in operation for more than 30 years and is the industry standard.
- Uniclass is a UK classification system for structuring product literature and project information, incorporating both Common Arrangement of Work Sections (CAWS) and EPIC.
- EPIC is a European-wide classification system and should be included especially if technical literature is to be used on a pan-European basis.

CI/SfB Construction index

CI/SfB is a library system used by the building industry and is suitable for the smallest or largest office.

CI = Construction Index
SfB = Samarbetskommitten för Byggnadsfrägor
      – a Swedish system of the late 1940s.

CI/SfB notation has four divisions: | 0 | 1 | 2 & 3 | 4 |

Table 0	= Physical environment
Table 1	= Elements
Tables 2 and 3	= Constructions and Materials
Table 4	= Activities and Requirements

The current CI/SfB edition was issued in 1976 and is still widely used. It was reviewed and the Uniclass system was developed as a result of this.

CI/SfB Tables

Table 0   Physical environment

0   Planning areas
01   Extra terrestrial areas
02   International, national scale planning areas
03   Regional, sub-regional scale planning areas
04
05   Rural, urban planning areas
06   Land use planning areas
07
08   Other planning areas
09   Common areas relevant to planning

1   Utilities, civil engineering facilities
11   Rail transport
12   Road transport
13   Water transport
14   Air transport, other transport
15   Communications
16   Power supply, mineral supply
17   Water supply, waste disposal
18   Other

2   Industrial facilities
21–25
26   Agricultural
27   Manufacturing
28   Other

3   Administrative, commercial, proactive service facilities
31   Official administration, law courts
32   Offices
33   Commercial
34   Trading, shops
35–36
37   Protective services
38   Other

4   Health, welfare facilities
41   Hospitals
42   Other medical
43
44   Welfare, homes
46   Animal welfare
47
48   Other

5   Recreational facilities
51   Refreshment
52   Entertainment
53   Social recreation, clubs
54   Aquatic sports
55
56   Sports
57
58   Other

6   Religious facilities
61   Religious centres
62   Cathedrals
63   Churches, chapels
64   Mission halls, meeting houses
65   Temples, mosques, synagogues
66   Convents
67   Funerary, shrines
68   Other

7   Educational, scientific, information facilities
71   Schools
72   Universities, colleges
73   Scientific
74
75   Exhibition, display
76   Information, libraries
77
78   Other

8   Residential facilities

81 Housing
82 One-off housing units, houses
83
84 Special housing
85 Communal residential
86 Historical residential
87 Temporary, mobile residential
88 Other

9   Common facilities, other facilities

91 Circulation
92 Rest, work
93 Culinary
94 Sanitary, hygiene
95 Cleaning, maintenance
96 Storage
97 Processing, plant, control
98 Other, buildings other than by function
99 Parts of facilities, other aspects of the physical environment, architecture, landscape

Table 1   Elements

(--) Sites, projects, building systems

(1–) Ground, sub-structure

(10)
(11) Ground
(12)
(13) Floor beds
(14)–(15)
(16) Retaining walls, foundations
(17) Pile foundations
(18) Other substructure elements
(19) Parts of elements (11) to (18), cost summary

(2–) Primary elements, carcass

(20)
(21) Walls, external walls
(22) Internal walls, partitions
(23) Floors, galleries
(24) Stairs, ramps
(25)–(26)
(27) Roofs
(28) Building frames, other primary elements
(29) Parts of elements (21) to (28), cost summary

(3–) Secondary elements, completion if described separately from (2–)

(30)
(31) Secondary elements to external walls, external doors, windows
(32) Secondary elements to internal walls, internal doors
(33) Secondary elements to floors
(34) Secondary elements to stairs
(35) Suspended ceilings
(36)
(37) Secondary elements to roofs: rooflights etc
(38) Other secondary elements
(39) Parts of elements (31) to (38), cost summary

(4–) **Finishes, if described separately**

(40)
(41) Wall finishes, external
(42) Wall finishes, internal
(43) Floor finishes
(44) Stair finishes
(45) Ceiling finishes
(46)
(47) Roof finishes
(48) Other finishes to structure
(49) Parts of elements (41) to (48), cost summary

(5–) **Services, mainly pipe and ducted**

(50)–(51)
(52) Waste disposal, drainage
(53) Liquids supply
(54) Gases supply
(55) Space cooling
(56) Space heating
(57) Air conditioning, ventilation
(58) Other piped, ducted services
(59) Parts of elements (51) to (58), cost summary

(6–) **Services, mainly electrical**

(60)
(61) Electrical supply
(62) Power
(63) Lighting
(64) Communications
(65)
(66) Transport
(67)
(68) Security, control, other services
(69) Parts of elements (61) to (68), cost summary

(7–) **Fittings**

(70)
(71) Circulation fittings
(72) Rest, work fittings
(73) Culinary fittings
(74) Sanitary, hygiene fittings
(75) Cleaning, maintenance fittings
(76) Storage, screening fittings
(77) Special activity fittings
(78) Other fittings
(79) Parts of elements (71) to (78), cost summary

(8–) ***Loose furniture, equipment**

(80)
(81) Circulation loose equipment
(82) Rest, work loose equipment
(83) Culinary loose equipment
(84) Sanitary, hygiene loose equipment
(85) Cleaning, maintenance loose equipment
(86) Storage, screening loose equipment
(87) Special activity loose equipment
(88) Other
(89) Parts of elements (81) to (88), cost summary

(9–) **External, other elements**

(90) External works
(98) Other elements
(99) Parts of elements, cost summary

    *   Use only **(7–)** if preferred

Table 2   Constructions

A*	Constructions, forms	N	Rigid sheets for overlapping
B*		O	
C*		P	Thick coating work
D*		Q	
E	Cast in situ work	R	Rigid sheets
F	Blockwork, blocks	S	Rigid tiles
G	Large blocks, panels	T	Flexible sheets
H	Section work, sections	U	
I	Pipework, pipes	V	Film coating & impregnation
J	Wirework, meshes	W	Planting, plants, seeds
K	Quilt work, quilts	X	Components
L	Flexible sheets (proofing)	Y	Formless work, products
M	Malleable sheets	Z	Joints

*   Used for special purposes e.g.: resource scheduling by computer

Table 3   Materials

a*		p	Aggregates, loose fills
b*		q	Lime & cement binders, mortars, concretes
c*			
d*		r	Clay, gypsum, magnesia & plastic binders, mortars
e	Natural stone		
f	Precast with binder	s	Bituminous materials
g	Clay (dried, fired)	t	Fixing & jointing materials
h	Metal	u	Protective & process/property modifying materials
i	Wood		
j	Vegetable & animal materials	v	Paints
k		w	Ancillary materials
l		x	
m	Inorganic fibres	y	Composite materials
n	Rubbers, plastics etc	z	Substances
o	Glass		

*   Used for special purposes e.g.: resource scheduling by computer

Tables 2 and 3 are positioned in the third division of the label, either separately or together as required,

e.g. | | | Ff | | = precast blocks

Table 4   Activities, requirements

Activities, aids
(A)   Administration & management activities, aids
(Af) Administration, organization
(Ag) Communications
(Ah) Preparation of documentation
(Ai) Public relations, publicity
(Aj) Controls, procedures
(Ak) Organizations
(Am) Personnel roles
(An) Education
(Ao) Research, development
(Ap) Standardization, rationalization
(Aq) Testing, evaluating

(A1) Organizing offices, projects
(A2) Financing, accounting
(A3) Designing, physical planning
(A4) Cost planning, cost control, tenders, contracts
(A5) Production planning, progress control
(A6) Buying, delivery
(A7) Inspection, quality control
(A8) Handing over, feedback, appraisal
(A9) Other activities, arbitration, insurance

(B)   Construction plant, tools
(B1) Protection plant
(B2) Temporary (non-protective) works
(B3) Transport plant
(B4) Manufacture, screening, storage plant
(B5) Treatment plant
(B6) Placing, pavement, compaction plant
(B7) Hand tools
(B8) Ancillary plants
(B9) Other construction plant, tools

(C)   *Used for special purposes*

(D)   Construction operations
(D1) Protecting
(D2) Cleaning, preparing
(D3) Transport, lifting
(D4) Forming, cutting, shaping, fitting
(D5) Treatment, drilling, boring
(D6) Placing, laying & applying
(D7) Making good, repairing
(D8) Cleaning up
(D9) Other construction operations

Requirements, properties
(E)   Composition
(F)   Shape, size
(G)   Appearance
(H)   Context, environment
(J)   Mechanics
(K)   Fire, explosion
(L)   Matter
(M)   Heat, cold
(N)   Light, dark
(P)   Sound, quiet
(Q)   Electricity, magnetism, radiation
(R)   Energy, side effects, compatability, durability
(S)
(T)   Application
(U)   Users resources
(V)   Working factors
(W)   Operation, maintenance factors
(X)   Change, movement, stability factors
(Y)   Economic, commercial factors
(Z)   Peripheral subjects: presentation, time, space

Sources: RIBA Enterprises Ltd, NBS Services

Uniclass

Uniclass (Unified Classification for the Construction Industry) was developed following a review of CI/SfB for the Construction Project Information Committee (CPIC) and the DoE Construction Sponsorship Directorate. The project was led by consultants from the National Building Specification (NBS) and is based on principles set out by the International Standards Organisation (ISO). The Construction Products Table is based on the work of Electronic Product Information Co-operation (EPIC).

It was designed for organizing information in libraries and projects, but can also be used for structuring files in databases. It is a faceted system which allows tables to be used independently or in combination with each other. It can be integrated with other information systems such as the Common Arrangement of Works Sections (CAWS), Civil Engineering Standard Method of Measurement (CESMM3) and the Building Cost Information Service (BCIS) Standard Form of Cost Analysis.

Uniclass consists of 15 tables:

A	Form of information
B	Subject disciplines
C	Management
D	Facilities
E	Construction entities
F	Spaces
G	Elements for buildings
H	Elements for civil engineering works
J	Work sections for buildings
K	Work sections for civil engineering works
L	Construction products
M	Construction aids
N	Properties and characteristics
P	Materials
Q	Universal Decimal Classification

Source: RIBA Publishing

2
Planning, Policy and Guidance

Planning and other permissions

Planning permission

Definitions

Original House:	The house as it was first built, or as it stood on 1 July 1948 if it was built before that date. House does not include flats.
Highway:	All public roads, footpaths, bridleways and byways, adopted or unadopted.
Article 4 Land:	Conservation Area, National Park, Area of Outstanding Natural Beauty and the Norfolk and Suffolk Broads, World Heritage Sites.
Volume:	Measured from external faces.

Summary of planning permissions

Planning permission is generally needed for the following work to houses and flats in England. Different rules apply in Wales, Scotland and Northern Ireland.

1   Dividing off part of a house for use as a separate dwelling.
2   Use of a caravan in a garden as a home.
3   Dividing off part of a house for business or commercial purposes.
4   Providing a parking place for a commercial vehicle or taxi.
5   Building something that goes against the terms of any planning permission.
6   Work which will involve a new or altered access to a trunk or classified road.
7   External alterations, additions or extensions to a flat or maisonette, including those converted from houses, excluding internal alterations which do not affect the

external appearance (Listed Building Consent could be required for internal alterations to flats or houses).

House extensions

8 Covering more than half the area of land around the original house with additions or other separate buildings including outbuildings.

9 Where the height of the altered house would be higher than the highest part of the roof of the original house.

10 Where the height of the eaves of the altered house would be higher than the eaves of the existing house. Separate rules apply to houses with different height eaves, on slopes or with flat roofs.

11 If the enlarged part of the house is closer to a highway than a wall which fronts the highway and forms the principle or side elevation of the original house. There are exceptions where the distance to the highway is 'substantial'.

12 If a single storey extension extends beyond the rear wall of the house by more than 4 m for a detached house and more than 3 m for any other house.

13 Where the enlarged house has more than one storey and extends beyond the rear wall of the house by more than 3 m.

14 If the enlarged house has more than one storey and is less than 7 m from any curtilage boundary opposite the rear wall of the house.

15 Where the enlarged part of the house is within 2 m of the boundary of the curtilage of the house and the height of the eaves of the enlarged part exceeds 3 m.

16 If the enlarged part of the house extends beyond the side elevation of the house, exceeds 4 m in height or has more than one storey or is greater in width than half the width of the original house. For extensions which affect both the side and rear wall both sets of restrictions apply.

Porches

17 Where the ground area of the porch structure exceeds 3 m^2.

18 Where any part of the porch structure is more than 3 m above ground level.
19 Where any part of the porch structure is within 2 m of the highway boundary.

Note: Where the house is on Article 4 Land the following will always require planning permission:

a Cladding any part of the exterior.
b Enlarging the house beyond the side elevation of the original.
c Enlarging the house by more than one storey beyond the original rear wall.

For Roof Extensions planning permission will be required:

20 Where the house is on Article 4 Land.
21 Where the height of the altered house would be higher than the highest part of the roof of the original house.
22 Where any part of the extension would extend beyond the plane of any existing roof slope on the principal elevation fronting a highway.
23 Where the resulting roof space exceeds the cubic content of the original roof space by 40 m^3 for a terraced house or 50 m^3 elsewhere.
24 Other alterations are permitted to enable the installation of rooflights without planning permission but conditions apply.

For Permitted Development Extension Schemes including Roof Extensions, the following conditions apply. If these are not met it may be necessary to apply for planning permission:

25 The materials used should be similar to those used for the exterior of the existing house except for conservatories.
26 Upper floor windows or rooflights must be obscured glazing.
27 Upper floor windows can only contain opening parts where they are more than 1.7 m above the floor of the relevant room.

28 Where the enlarged part of the house is more than one storey the roof pitch should, as far as practicable, be the same as the original house.

29 The closest edge of the eaves of a roof extension should be not less than 20 cm from the eaves of the original roof.

Under some circumstances the following may require planning permission:

30 The construction of a veranda, balcony or raised platform.

31 The installation, replacement or alteration of a microwave antenna.

32 The installation, alteration or replacement of a chimney, flue or soil pipe.

Separate new buildings on the land around the house will require planning permission where:

33 Any building, enclosure or container is to be used other than for domestic purposes or which exceeds condition 9 above.

34 Any building, enclosure or container would be on land in front of the principle elevation of the house.

Any building, enclosure or container would be more than a single storey

Any building, enclosure or container would be within 2 m of the boundary which is more than 2.5 m high. Any building, enclosure or container more than 4 m high with a dual pitched roof or 3 m high in any other case.

Any building, enclosure or container where the eaves height exceeds 2.5 m.

35 Any building, enclosure, pool or container in the grounds of a Listed Building.

36 Any container with a capacity greater than 3500 litres.

37 In National Parks, Areas of Outstanding Natural Beauty and the Norfolk and Suffolk Broads or World Heritage Sites any building enclosure or container in excess of 10 m^2 if situated more than 20 m from any wall of the house.

Erecting fences, walls and gates require permission:

38 If a house is a Listed Building.

39 If over 1 m high where next to a road or over 2 m elsewhere.

Chimneys, Flues, Soil and Vent Pipes

Apart from on Article 4 Land these are permitted unless they exceed the highest part of the roof by 1m or more.

Planting hedges or trees

41 If a condition was attached to the planning permission of the property which restricts such planting.

Erecting a satellite dish or antenna

Other than normal TV or radio aerials. There is a general permission to install antenna up to a specific size on property without the need for planning permission but there are conditions which apply and should be checked.

Driveways

42 If a new or wider access is made onto an adopted road. Approval of the highways department of the local council will also be needed if a new driveway crosses a pavement or verge.

Planning permission is not required for

Sheds, garages, greenhouses, domestic pet houses, summer houses, swimming pools, ponds, sauna cabins or tennis courts, although there are restrictions on the size and the location within the curtilage.

Creation or replacement of patios, hard standings, paths and driveways unless used for parking a commercial vehicle or taxi. If in front of the principal elevation or exceeding 5 m^2, however, the hard surface must direct water to a permeable or porous area within the curtilage.

Normal domestic TV and radio aerials – but see under 'Erecting a satellite dish or antenna' above.

Repairs, maintenance or minor improvements such as redecorating or replacing windows, insertion of windows, skylights or rooflights – but see the next section on Listed Buildings and Conservation Areas, where consents may be needed.

Other consents

Listed Buildings
See websites for advice in Wales, Scotland and Northern Ireland.

A Listed Building includes the exterior and interior of the building and, with some exceptions, any object or structure within the curtilage of the building, including garden walls.

Listed Building Consent is needed to demolish a Listed Building, or part of one, or to alter or extend it in any way inside or out which would affect its architectural or historic character.

Certain minor works such as plumbing, electrical installations, and fitted furniture and appliances, as for kitchens and bathrooms, MAY be considered 'de minimis' and not require consent if the work is both non-destructive and reversible, but it is unwise to assume this. Check with the council first. It is a criminal offence to carry out any work without consent. No application fees are required.

See also p. 54.

Conservation Areas
Consent is needed to demolish any building in a Conservation Area with a volume of more than $115\,m^3$ or a gate or fence more than 1 m high where abutting a highway, or more than 2 m high elsewhere.

No application fees are required.

National Parks, Areas of Outstanding Natural Beauty and the Broads, World Heritage Sites
Generally permissions to carry out building work in these areas are more limited, so check with the appropriate body first.

Trees and high hedges

Many trees have Tree Preservation Orders which mean consent is needed to prune or fell them. Most trees are protected in Conservation Areas. In Conservation Areas, notice is required for works to trees that have a trunk diameter of more than 75 mm when measured at 1.5 m from ground level.

Tall evergreen hedges over 2 m high may be subject to the Anti-Social Behaviour Act 2003 (Part 8).

Building Regulations approval

Almost all new building must comply with the Building Regulations except small, detached buildings without sanitary facilities such as sheds and garages. The Regulations are available in full on the internet.

Rights of way

If a proposed building would obstruct a public path then consult with the local authority at an early stage. If they agree to the proposal then an order will be made to divert or extinguish the right of way. No work should proceed until the order has been confirmed.

Advertising

Displaying an advertisement larger than $0.3 m^2$ outside a property may need consent. This can include house names, numbers or even 'Beware of the Dog'. Temporary notices up to $0.6 m^2$ relating to local events may be displayed for a short time.

Wildlife

If the proposed new building or alterations will involve disturbing roosts of bats or other protected species, then Natural England (NE), the Countryside Council for Wales (CCW) or Scottish Natural Heritage (SNH), whichever is appropriate, must be notified. The possible delays and costs involved in dealing with protected species, for example in avoiding disturbance during breeding or hibernation and in obtaining the necessary licences and carrying out mitigation works, can be severe.

Source: *Permitted development for householders. DCLG*
        August 2010
        www.planningportal.gov.uk

Planning appeals

The following relates to appeals in England. Similar processes
are in place in Scotland, Wales and Northern Ireland.

Considering an appeal

It is possible to appeal against a Local Planning Authority
(LPA) which has refused Planning Permission, whether outline
or full; or if they have given permission but with conditions
which seem to the Appellant to be unreasonable; or if a decision has not been made within the time laid down, which is
normally 8 or 13 weeks from registration. However, before
lodging an appeal, the Appellant should consider modifying
the scheme if this could meet the objections. Generally if a
revised scheme is presented within 1 year of the refusal date,
no extra planning fee is requested. Appeals should be a last
resort. They take time and cost money. The majority of appeals
are not successful. Inspectors must take their decisions based
on relevant facts and material planning considerations. They
consider the planning merits of the case and personal considerations are unlikely to outweigh strong planning objections.

Making an appeal

Appeals must be lodged within 6 months of the date of
the decision. The Secretary of State (SoS) can accept a late
appeal, but will do so only in very exceptional circumstances.
Most appeals are decided on the basis of written represen-
tations and a visit to the site by the planning inspector. The
Inspectorate may agree to or require a Hearing or a Public
Inquiry. Appeals against Planning Permission, Listed Building
Consent or Conservation Area Consent can be submitted online via the Planning Portal or on forms which can
be obtained from the Planning Inspectorate in England and
Wales, the Scottish Executive (SEIRU) in Scotland and the
Planning Appeals Commission in Northern Ireland. In England
there is an expedited procedure for householder appeals.

Currently (other than in Northern Ireland) appeals can only be made by the applicant not by any interested third party.

Written representation

The appeal form stating the grounds of appeal together with documents and plans should be sent to the Planning Inspectorate (PI). The LPA will send their case to the PI, copies of which will be sent to the Appellant who is allowed to make comments. Interested people such as neighbours and environmental groups will be notified of the appeal and are also able to comment. When the Inspector is ready, a site visit is arranged. This may be an unaccompanied visit if the site can be viewed from public land or an accompanied visit when the site is on private land and where both the Appellant, or a representative, and the LPA must be present, although only factual matters can be pointed out; no discussion is entered into.

Hearings

Hearings are less formal and therefore less expensive than a public inquiry and legal representatives are not normally used. This method is not suitable where there is a considerable amount of public interest in a case.

Local inquiry

This procedure is used where requested by the LPA, the Appellant or the Inspectorate and when the Inspectorate agree to this procedure. The procedure is more formal and strict deadlines for the submission of evidence are imposed.

All witnesses or representatives may be questioned or cross-examined. At the inquiry, anyone involved may use a lawyer or other professional to put their case. The Inspector will make visits to the site usually alone, before the inquiry and accompanied as part of the Inquiry.

Costs

The Appellant and the LPA will normally pay their own expenses, whichever procedure is used. However either side can make a submission for the payment of costs where they consider that the behaviour of other party has been unreasonable and therefore put them to unnecessary expense.

The decision

Where new evidence emerges before the decision is issued which may put new light on the subject, both parties will have a chance to comment before a decision is made and the inquiry may be re-opened. The Inspector sends the decision to the Appellant with copies to the LPA and anyone else entitled or who asked for a copy. In some cases the Inspector does not make the decision but makes a recommendation to the SoS who considers the merits and makes the final decision.

The High Court

The only way an appeal can be made against the Inspector's decision is on legal grounds in the High Court. This challenge usually has to be made within 6 weeks of the date of the decision. For right of appeal to the High Court to succeed, it must be demonstrated that the Inspectorate or the SoS has exceeded their powers or that proper procedures were not followed. If the High Court appeal succeeds it only means that the case has to be heard again it may not change the ultimate outcome.

Source: *Planning Portal: www.planningportal.gov.uk*
Procedural Guidance: Planning appeals and called-in planning applications (PINS 01/2009)
Procedural Guidance: Enforcement appeals and determination of appeal procedure (PINS 02/2009)

Party wall awards

The Party Wall etc Act 1996 has effect throughout England and Wales and involves the following proposed building work:

1   Work to an existing party wall, such as taking support for a new beam, inserting full-width DPCs, underpinning, raising, rebuilding or reducing the wall.
2   Building a new party wall on or astride a boundary line between two properties.

3   Constructing foundations for a new building within 3 m of a neighbouring building, where the work will go deeper than the neighbouring foundations.

4   Constructing foundations for a new building within 6 m of a neighbouring building where the work will cut a line drawn downwards at 45° from the bottom of the neighbour's foundations.

Notices must be served by the *building owner* to the *adjoining owner* or owners, which may include landlords as well as tenants, at least 2 months before the work starts or 1 month in advance for new work as described in 3 and 4 above. There is no set form for the Notice, but it should include: the owner's name and address; the address of the building (if different); full detailed drawings of the proposed work; and the starting date. It may also include any proposals to safeguard the fabric of the adjoining owner's property. The adjoining owner cannot stop someone exercising their rights given them by the Act, but can influence how and when the work is done. Anyone receiving a notice may give consent within 14 days, or give a counter-notice setting out modifications to the proposals. If the adjoining owner does not reply, a dispute is assumed to have arisen.

The Award

The Party Wall Act is in force to safeguard the interests of the wall. It is there to prevent confrontation between neighbours and although the Adjoining Owner can 'dissent' to the work that does not give them a veto to prevent the work being carried out.

When consent is not received the two owners agree to appoint one surveyor to act for both sides, or two surveyors, one to act for each side. Surveyors appointed must take into account the interests of both owners. The surveyors draw up and supervise the *Award*, which is a statement laying down what work will be undertaken and how and when it will be done. It should include a *Schedule of Condition*, which describes in detail the state of the wall viewed from the adjoining owner's side. The Award will also specify who pays the construction costs and the surveyors' fees – usually the owner who initiates the work. The Award is served on all relevant owners, each of whom is bound by the Award unless appeals are made within 14 days to the county court.

Sources: *A Short Guide to the Party Wall Act 1996*
The Party Wall etc. Act 1996: Explanatory Booklet
Available online from www.communities.gov.uk

Listed Buildings

All applications for the inclusion of a building, site or other Heritage Asset on a statutory list must be submitted to English Heritage (EH) who carry out all the consultation and research. A Listing Schedule is produced (the official signed document, essentially the list entry) and this is signed by an English Heritage official although the Secretary of State for DCMS has to agree with the EH recommendations.

Buildings may be listed because of age, rarity, architectural merit, method of construction and occasionally because of an association with a famous person or historic event. Groups of buildings may be listed for their collective merit.

All buildings largely in their original condition before 1700 are likely to be listed, as are most between 1700 and 1840. Later on the criteria became tighter with time, so that post-1945 only exceptional buildings are listed.

Grades

Listed Buildings are graded as follows:

- Grade I buildings are of exceptional interest
- Grade II* buildings are particularly important buildings of more than special interest
- Grade II buildings comprise over 92% of Listed Buildings; they are nationally important and of special interest.

Listing applies to the entire building, including anything fixed to the building or in the grounds before 1 July 1948.

See p. 44 for permissions needed to add, alter or demolish a Listed Building.

Some grants are available for the repair and conservation of the most significant historic buildings, monuments and designed landscapes. These are mainly for urgent repairs or other work required to prevent loss or damage to important architectural, archaeological or landscaping features.

Work to residential Listed Buildings may be VAT zero-rated for approved alterations. See Notice 708 Buildings and Construction from H M Revenue and Customs.

For advice on how to get a building listed or other information, consult the Local Authority and English Heritage website. The responsibility for issuing Consent for altering or extending a Listed Building lies with local planning authorities and ultimately with the DCMS acting on the advice of EH.

For Listed Buildings in Scotland, Northern Ireland and Wales, consult Historic Scotland, CADW, and Historic Buildings and Monuments Belfast respectively.

Sources: *English Heritage – www.english-heritage.org.uk/*
Cadw: www.cadw.wales.gocvv.uk
www.historic-scotland.gov.uk
www.nidirect.gov.uk
Department for Culture Media and Sport –
www.culture.gov.uk
H M Revenue and Customs – www.hmrc.gov.uk

Building Regulations 2000

The approved documents

These documents are published as *practical guidance* to the Building Regulations, i.e. they are not the Building Regulations as such.

The mandatory **Requirement** is highlighted in green near the beginning of each document. The remaining text is for guidance only.

The Building Inspectorate accept that if this guidance is followed then the requirement is satisfied. There is no obligation to comply with these guidelines providing evidence is produced to show that the relevant requirement has been satisfied in some other way.

The purpose of the Building Regulation is to secure reasonable standards of health, safety, energy conservation and the convenience of disabled people.

A separate system of control applies in Scotland and Northern Ireland.

The regulations are published by the NBS and are available from RIBA Bookshops and online.

Approved documents

Part A
Approved Document A – Structure (2004 edition)

Part B
Approved Document B (Fire safety) – Volume 1: Dwelling houses (2006 Edition)

Approved Document B (Fire safety) – Volume 2: Buildings other than dwelling houses (2006 Edition)

Part C
Approved Document C – Site preparation and resistance to contaminates and moisture (2004 edition)

Part D
Approved Document D – Toxic substances (1992 edition)

Part E
Approved Document E – Resistance to the passage of sound (2003 edition)

Part F
Approved Document F – Ventilation (2006 edition)

Part G
Approved Document G – Sanitation, hot water safety and water efficiency (2010 edition)

Part H
Approved Document H – drainage and waste disposal (2002 edition)

Part J
Approved Document J – Combustion appliances and fuel storage systems (2002 edition)

Part K
Approved Document K – Protection from falling collision and impact (1998 edition)

Part L – Dwellings
Approved Document L1A: Conservation of fuel and power (New dwellings) (2010 edition)
Approved Document L1B: Conservation of fuel and power (Existing dwellings) (2010 edition)

Part L – Buildings other than dwellings
Approved Document L2A: Conservation of fuel and power (New buildings other than dwellings) (2010 edition)
Approved Document L2B: Conservation of fuel and power (Existing buildings other than dwellings) (2010 edition)

Part M
Approved Document M – Access to and Use of Buildings (2004 edition)

Part N
Approved Document N – Glazing (1998 edition)

Part P
Approved Document P – Electrical safety – Dwellings (2006 edition)

Regulation 7
Approved Document for Regulation 7 (1992 edition)

Construction Design and Management Regulations

In the mid-1990s, fatal accidents in the construction industry were five to six times more frequent than in other areas of manufacture. Also, all construction workers could expect to be temporarily off work at least once in their working life as a result of injury. The Construction Design and Management Regulations (CDM) 1994, effective from 31 March 1995, were drafted to try and improve these statistics. The regulations were revised and clarified in 2007 and are explained in the Approved Code of Practice 'Managing health & safety in construction'.

'Designers are required to avoid foreseeable risks "so far as is reasonably practicable, taking due account of other relevant design considerations." The greater the risk, the greater the weight that must be given to eliminating or reducing it.'

For all projects, designers should check that clients are aware of their duties, and before they start design work on 'notifiable projects', they should ensure that clients have appointed a CDM Co-ordinator.

The key aims of the CDM Regulations 2007 are to integrate health and safety into the management of the project and to encourage everyone involved to work together to:

- improve the planning and management of projects from the very start;

- identify hazards early on, so they can be eliminated or reduced at the design or planning stage and the remaining risks can be properly managed;
- target effort where it can do the most good in terms of health and safety; and
- discourage unnecessary bureaucracy.

Revisions to the regulations have been focussed on clarifying the client's responsibilities as the primary instigator of compliance with the regulations, and warning against inappropriate bureaucracy, which tends to obscure the real health and safety issues.

The Planning Supervisor has been renamed as the CDM Co-ordinator – a more accurate description of the role. To implement the regulations for any 'notifiable project', a CDM Co-ordinator (CC) must be appointed by the client. This can be anyone competent, and may be a member of the design team, contractors or even the client. For smaller projects, it simplifies procedures if the CC is also part of the design team, such as the architect or engineer.

The CC must advise and assist the client with their duties; notify the HSE of a 'notifiable project'; co-ordinate health and safety aspects of design work and co-operate with others involved with the project; facilitate good communication between client, designers and contractors; liaise with the principal contractor regarding ongoing design; identify, collect and pass on pre-construction information; prepare/update the Health & Safety file for the client on completion. They may also, if requested by a client, advise on the appointment of consultants and contractors as to their competence and resources in regard to CDM matters. If architects are to act as CDM Co-ordinators they must ensure that they receive certified HSE training, as failure to comply with the regulations could lead to criminal prosecution.

When CDM regulations are not applicable in full – 'not notifiable'

Listed below are situations where the CDM regulations need not apply in full. However, the designer is still legally obliged to avoid foreseeable risks; give priority to protection for all; and include adequate H & S information in the design.

- Work carried out for domestic householders, on their own residences, used solely as a private dwelling (e.g. not as an office as well as a home).
- Work which is for 30 days or less duration and involves less than 500 person days on site and does not involve demolition or dismantling of a structure.

There are a number of construction-related activities that are listed as 'not construction' for the purposes of the regulations, including erecting and dismantling marquees, lightweight movable partitions as used for office screens, exhibition displays, etc; tree planting and general horticultural work; surveying including 'examining a structure for faults', and off-site manufacture of construction components, e.g. roof trusses, precast concrete and bathroom pods. CDM, therefore, does not apply to these works.

Source: *Managing Health and Safety in Construction HSE 2007*

Standards – in the construction industry

Efforts are being made to harmonize standards throughout Europe so as to open up the single market for construction products. It is still something of a minefield, as harmonization at the beginning of the twenty-first century is not complete. Listed alphabetically below are the organizations and standards involved, which may help to clarify the current situation.

BBA – British Board of Agrément. This organization assesses and tests new construction products and systems which have not yet received a relevant BS or EN. It issues Agrément Certificates to those that meet their stand-

ards. The Certificate gives an independent opinion of fitness for purpose. Holders are subject to 3-yearly reviews to ensure standards are maintained. The BBA represents the UK in the UEAtc and is designated by the government to lead the issuing of ETAs.

BSI – British Standards Institution. This was the first national standards body in the world. It publishes British Standards (BS) which give recommended minimum standards for materials, products and processes. These are not mandatory, but some are quoted directly in the Building Regulations (see

also EN below). All materials and components complying with a particular BS are marked with the BS kitemark together with the relevant BS number. BSI also publishes codes of practice (CP) which give recommendations for good practice in relation to design, manufacture, construction, installation and maintenance, with the main objectives being safety, quality, economy and fitness for purpose. Drafts for Development (DD) are issued when there is insufficient information for a BS or a CP. These are similar to ENVs.

CE mark – Communauté Européenne mark. This mark was introduced by the CPD, and is a symbol applied to products by their manufacturers to indicate their compliance with European member state regulations. It has nothing to do with quality or safety (unlike the BS kitemark). If the CE mark has a number attached, this signifies that the product has been independently tested.

CEN – Comité Européen de Nationalisation (also known as the European Committee for Standardisation). Its main aims are to harmonize national standards; promote implementation of the ISO; prepare ENs; co-operate with EFTA and other international governmental organizations and CENELEC (the electrotechnical counterpart of CEN). The BSI is a member of CEN.

CPD – Construction Products Directive. This is a directive produced by the European Commission introducing the CE mark.

EN – Euronorm (also known as European Standard) and **Eurocodes.** European Standards are published by the CEN for a wide range of materials. A full EN, known in the UK as a BS EN, is mandatory and overrules any conflicting previous BS, which must be withdrawn. Prospective standards where documentation is still in preparation are published as European prestandards (ENV). These are normally converted to full ENs after a 3-year experimental period. See Chapter 3.

EOTA – European Organization for Technical Approvals. Members of this organization issue ETAs. The UK is represented in EOTA by the BBA. EOTA polices organizations nominated by member states to make sure they all apply the same tests and level of expertise when preparing ETAs.

ETA – European Technical Approval. ETAs are issued by members of EOTA. They are available for products whose performance or characteristics fall outside the scope of a European Standard (EN) mandated by the EC, and are based upon assessment methods known as ETAGs (European Technical Approval Guidelines). Both ETAs and ENs enable products to which they refer to be placed in the single European market.

ISO – International Organization for Standardization. This organization prepares International Standards for the whole world. They are prefixed ISO and many are compatible and complement British Standards. In the UK, BSs and ENs that are approved by the ISO are prefixed BS ISO or BS EN ISO.

MOAT – Method of Assessment and Testing. These are the criteria and methods used by the BBA when testing products. Many MOATs have been developed in consultation with the European Agrément organizations under the aegis of the UEAtc.

QA – Quality Assurance. BS EN 9001 lays down procedures for various organizations to conform to a specification and thus acquire QA for a production or a service. RIBA Chartered Architects are required to adopt appropriate QA for their type and scale of work. BS EN 14001 2004 is the environmental equivalent standard that specifies requirements for an environmental management system for an organization to control and improve its environmental impacts and performance.

UEAtc – European Union of Agrément technical committee. A technical committee to which all European Agrément institutes belong, including the BBA for the UK. Its principal function is to facilitate trade in construction products between member states, primarily through its Confirmation process, whereby an Agrément Certificate issued by a UEAtc member in one country can be used to obtain a Certificate in another.

Costs and law

Costs and legal issues are described in principle and in outline only since both contract values and case law change too frequently for actual figures and legal detail to have lasting value.

Costs

The architect's role both as a cost advisor and as a certifier of contractors' valuations varies with the scale of projects. For most small projects and many of the simpler medium scale ones, the architect is both the client's cost advisor and responsible for checking as well as certifying payments to the contractor: awareness of current costs is therefore vital to architects working at this level with local experience usually the best guide, though several price books are available including those covering small works and refurbishment.

The simplest rule in estimating costs is that they decrease as scale increases and increase with complexity; time is also an issue but the most economic length of time for a construction project will vary for different contractors and circumstances; either forcing the pace for an earlier completion or slowing progress artificially may increase costs.

Project costs can be lower in the early stages of simpler, less skilled work and cheaper materials and increase sharply towards completion as more skilled trades are required for services and finishing and more expensive components are fitted such as joinery, electrical and sanitary fittings.

Labour costs have grown steadily as a proportion of construction costs which is reflected in the growth of prefabrication and pre-finishing both of components such as windows, kitchens and bathroom pods, and of material elements such as wall, roof and floor panels; recently renewed enthusiasm for prefabrication has coined the term 'Modern Methods of Construction'.

Preliminary cost estimating for most projects is done on a pounds per square metre of internal floor area basis; the rates for different types and scales of buildings vary sharply, so that for example, a simple industrial shed may cost half as much per square metre as speculative housing which in turn may cost half as much per square metre as a hospital. Despite the decades since metrication, many in the commercial development world still work in square feet for both rents and build costs (10.67 sq ft = 1 sq metre).

For smaller projects, where the architect is often the client's only cost advisor, the work is typically tendered on the basis of drawings and a specification or schedule of works. The architect will agree the list of contractors with the client, issue the tenders, advise the client on the relative merits of the tenders received, negotiate any cost savings needed and arrange the contract between client and contractor; once the work starts, the architect will administer the contract on behalf of both parties, value the contractor's work – usually at monthly intervals – and prepare certificates for the client to pay, including where necessary any variations in the work covered by the architect's certificates. After completion the architect negotiates the final account with the contractor.

Larger projects – and especially those where the client wants detailed and explicit cost estimating, monitoring and control – usually include a Quantity Surveyor in the consultant's team who may provide a series of estimates and carry out value engineering exercises during the briefing and design process, and then prepare a Bill of Quantities during the working drawings stage which describes the works in sufficient numeric detail so that tenderers can quote precisely against the Bill.

The QS advises the client on tenders received and prepares valuations during the contract as a basis for the architect's certificates, as well as dealing with the final account.

Whether or not a QS is involved, the architect is still responsible under most forms of contract for certifying payments and takes on the additional role of 'administering the contract';

in which role they are required to act fairly and impartially to both client and contractor in matters of cost, timing, quality, etc. It is important that architects make this clear to inexperienced clients at the outset.

One of the architect's most important duties relates to assessing extensions of time which can have substantial cost consequences – both in terms of contractors' claims for loss and expense, and reductions of clients' rights to liquidated damages.

Fees

There are no set fee scales for architects and the only advice that RIBA is allowed to give on fee levels is based on average fees charged, broad band graphs of which are included in their advice to clients.

For larger projects, fees are often charged on a percentage of final construction cost; smaller projects may be carried out on a time basis or against a lump sum quotation.

As for construction costs, fees tend to decrease with increasing project scale and increase with complexity, so, for example, fees for a large new build warehouse on a greenfield site may be below 5% whereas the restoration and conversion of a small Grade 1 Listed Building to a private home might involve fees as high as 20%.

RIBA's appointment documents advise what standard services are normally included within an architect's fee and what special services need to be separately negotiated.

Where several consultants work on a project, their fees will be individually negotiated with the client but it is important that each consultant's scope of work is clearly defined, so that there are neither gaps nor duplication in the service to the client.

For a project with an overall fee of 15%, the split between consultants might be: architect 7%; landscape architect 1.5%; structural engineer 2.5%; services engineer 1.5%; quantity surveyor 2% and CDM co-ordinator 0.5% – though projects can involve very different relative demands for consultants' skills.

Each consultant is typically appointed directly by the client; where clients require a single appointment, for example of an architect who then subcontracts other consultants, the architect needs to clear such an arrangement with their professional indemnity insurer.

Law

Architects' role in construction contracts is their main area of legal involvement but they may be asked by clients for legal advice in relation to Planning, Listed Buildings and Building Regulations, or in connection with health and safety under the CDM regulations (see p. 54), or boundary matters under the Party Wall Act (see p. 48), or a number of other relevant items of legislation such as Health & Safety at Work Act, Offices Shops & Railway Premises Act, etc. It is important that architects do not give clients advice beyond their expertise in legal matters and recommend their clients consult legal advisors when appropriate.

Legal disputes, particularly where litigation and arbitration are involved tend to be time-consuming and costly; The Construction Act (Housing Grants, Regeneration and Construction Act Part II 1996) introduced adjudication as a simpler and swifter method of dispute resolution but it has its own rules and timetables of which architects need to be aware, particularly as timescales can be very tight.

For private householders, contracts can be amended to exclude the adjudication provisions of the Construction Act. Some clients and some PI insurers may prefer to rely on legal proceedings as the only formal recourse in disputes.

Architects should also remember that their own appointments with their clients are classed as construction contracts under the Construction Act, and they can, therefore, avail themselves of such remedies as the Act provides, such as adjudication, suspension of services, right to staged payments, etc.

Disputes often arise between client and contractor over the architect's extension of time award.

Architects will need to consult their professional indemnity insurers or brokers when a dispute arises that might involve a claim against them. It may be more helpful to consult a professional contractual consultant in the first instance rather than a lawyer for advice on contractual disputes or claims.

Registered architects – and practising members of RIBA – are required to carry appropriate levels of professional indemnity insurance so that there is assurance of redress for clients – or others – who may suffer financially as a result of an architect's mistakes.

Contracts between the architect and their insurer involve the usual conditions and most critically that the architect informs their insurer as soon as possible of any 'circumstance likely to lead to a claim'. Since this condition is open to wide interpretation, it is helpful for architects to establish a positive advisory relationship with their broker or insurer.

Sustainability, energy saving and green issues

Matters which are considered relevant at the beginning of the twenty-first century.

Architects' responsibilities

Architects have responsibilities to their clients, their building users, the community and the wider world, as well as to their builders and consultants. Excessive resource – and especially energy – consumption and CO_2 generation are the most pressing problems facing the world: responsibility for resolving these problems lies most heavily on the industrialized world that has largely created them.

Around half the UK's CO_2 emissions are from building and buildings, two-thirds of which are from housing. It is stated government policy that by 2016 all new housing must be built to even higher carbon neutral standards or 'Level 6' in the Code for Sustainable Homes. This effectively means that the house is designed to need virtually no space heating or cooling (the German Passivhaus standard), and that residual energy use including water heating, cooking, lighting and other appliances is balanced by at least as much ambient energy generated on site, for example by photovoltaic panels or wind turbines.

The four keys to successful passivhaus design are:

- Super-insulation of fabric and glazing – for example 400 mm of cellulose fibre or 200 mm of phenolic foam insulation, with triple, low-e coated, gas-filled glazing.
- Effectively airtight construction to bring air leakage down to less than 0.6 air changes/hour rather than 10 AC/hr more typical of UK construction.
- Design for effective control of internal and external heat gains – for example in passive solar design, heat reclaim ventilation, etc., with a residual heating (or cooling) load of no more than 15 kWh per square metre per annum.
- Incorporation of available thermal mass – for example in dense floor and internal wall materials to absorb and even out heat gains.

The Code for Sustainable Homes is a voluntary standard for new housing, except for Housing Associations where Level 3 is a mandatory requirement, which assesses the standard of the building under nine criteria: Energy, Waste, Water, Materials, Surface Water Run Off, Management, Pollution, Heath & Wellbeing, and Ecology. Now, only four levels are applicable; from Level 3 to 6, each category has a minimum level of achievement before any credits are awarded, some having mandatory sections before any additional credits can be given. It's a flexible assessment; not every category needs to be achieved to gain an overall rating.

Due into the regulations in 2013, but already incorporated into the Code for Sustainable Homes, is the Fabric Energy Efficiency Standard (FEES). This is a standard that will cover in total the energy efficiency of the building's walls, floor, roof, windows, thermal bridging and air permeability into a single $kWh/m^2/yr$ figure.

New buildings are only a small fraction of the national stock: although designing new buildings to high standards is vital, the bulk of the problem lies with the poor standards of existing buildings.

The vast amount of alteration and refurbishment work represents the major opportunity that most people have to improve the environment and their own future. A number of organizations are researching the most appropriate sustainable refurbishment for old properties. The Energy Saving Trust have produced a number of useful documents covering sustainable refurbishment.

Constraints on maximizing environmental improvements to some existing buildings include poor siting, overshadowing and historic building restrictions; the one advantage that many existing buildings have is substantial thermal mass – increasingly valuable in an age of global warming.

Land use planning and transport

New development should increase density and integrate uses to minimize transport (which accounts for over 30 per cent of UK CO_2); planning and facilities to encourage public transport, electric vehicles and cycle use should be included. Food and biomass production should ideally be allowed for locally. Site layouts should be solar oriented and minimize overshadowing.

Landscape design

• Direct enhancements of the environmental performance of buildings: shelter planting both for wind breaks and climbers attached to buildings; deciduous planting for seasonal shade (planted pergolas are more controllable than tree planting which may grow to shade solar panels and PVs); planted roofs for micro-climate, insulation and membrane protection; water conservation ponds for reuse and amenity; reed bed sewage treatment; biofuel cropping.

- Indirect enhancements in terms of the quality of life and the biosphere: planted roofs, permeable/informal pavings and sustainable drainage systems to minimize flooding; indigenous and site specific planting; allotments; composting provision; wildlife supportive planting to improve habitats and biodiversity.
- Process enhancements to minimize construction damage: thorough landscape surveys followed by enforceable wildlife and planting protection plans; pollution control during construction; high quality and motivated site management to prevent damage and promote landscape protection.

Environmental building design

Principal glazed elevations should be oriented south or between SW and SE to maximize useful solar gain passively and actively, without shading or obstruction of low angle winter sun but – and this is vital as the climate warms – with adequate secure ventilation and shading against high angle summer sun to prevent overheating; deciduous planting can provide seasonally adjusting shade at low cost. Northerly elevations for housing should have least glazing, though for some building types with high internal heat gains, such as offices, maximizing daylight via north lights may be a more effective energy saving measure.

New glazing should be to the best standards, for example triple, soft-coat low-e glazing, gas-filled, with thermal-spacers to centre pane U-values below 0.7 $Wm^2°C$.

Window location and design should allow for cross flow and high and low level ventilation including secure night ventilation to make best use of thermal mass.

Housing should be planned to provide principal spaces towards the south and 'buffer spaces' – usually service areas that can be heated to a lower temperature – to the north.

Super-insulated walling and roofing should be combined with dense internal linings, structure, floors and partitioning to provide appropriate thermal mass.

Conservatories can be used effectively as passive solar sunspaces but should not be substituted for basic space; they should be separated by insulated walling and glazing from other parts of the building. If they are heated at all, for frost protection of plants for example, they need to be separately thermostatically controlled so that lower temperatures are maintained; they need to be securely vented at high and low level to prevent overheating in summer and south facing sunspaces will need external shading or solar control glass in addition.

Building services

The objective should be to simplify and reduce building services to a minimum.

Complex services tend to increase both capital and maintenance costs and reduce user satisfaction through lack of understanding and control.

Where heating or cooling systems are necessary in existing buildings, radiant types such as underfloor water heating pipework tend to be most efficient for the majority of building types, especially high spaces. Local controls, such as thermostatic radiator valves, are important to allow for varying conditions and to avoid wasted heating; efficiency of existing systems can be improved by more specific control systems allowing for different temperatures in different zones and weather compensation.

Air conditioning should not be needed for normal occupation and should be excluded from new building designs.

Hot water services should be concentrated around heat sources and storage to minimize heat loss from pipework; wherever possible, hot water should be preheated by solar panels with high capacity super-insulated storage so as to avoid fuel use during summer.

Subject to site and planning restrictions, wind turbine installations should be considered with photovoltaics as a more costly, though more adaptable, alternative for providing site generated electricity which can also be grid connected – all the more attractive financially since the introduction of the Feed In Tariff (FITs) .

Where substantial heating is required in larger existing buildings, combined heat and power (CHP) systems can provide heat and electrical generation simultaneously at high efficiency; biofuel boilers using wood pellets, wood chips, straw, logs, etc. are available to very high efficiencies and levels of automation, though local fuel availability and maintenance issues need to be resolved.

Ventilation systems are likely to be required because of the very high standards of airtightness required in new buildings; humidity-sensitive passive or wind-driven stack systems minimize energy use while powered heat reclaim vent systems at efficiencies up to 90% minimize ventilation heat losses.

Daylighting and artificial lighting should be considered together. High levels of daylight will reduce electrical consumption for lighting but glare may need to be controlled; use of horizontal blinds, light shelves, etc. can improve daylighting in deep plan spaces while reducing glare at the perimeter. Artificial lighting should be high efficiency, i.e. LED, fluorescent or discharge lamps, and should be locally controlled or daylight/occupancy-sensor controlled in larger buildings. Both light fittings and window glazing need to be regularly cleaned to maintain efficiency.

Water consumption should be reduced by use of low water use appliances such as spray, percussive or electronic taps, low flush cisterns, fine spray showers, etc. Where site conditions permit, installation of below ground rainwater cisterns to collect roof drainage for use in WC flushing, external taps, etc., plus washing machine and bathing use if appropriately filtered, can be cost-effective due to savings on both water metering and sewerage charges. Grey water systems filter and recycle waste water from showers, baths and washing machines and need less tank space but require more maintenance than rainwater systems.

Materials

Environmental concerns should figure prominently alongside issues of function, aesthetics and cost in the selection of materials by architects. The environmental implications of particular materials specification are often complex and it may prove most practical to refer to the guides available such as 'BRE Green Guide to Specification'.

There are three main areas for environmental consideration:

- Embodied energy – the sum of all energy used in the extraction, processing, manufacture and delivery of a material. One of the best known high embodied energy materials is aluminium whose extraction and processing from bauxite requires very high energy input, though recycling and the use of 'green' hydro-electric power for smelting immediately complicate the picture. Arguably, embodied energy concerns can be offset in the consideration of energy conservation materials.
- Toxicity – toxic pollution arising from extraction, processing and manufacture: toxins emitted in the installation and use of a material; toxins emitted in the decay, demolition and disposal of a material. PVC is probably the most notorious building material in this respect with both its manufacture and disposal at risk of being seriously toxic. Many materials including solvents (paints, preservatives, liquid tanking, etc.) and glues containing formaldehyde (as in chipboard,

MDF, etc.) are best known for emitting toxic pollution in application and during occupation of buildings.

• Sourcing – the environmental implications of obtaining a material from a particular source or type of supplier. The best publicized issue in this respect is the one regarding unsustainable forestry where the use of timber (generally an environmentally benign material), extracted in a non-environmental way, has led to widespread bans on its use without third party certification. The most respected certifier is the Forestry Stewardship Council (FSC) who have sustained independent probity over many years; the PEFC (Programme for Endorsement of Forest Certification) is also worthy of consideration.

In virtually all cases, there are more acceptable substitutes for environmentally damaging materials, though in some cases the substitutes may be less widely available or more costly. Some examples are given below:

Cement	Lime in place of cement or cement reduction by PFA in mix
Chipboard, MDF, etc.	Timber/oriented strand board(OSB)/softwood plywood/vapour-permeable sheathing boards
Fibreglass/mineral wool	Cellulose fibre/sheep's wool/ flax & hemp/recycled plastic
Lead sheet roofing	Tin-coated stainless steel or titanium zinc
Oil-based insulation foams	Cork/foamed glass
PVC rainwater goods	Galvanized steel
PVC drainage goods	Clayware/polypropylene/ Polythene/Stainless steel
PVC roof membranes	EPDM, TPO, etc.
PVC-sheathed cables	Rubber-sheathed cables
Rainforest hardwoods	FSC Certified/temperate sourced hardwoods
Solvent-based paints, etc.	Waterbased/eco paints

| Timber preservatives | No preservative/Boron preservatives |
| Vinyl flooring | Linoleum/natural rubber |

In few cases are the substitutes either a perfect substitute or entirely free of adverse environmental consequences; the guides referred to above provide more details.

In some cases, there are serious practical disadvantages to the substitutes, for example there are no benign insulants to compare in performance for an equivalent thickness to the high performance petro-chemical foams such as phenolic foam and isocyanurate, which are nearly twice as effective as cellulose fibre or sheep's wool. Architects and their clients may decide that this is a more environmentally acceptable use of petroleum, rather than as petrol, and that the space saving is worth achieving.

Finishes

Reducing the use of finishes is generally environmentally beneficial: unfinished materials tend to be better quality, less processed, last longer and require less maintenance, thus reducing future environmental burdens; their higher capital cost is quickly offset once cycles of redecoration or renewal are considered. For example, a stone finish may cost more than a good quality carpet on a screeded floor but once the carpet requires replacement, the stone is quickly seen to have been the economic choice.

Unfinished materials are easier and more valuable to recycle or reuse since their lack of finishes makes them both easier to inspect and simpler to process.

Sources: *Green Guide to the Architect's Job Book*
BRE Green Guide to Housing Specification

Anthropometric data

Standing

Dimensions given are the average for British men and women. They include an allowance for clothing and shoes.

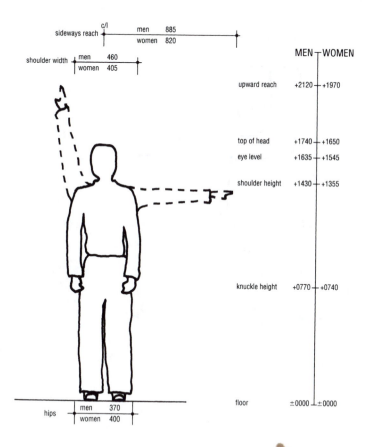

Sitting

Dimensions given are the average for British men and women. They include an allowance for clothing and shoes.

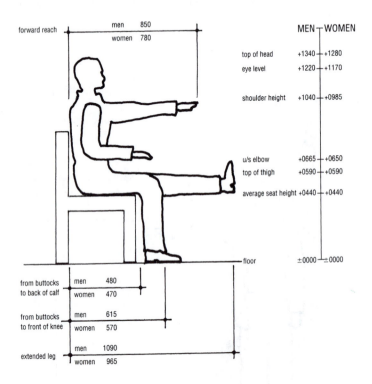

	men	850
forward reach	women	780

	MEN	WOMEN
top of head	+1340	+1280
eye level	+1220	+1170
shoulder height	+1040	+0985
u/s elbow	+0665	+0650
top of thigh	+0590	+0590
average seat height	+0440	+0440
floor	±0000	±0000

from buttocks to back of calf	men	480
	women	470
from buttocks to front of knee	men	615
	women	570
extended leg	men	1090
	women	965

Wheelchair

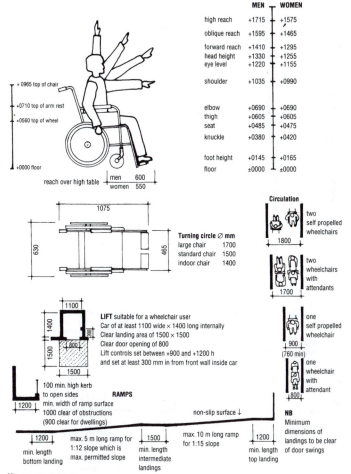

	MEN	WOMEN
high reach	+1715	+1575
oblique reach	+1595	+1465
forward reach	+1410	+1295
head height	+1330	+1255
eye level	+1220	+1155
shoulder	+1035	+0990
elbow	+0690	+0690
thigh	+0605	+0605
seat	+0485	+0475
knuckle	+0380	+0420
foot height	+0145	+0165
floor	±0000	±0000

+ 0965 top of chair
+0710 top of arm rest
+0560 top of wheel
+0000 floor

reach over high table
| men | 600 |
| women | 550 |

1075
630
465

Turning circle ⌀ mm
large chair	1700
standard chair	1500
indoor chair	1400

Circulation

two self propelled wheelchairs
1800

two wheelchairs with attendants
1700

one self propelled wheelchair
900 (760 min)

one wheelchair with attendant
800

1100
1400
300
800
1500
1500

LIFT suitable for a wheelchair user
Car of at least 1100 wide × 1400 long internally
Clear landing area of 1500 × 1500
Clear door opening of 800
Lift controls set between +900 and +1200 h
and set at least 300 mm in from front wall inside car

100 min. high kerb
to open sides   **RAMPS**
1200   min. width of ramp surface
1000 clear of obstructions
(900 clear for dwellings)

non-slip surface ↓

NB
Minimum dimensions of landings to be clear of door swings

1200
min. length bottom landing
max. permitted slope

max. 5 m long ramp for 1:12 slope which is max. permitted slope

1500
min. length intermediate landings

max. 10 m long ramp for 1:15 slope

1200
min. length top landing

All measurements in mm

Wheelchair access

Entrance lobbies & corridors – not in dwellings

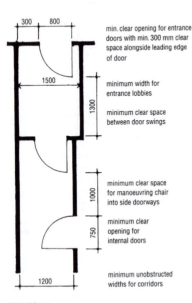

min. clear opening for entrance doors with min. 300 mm clear space alongside leading edge of door

minimum width for entrance lobbies

minimum clear space between door swings

minimum clear space for manoeuvring chair into side doorways

minimum clear opening for internal doors

minimum unobstructed widths for corridors

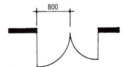

Double doors to have at least one leaf with 800 mm clear opening

NB:
Minimum clear opening for doorways means clear of door thickness, doorstops and any full length pull handle.
In practice this requires a 1000 mm doorset to achieve a minimum 800 mm clear opening.

Principal entrance doors, doors in frequent use and doors across circulation routes should have glazed panels at least between heights of +0900 and +1500 but preferably with the u/s at +0450.

NOTE
No frameless glass doors. No revolving doors unless very large as in airports. Door pulls and lever handles for easy opening. Any door closers to be adjusted to open with minimum force and close slowly.

Means of Escape
See Approved Document B of the Building Regulations and BS 5588: Part 8: 1999

Audience & Spectator Seating
Six wheelchair spaces or 1/100th of spectator seating whichever is greater should be provided.
Each space to be 1400 × 900 with unobstructed view and adjacent to seated companions. The space may be created by readily removing seats for the occasion.

DWELLINGS
NOTE; Part M of the Building Regulations applies only to NEW DWELLINGS, not to existing dwellings nor extensions to existing dwellings.

ENTRANCE DOORS to have min clear opening 775 mm
DOORWAYS in relation to CORRIDORS as table below:

Doorway – clear opening mm	Corridor – minimum width mm
750 or wider	900 when approach head-on
750	1200 when approach not head-on
775	1050 when approach not head-on
800	900 when approach not head-on

A WC must be provided in the entrance storey of a dwelling – or the principal storey if there are no habitable rooms at the entrance level.

This WC compartment must be min. 900 wide with an opening-out door and a clear space 750 deep in front of the pan clear of any wash basin. This WC may be part of a bathroom.

ACCESS to dwellings not steeper than 1:20 or ramps as shown on opposite page with dropped kerbs to any pavements.

ELECTRICAL SWITCHES & SOCKETS
Height of switches, socket outlets, bell pushes, telephone jacks, TV aerial sockets, etc. to be positioned between +0450 and +1200 above FFL.

Sources:
Approved Document M of the Building Regulations 2004
Metric Handbook
Designing for Accessibility

Furniture and fittings data

Living room

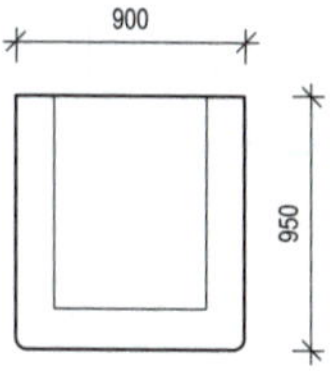

900
950
armchair

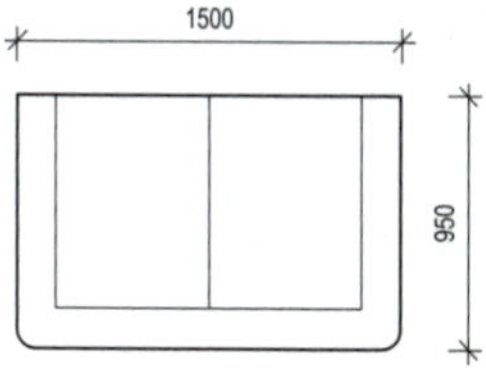

1500
950
two seater sofa

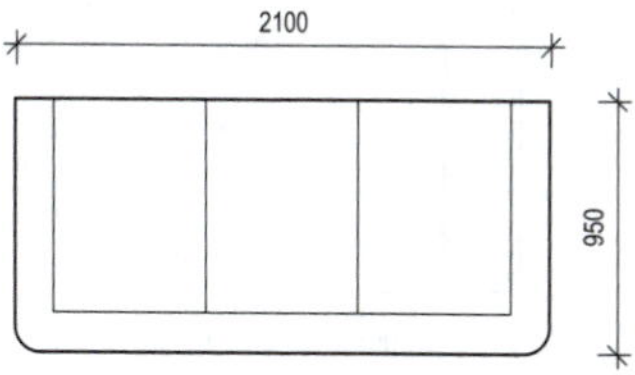

2100
950
three seater sofa

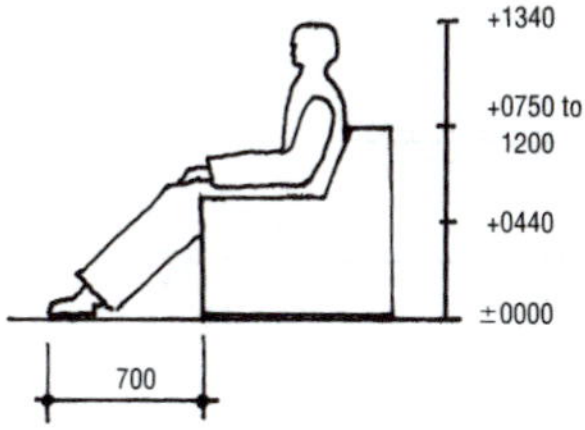

+1340
+0750 to 1200
+0440
±0000
700

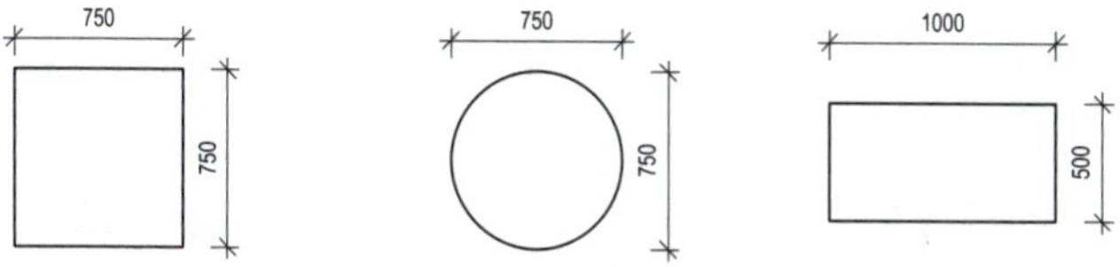

750
750
coffee tables – 400 (h)

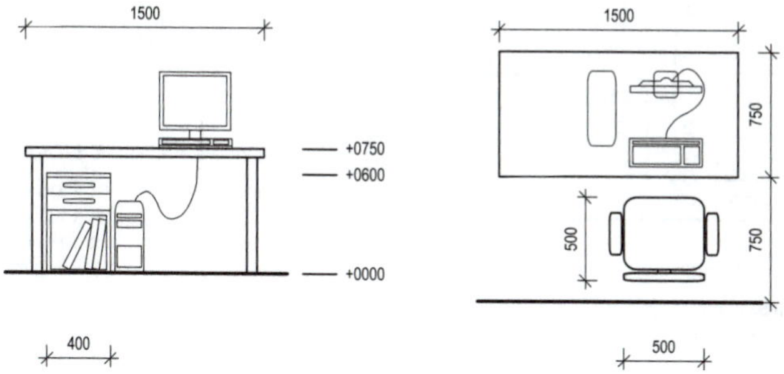

750
750

1000
500

1500
+0750
+0600
+0000
400

1500
750
500
750
500
home office desk and chair

All measurements in mm

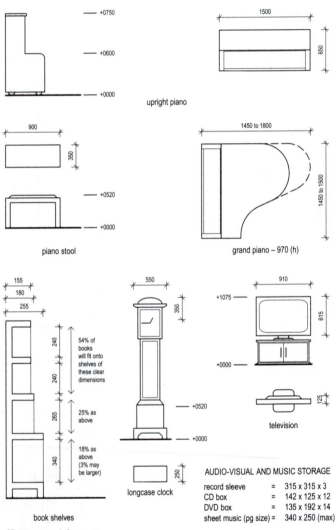

+0750
+0600
+0000

upright piano

1500
650

900
350
+0520
+0000

piano stool

1450 to 1800
1450 to 1500

grand piano – 970 (h)

155
180
255
240
240
265
340

54% of books will fit onto shelves of these clear dimensions

25% as above

18% as above (3% may be larger)

book shelves

550
350
+0520
+0000

longcase clock

250

910
+1075
615
+0000

television

125

AUDIO-VISUAL AND MUSIC STORAGE

record sleeve	=	315 x 315 x 3
CD box	=	142 x 125 x 12
DVD box	=	135 x 192 x 14
sheet music (pg size) =		340 x 250 (max)

All measurements in mm

Kitchen

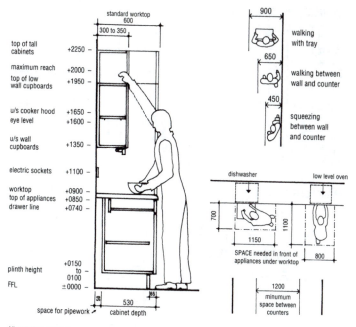

standard worktop
600

300 to 350

top of tall cabinets   +2250 –

maximum reach   +2000 –
top of low wall cupboards   +1950 –

u/s cooker hood   +1650 –
eye level   +1600 –

u/s wall cupboards   +1350 –

electric sockets   +1100 –

worktop   +0900 –
top of appliances   +0850 –
drawer line   +0740 –

plinth height   +0150 to 0100 –

FFL   ±0000 –

space for pipework ➚   cabinet depth

530

65

50

All measurements in mm

900

walking with tray

650

walking between wall and counter

450

squeezing between wall and counter

dishwasher   low level oven

700   1100

1150

SPACE needed in front of appliances under worktop   800

1200

minumum space between counters

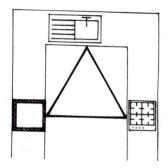

KITCHEN TRIANGLE
To achieve a compact yet workable kitchen the triangle formed by lines linking sink to cooker and refrigerator should total between 3.6 m and 6.6 m long with a maximum of 7.0 m. Avoid circulation through the triangle – particularly between sink and cooker which should not be more than 1.8 m apart.

Allow a minimum 400 mm between hob and sink and any tall cupboards for elbow room.

Cooker should not be positioned near door or in front of window.

Keep electric sockets well away from sink area.

Provide lighting over worktops.

Install extractor fan over hob.

CABINETS width dimensions

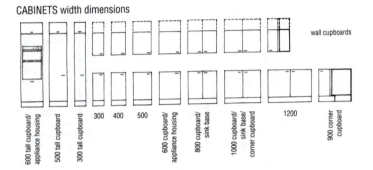

APPLIANCES

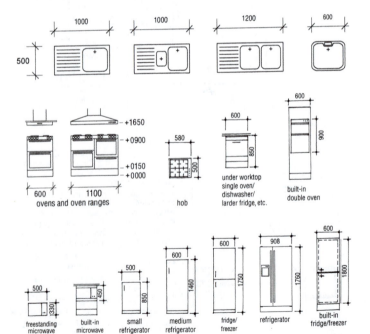

All measurements in mm

Dining room

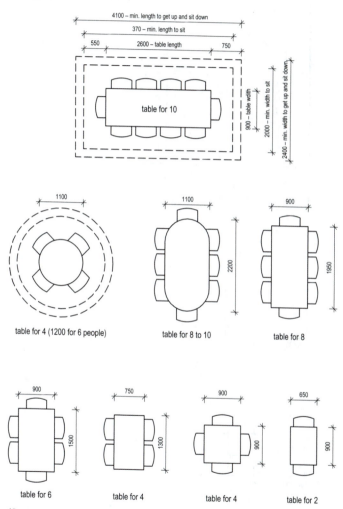

table for 4 (1200 for 6 people)

table for 8 to 10

table for 8

table for 6

table for 4

table for 4

table for 2

All measurements in mm

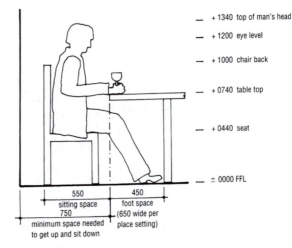

+ 1340 top of man's head

+ 1200 eye level

+ 1000 chair back

+ 0740 table top

+ 0440 seat

± 0000 FFL

550	450
sitting space	foot space
750	(650 wide per
minimum space needed	place setting)
to get up and sit down	

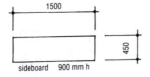

1500

450

sideboard   900 mm h

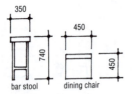

350

740

bar stool

450

450

dining chair

All measurements in mm

Bedroom

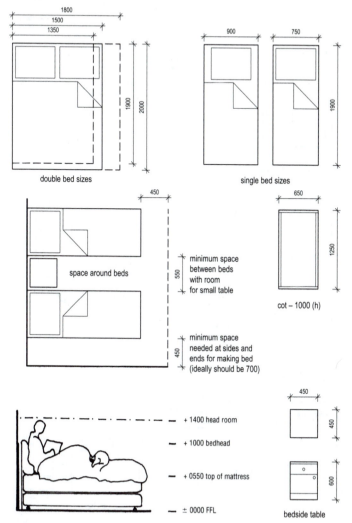

double bed sizes

single bed sizes

space around beds

minimum space between beds with room for small table

minimum space needed at sides and ends for making bed (ideally should be 700)

cot – 1000 (h)

+ 1400 head room

+ 1000 bedhead

+ 0550 top of mattress

± 0000 FFL

bedside table

All measurements in mm

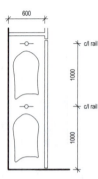

short clothes hanging space

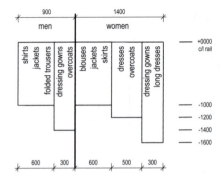

hanging clothes – average space requirements

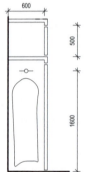

blanket
and hat
space

a rail at this
height will
accommodate
the longest
garment while
leaving space
under shorter
clothes for
shoes

long clothes hanging space

chest of drawers
900 (h)

wardrobe
1700 – 2100 (h)

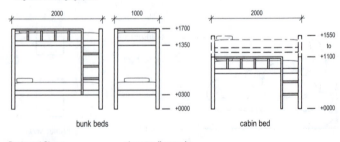

bunk beds

cabin bed

Boots and Shoes	size overall per pair
men's wellington boots	330 × 240 × 430 h
men's walking shoes	330 × 240 × 120 h
women's high heeled shoes	280 × 180 × 150 h
women's flat shoes	280 × 180 × 90 h

All measurements in mm

Bathroom

Bathroom

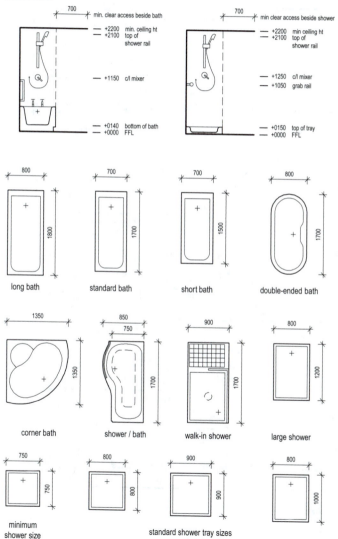

700 min. clear access beside bath	700 min clear access beside shower
+2200 min. ceiling ht	+2200 min ceiling ht
+2100 top of shower rail	+2100 top of shower rail
+1150 c/l mixer	+1250 c/l mixer
	+1050 grab rail
+0140 bottom of bath	+0150 top of tray
+0000 FFL	+0000 FFL

long bath — 800 × 1800

standard bath — 700 × 1700

short bath — 700 × 1500

double-ended bath — 800 × 1700

corner bath — 1350 × 1350

shower / bath — 850 / 750 × 1700

walk-in shower — 900 × 1700

large shower — 800 × 1200

minimum shower size — 750 × 750

standard shower tray sizes — 800 × 800, 900 × 900, 800 × 1000

All measurements in mm

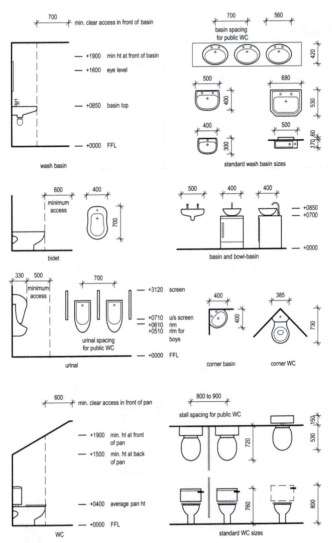

wash basin

standard wash basin sizes

bidet

basin and bowl-basin

urinal

corner basin   corner WC

WC

standard WC sizes

All measurements in mm

Miscellaneous data

Laundry and utility

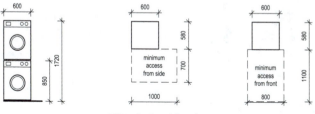

washing machine, dryer and other appliances

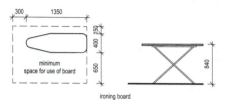

ironing board

Cleaning and refuse

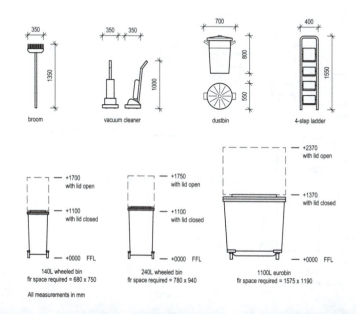

broom

vacuum cleaner

dustbin

4-step ladder

140L wheeled bin
flr space required = 680 x 750

240L wheeled bin
flr space required = 780 x 940

1100L eurobin
flr space required = 1575 x 1190

All measurements in mm

Hall and shed

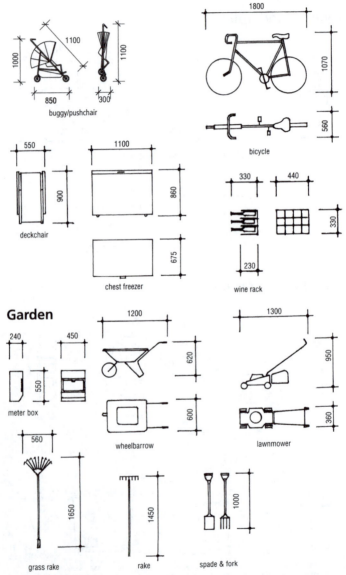

buggy/pushchair

bicycle

deckchair

chest freezer

wine rack

Garden

meter box

wheelbarrow

lawnmower

grass rake

rake

spade & fork

All measurements in mm

Domestic garages

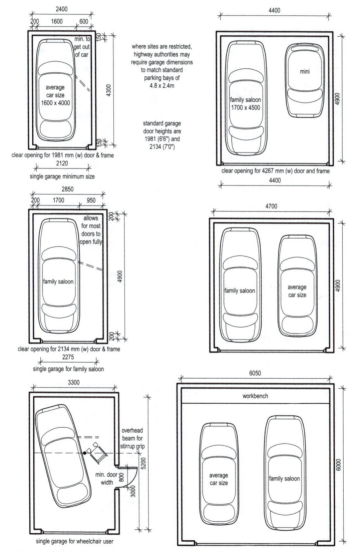

where sites are restricted, highway authorities may require garage dimensions to match standard parking bays of 4.8 x 2.4m

standard garage door heights are 1981 (6'6") and 2134 (7'0")

Single garage minimum size
2400 (200 / 1600 / 600)
average car size 1600 x 4000
4300
min. to get out of car
clear opening for 1981 mm (w) door & frame
2120

Single garage for family saloon
2850 (200 / 1700 / 950)
family saloon
4900
allows for most doors to open fully
clear opening for 2134 mm (w) door & frame
2275

Single garage for wheelchair user
3300
5200
overhead beam for stirrup grip
min. door width 800
3000

family saloon 1700 x 4500 / mini
4400
4900
clear opening for 4267 mm (w) door and frame
4400

family saloon / average car size
4700
4900

workbench
average car size / family saloon
6050
6000

All measurements in mm

Vehicle sizes and parking bay

VEHICLE	l	w*	h	radius
wheelchair – standard	1075	630	965	1500
bicycle	1800	560	1070	–
motor bicycle	2250	600	800	–
small car (Mini)	3050	1400	1350	4800
average sized car	4000	1600	1350	5250
family saloon	4500	1700	1460	5500
caravan – average touring	4500	2100	2500	–
Rolls Royce	5350	1900	1670	6350
hearse	5900	2000	1900	–
skip lorry	7000	2500*	3350	8700
dustcart – medium capacity	7400	2290*	4000	7000
fire engine – medium size	8000	2290*	4000	7600
furniture van	11 000	2500*	4230	10 050

The standard parking bay is 2400 x 4800 which will accomodate most European cars.

2800 x 5800 will accommodate American and other large cars.

3300 x 5200 is the required minimum for a disabled parking bay.

*widths exclude wing mirrors which may add 600 to 800 mm to the body width

Radii should not necessarily be considered as turning circles. Turning circles depend upon the speed the vehicle is travelling, the hand of the driver (left hand differs from right), and overhang, particularly at front and back of vehicle. Allow 1.2 m clear space both sides of carriageway to accommodate overhang.

Bicycle parking

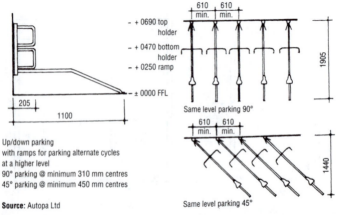

Up/down parking
with ramps for parking alternate cycles
at a higher level
90° parking @ minimum 310 mm centres
45° parking @ minimum 450 mm centres

Source: Autopa Ltd

All measurements in mm

Sanitary provision for public buildings

Summary of *minimum* facilities

There should be separate facilities for men and women.

Generally washbasins should be provided in equal numbers to WCs with one for every five urinals.

In most public buildings, a minimum of two WCs should be provided so that one may act as a reserve if the other is out of order.

Disabled toilets

Where there is space for only one toilet in a building, it should be a wheelchair accessible unisex toilet, wide enough to accommodate a standing height wash basin.

At least one wheelchair accessible WC should be provided at each location in a building where sanitary facilities are provided.

At least one WC cubicle should be provided in separate sex toilet accommodation for use by ambulant disabled people. In addition, where there are four or more WC cubicles in separate sex toilet accommodation, one of these should be an enlarged cubicle for use by people who need extra space.

Offices and shops

No. of persons	No. of WCs and basins
Up to 15	1
16–30	2
31–50	3
51–75	4
76–100	5
over 100	1 extra for each additional 25

There is no specific requirement for urinals, but if provided men's facilities may be reduced to:

No. of persons	No. of WCs and basins
Up to 20	1
21–45	2
46–75	3
76–100	4
over 100	1 extra for each additional 25

Factories

WCs	1 per 25 persons
Urinals	No specific requirement
Basins	1 per 20 persons for clean processes 1 per 10 persons for dirty processes 1 per 5 persons for injurious processes

Restaurants

	Men		*Women*	
WCs	Up to 400:	1 per 100	Up to 200:	2 per 100
	Over 400:	1 extra for each additional 250 or part thereof	Over 200:	1 extra for each additional 100 or part thereof

Urinals 1 per 25 persons

Basins 1 per WC and 1 per 5 urinals   1 per 2 WCs

Concert halls, theatres and similar buildings for public entertainment

	Men		*Women*	
WCs	Up to 250:	1	Up to 50:	2
	Over 250:	1 extra for each additional 500 or part thereof	50–100:	3
			Over 100:	1 extra for each additional 40 or part thereof

Urinals Up to 100: 2
       Over 100: 1 extra for each
       additional 80 or
       part thereof

Cinemas

	Men			*Women*	
WCs	Up to 250:	1		Up to 75:	2
	Over 250:	1 extra for each additional 500 or part thereof		76–100:	3
				Over 100:	1 extra for each additional 80 or part thereof

Urinals Up to 200: 2
       Over 200: 1 extra for each
       additional 100 or
       part thereof

WC compartments for disabled people

Wheelchair user

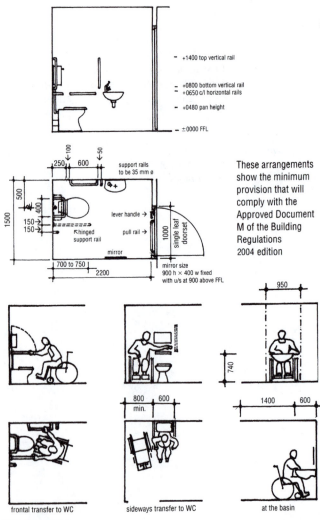

+1400 top vertical rail

+0800 bottom vertical rail
+0650 c/l horizontal rails

+0480 pan height

±0000 FFL

support rails to be 35 mm ø

lever handle →

pull rail →

single leaf doorset

↖hinged support rail

mirror

mirror size 900 h × 400 w fixed with u/s at 900 above FFL

These arrangements show the minimum provision that will comply with the Approved Document M of the Building Regulations 2004 edition

frontal transfer to WC

sideways transfer to WC

at the basin

All measurements in mm

Ambulant disabled user

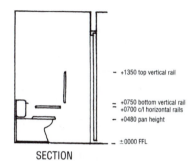

— +1350 top vertical rail

= +0750 bottom vertical rail
— +0700 c/l horizontal rails
— +0480 pan height

— ±0000 FFL

SECTION

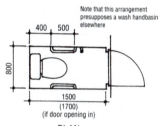

Note that this arrangement
presupposes a wash handbasin
elsewhere

400   500

800

1500
(1700)
(if door opening in)

PLAN

480

WC height

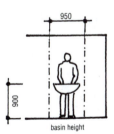

950

900

basin height

All measurements in mm

Trees for towns

Name	Ht m 25 yrs	Ht m mature	Location	Description
Acacia – false *Robinia pseudoacacia*	14	21	S	Open headed, rugged bark, thorny twigs. Ornamental and very drought and pollution tolerant
Ailanthus *Altissima* (tree of heaven)	18	21	S	Fast growing, imposing, with ash-like leaves. Female trees produce spectacular red fruit. Tolerant of industrial pollution
Almond *Prunus dulcis*	7	8	S	Pink or white flowers early spring, before dark green finely-toothed leaves and velvety green fruit
Birch – Himalayan *Betula utilis jaquemontii*	10	18	R	Vivid white bark, very strong upright stem. Forms a striking avenue. Casts only light shade
Catalpa *Bignonioides* (Indian bean)	10	12	P	Wide, domed crown, heart-shaped leaves, white flowers July, with beans in hot weather. Avoid cold/exposed sites. Good specimen tree
Cherry – gean* *Prunus avium* 'Plena'	12	15	S	One of the loveliest cherries, hardy, invariably producing masses of pure white drooping double flowers
Cherry – bird* *Prunus padus* 'Albertii'	7	14	S	Upright form of native 'bird cherry'. Racemes of white flowers in May, ideal for street planting
Chestnut – red *Aesculus × carnea* 'Briottii'	7	12	A	Slow growing, compact form with deep crimson flowers in June. Especially suitable for streets and avenues
Crab apple – *Malus floribunda*	5	9	S	Arching branches with early crimson flowers opening to white. Popular in streets and gardens. Scab and mildew resistant
Crab apple *Malus tschonoskii*	6	12	S	Strong growing conical habit, good for narrow streets. Flowers tinged pink. Excellent autumn colour
Hawthorn (May) *Crataegus × lavellei*	6	8	S	Dense headed, with long glossy dark green leaves until December. Orange fruit persisting until January
Lime – silver *Tilia tomentosa*	10	18	R	Pyramidal dense habit, with large dark green leaves with white felted undersides. Aphid-free, so no drips – good for car-parking areas
Maidenhair *Ginko biloba*	7	30	P	Slow growing superb specimen tree, pale green, small, fan-shaped leaves turning yellow in autumn. Pollution tolerant
Maple – field* *Acer campestre* 'Streetwise'	7	10	S	Neat form with dominant central leader and balanced crown. Brilliant autumn colour, very hardy

Trees for towns – continued

Name	Ht m 25 yrs	Ht m mature	Location	Description
Maple – silver *Acer saccarinum* 'Laciniatum'	15	25	R	Fast growing with pale green deeply cut leaves turning clear yellow in autumn. Good for wide roadsides. Not for windy sites
Mountain ash* *Sorbus* *aucuparia*	7	8	S	Strong growing with neat upright habit. Abundant bright orange berries in autumn. Good for street planting in grass verges
Oak – evergreen *Quercus ilex* (Holm oak)	7	28	P	Slow growing, broad-leaved evergreen specimen tree for parks. Good for coastal regions but not for coldest inland areas
Oak – scarlet *Quercus coccinea* 'Splendens'	15	18	P	Superb tree for large parks, with shiny dark green leaves. Spectacular crimson leaf colour in autumn. Requires lime-free soil
Plane – London *Platanus* × *hispanica*	12	28	S	Large, fast growing with boldly lobed leaves and flaking bark. Good street tree, tolerant of atmospheric pollution
Sycamore *Acer* *pseudoplatanus*	12	25	R	Fast growing. Wide-headed tree. Good for quick shelter in difficult situations and maritime sites. Tolerant of pollution
Tulip tree *Liriodendron* *tulipifera*	12	30	A	Fast growing, three-lobed leaves turning butter yellow. Good for avenues. Green/white July flowers on mature trees. Smoke tolerant
Whitebeam* *Sorbus aria* 'Majestica'	7	12	S	Handsome round head, large bright green leaves with vivid white undersides. Very hardy and smoke resistant

* = native tree
A = avenue
P = park
R = roadside
S = street

Trees listed above are recommended for various urban situations. Other varieties may be equally suitable, but check that they do not have invasive root runs, surface roots, brittle branches or cannot tolerate pollution.

All the trees listed, except the evergreen oak, are deciduous. Conifers are generally too large for most urban situations, and very few can cope with atmospheric pollution.

Sources: *The Hillier Designer's Guide to Landscape Plants*
Tree Planting Year 1973

Hedges

Name	Leaves	Flowers	Growth	Prune	Site	Description
Beech* *Fagus silvatica*	D	–	fast	Aug	W, C	Pale green leaves in spring turning to rich copper, persisting through winter
Berberis *Berberis darwinii*	E	✲	fast	July	Sh	Shiny dark green prickly foliage, orange flowers in May followed by blue berries
Box – common* *Buxus sempervirens*	E	–	slow	Aug–Sep	Sh	Bushy shrub with glossy dark green leaves. Use the variety 'Suffruticosa' for dwarf edging
Cotoneaster *Cotoneaster sinosii*	SE	✲	medium	Feb–Aug	Sh	Leathery deep green leaves, small white flowers in June and persistent red berries in autumn
Eleagnus *Eleagnus pungens* 'Maculata'	E	–	fast	April	W, Sh	Leathery leaves with bright gold splash on slightly prickly twigs making dense hedge
Escallonia *Escallonia* 'C. F. Ball'	E	✲	medium	Oct	St, W	Glossy dark green leaves and crimson flowers June–Oct. Good for seaside. Not for cold areas
Firethorn *Pyracantha* 'Watereri'	SE	✲	fast	May–July	Sh	Dense prickly stems, clusters of small white flowers in June and bright red fruits in autumn
Hawthorn (May)* *Crataegus monogyna*	D	✲	fast	July–Mar	W, Wet	Very thorny, white or pink blossom with small red haws in autumn
Holly* *Ilex aquifolium*	E	–	slow	Aug	Sh, W	Very dense prickly dark green leaves, bright red berries if both male and female plants adjacent
Hornbeam* *Carpinus betulus*	D	–	medium	Aug	Wet, Sh	Similar to beech, retaining coppery leaves in winter. Good for frost pockets and pleaching
Laurel *Prunus laurocerasus*	E	✲	medium	Aug	W, Sh	Large leathery glossy green leaves, long white flower spikes in April if buds not pruned
Photinia *P. × fraserii* 'Red Robin'	E	–	medium	Mar	–	Brilliant red new growth persisting until summer, reverting to dark green in winter
Privet *Ligustrum ovalifolium*	SE	–	fast	as nec.	Sh	Dense hedge with medium-sized green leaves, clusters of creamy white flowers in July
Yew* *Taxus baccata*	E	–	slow	Aug	W, C, Sh	Very hardy, dense dark green needles with bright red fruits attractive to birds

* = native species; E = evergreen; D = deciduous; SE = semi-evergreen; W = wind resistant;
C = will grow on chalk; Sh = will tolerate shade; St = will tolerate salt–laden winds.

Sources: Buckingham Nurseries Hedging catalogue
The Right Hedge for You

3
Structures

A good relationship is essential between an Architect and a Structural Engineer. In very rough terms, an architect says what a building looks like and the Structural Engineer make sure it doesn't fall down! There should be a feeling of a team, with both working to the same aim. An Architect needs to appreciate the structural challenges that the scheme imposes. An Engineer needs to appreciate the Architect's requirement for form and function. Both consultants aim to provide the client with what they want and within the budget available.

Design of structural elements can be carried out by permissible stress or ultimate limit state (ULS). Permissible stress limits the loading to a predetermined safe working stress, commonly known as elastic design as deformation of the element is recoverable (elastic). ULS factors the loads (partial safety factors) to be carried and the design is related to the potential ultimate failure of the structural element. Deflection of the structural element is limited to the elastic deformation of the material and the effect on what is being carried. There are different deflection limits for different materials.

Structural members are now generally designed to Eurocodes and are more suited for computer applications.

The structural Eurocodes are pan-European structural design codes for building and civil engineering works. They are replacing national standards.

Eurocodes are designed to create a unified approach throughout Europe with regards to construction design. Each Eurocode has a corresponding National Annex document. This documents and clarifies laws or standards applicable to each particular country.

Eurocodes

Eurocode 0	Basis of structural design	EN1990
Eurocode 1	Actions on structures	EN1991
Eurocode 2	Design of concrete structures	EN1992
Eurocode 3	Design of steel structures	EN1993
Eurocode 4	Design of composite steel and concrete structures	EN1994
Eurocode 5	Design of timber structures	EN1995
Eurocode 6	Design of masonry structures	EN1996
Eurocode 7	Geotechnical structures	EN1997
Eurocode 8	Design of structures for earthquake resistance	EN1998
Eurocode 9	Design of aluminium structures	EN1999

Examples given are using the less complicated permissible stress design based on Codes of Practice and British Standards that are being withdrawn in favour of the Eurocodes.

Information given is for guidance only and should give an indication of the size of structural members required to assist with developing a scheme. All structural elements should be checked by a qualified Chartered Structural Engineer for Building Regulation and construction purposes. Consultation with a Chartered Structural Engineer is advised at an early design stage to ensure structural feasibility of the proposals.

Foundation types

When determining the type and depth of foundations required for a low rise residential project it is necessary to take into account the founding material and type and distance of trees – both existing and proposed. Simple trial holes can sometimes be sufficient to determine the depth to a suitable bearing level. The usual minimum acceptable depth to the formation level of foundations is 1m, to be below the level of frost susceptibility. If the founding material is clay and there are trees close by it will be necessary to determine the potential for shrinkage/swelling of the clay (as the trees affect the moisture content of the clay) and compare this with the height and variety of trees. This can increase the depth of the foundations significantly.

Ground that is liable to swell following removal of existing trees can damage foundations and measures to protect footings and slab need to be put in hand. The use of a compressible layer against the face of the foundations is usual, as is provision of a void below the slab.

An experienced engineer will be able to advise of the type of foundations and any protection measures required.

Simple strip/trench fill foundations

This style of foundation is suitable for depths up to 2.5m (subject to stability of the sides of the excavations). It is recommended that trench fill be used for foundations deeper than a metre so that the concrete level for laying blocks, etc. is high enough not to require protection against collapse of the excavation sides.

Piled foundations

This style of foundation is suitable for building on filled or soft ground or ground requiring deep foundations to overcome the problems of swelling/shrinkage. Detailed site investigations are required to determine the ground conditions at depth and are best undertaken by a specialist geotechnical firm. The piles are used to support reinforced ground beams and/or slab.

Raft foundations

Rafts are used when the ground conditions are such that strip footings would need to be very wide or there is high risk of settlement. The raft distributes the loads over a very large area. It is essential that the ground conditions are uniform under the raft to eliminate the risk of differential settlement. It is necessary to ensure services entering or leaving have a flexible connection – such as rocker pipe in the foul drains.

Masonry structures

The majority of the existing building stock in the UK is masonry built and a large proportion of smaller scale new buildings are still built in masonry. Timber frame structure has a growing share, even though much is masonry clad.

Masonry structural design is based on Eurocode 6 BSEN 1996-1-2, partly derived from BS 5628.

Masonry structural solutions for small buildings include:

1 Insulated cavity walling: traditional cavity walls with masonry inner and outer leaves and tied cavities with full or partial insulation.
2 Insulated solid walling: usually aerated concrete or hollow clay block walling with external or internal insulation in addition.
3 Concrete-filled insulated shuttering systems (a masonry/ monolithic hybrid): tied shuttering 'blocks' of polystyrene or woodwool slab assembled dry and filled with pumped concrete; should maximize insulation externally to achieve some degree of thermal mass internally.

Masonry walling relies on bonding of the individual blocks or bricks to distribute loading and provide continuity in the wall, and on the mortar to distribute stress between individual units.

Traditional masonry design relies on 'normal' arrangement and proportions of solid walling to window and door openings; where design requirements require departures to achieve cantilevers, open corners, or simply very large openings, masonry design is hybridized usually with steel – occasionally concrete – beams and posts. Long panels of masonry may need stiffening with wind posts within the wall construction in order to resist lateral loads. Where floor joists span parallel to external walls (i.e. not built-in) it is necessary to strap the walls to the floors in order to give lateral stability against wind loads. Sometimes movement joints are introduced to control thermal and shrinkage movement. These joints need to be supported laterally – by wind posts or return walls. As a general rule movement joints should be at 6 m centres in blockwork and 12 m in clay brickwork.

The use of lime mortars can increase the flexibility of masonry construction and reduce the need for movement joints, but also reduces the strength of the wall panels for vertical and horizontal loads.

Timber frame construction

Timber frame is a method of construction, not a system of building. Timber frame construction uses softwood vertical studs and horizontal rails, and a wood-based panel sheathing to form a structural frame and transfer them to the foundations. The sheathing provides resistance to lateral wind loads (known as racking resistance). At openings, such as doors and windows, the vertical loads are carried by timber lintels over the opening and through additional supports, known as cripple studs, at each end of the lintel. The outer cladding provides decoration and weather protection. The exterior cladding is non-load bearing, although it may contribute to wind resistance; it is used to weatherproof the building and provide the desired external appearance. Thermal insulation is usually incorporated in the spaces between the studs of external walls and various protective membrane materials may also be required, depending on the design of the wall.

Wall panels in the UK are usually factory-produced. Their size and degree of prefabrication varies between:

- Open panels comprising studs, rails, sheathing and an external breather membrane. The thermal insulation, internal vapour control membrane (where needed) and lining are all installed on site, and
- Closed panels as above but with insulation, protective membranes, linings, external joinery and sometimes even services already installed.

Additional layers of insulation and board materials are added to provide higher levels of sound insulation and additional fire protection where required, e.g. party walls between houses and party walls between flats.

The choice of floor and roof construction for timber frame is the same as for other building types. Ground floors can be of concrete or timber. Intermediate floors are of timber joists or prefabricated panels. The joists or prefabricated panels are usually installed on top of the wall panels and provide a platform from which to build subsequent storeys – hence the term *platform frame*.

Roofs are frequently trussed rafters, but other types are also suitable, including prefabricated panel types.

Completion of a weatherproof shell for a two-storey house using manual erection with a team of four men typically can be achieved within a working week and using crane erection, in one or two days. Once the timber frame shell is completed, work can continue inside the building regardless of weather conditions. Depending upon the degree of prefabrication of the timber frame panels, this may comprise installation of:

insulation, vapour control layer and wall linings in external walls; internal non-load bearing walls; floor decking and ceilings; internal joinery; services and fittings

Externally, the cladding is applied. Brick or stone cladding is erected as a separate skin, linked to the timber frame studs by stainless steel wall ties. Differential movement is likely to occur between the timber frame and brick or block cladding and the design detailing must make allowance for this. Tile and timber cladding is fixed on timber battens fixed through to the studs of the wall panels.

External joinery is fixed into openings in the timber frame, not into the cladding.

Roof slates or tiles are fixed to tiling battens and external works completed.

Source: *Timber Frame Construction, TRADA. www.trada.co.uk*

Weights of materials (for further information, see BS 648)

Material	Description	Quantity of unit	kg/m²	kg/m³
aluminium	cast			2770
aluminium roofing	longstrip	0.8 mm	3.70	
asphalt roofing	with vapour barrier	20 mm	47.00	
ballast	loose, graded			1600
bituminous felt roofing	3 layers + vapour barrier		11.10	
blockboard	sheet	18 mm	10.50	
blockwork	high strength	100 mm	220.00	
	aerated	100 mm	64.00	
	lightweight	100 mm	58.00	
	foundation	255 mm	197.00	
brass	cast			8425
brickwork	blue	115 mm	276.60	2405
	engineering	115 mm	250.00	2165
	sand/cement	115 mm	240.00	2085
	London stock	115 mm	212.00	1845
	fletton			1795
calcium silicate board	sheet	6 mm	5.80	
cement				1440
chalk				2125
chipboard	flooring grade C4	18 mm	13.25	
	furniture grade C1A	18 mm	11.75	
chippings	flat roof finish	1 layer	4.75	
clay	undisturbed			1925
concrete	reinforced 2% steel			2400
	plain			2300
concreting ballast				1760
copper	cast			8730
copper roofing	longstrip	0.6 mm	5.70	
cork	granulated			80
cork flooring	tiles	3.2 mm	3.00	
cork insulation	board	50 mm	6.50	
felt	roofing underlay		1.30	
glass	clear float	4 mm	10.00	
	clear float	6 mm	15.00	
	clear float	10 mm	25.00	
glass wool	quilt	100 mm	1.02	
gravel	loose			1600
hardboard	medium	6.4 mm	3.70	
hardboard	standard	3.2 mm	2.35	

Weights of materials – continued

Material	Description	Quantity of unit	kg/m²	kg/m³
hardwood	greenheart			1040
	oak			720
	iroko, teak			660
	mahogany			530
hardwood flooring	boards	23 mm	16.10	
iron	cast			7205
lead	cast			11322
	sheet	code 4	20.40	
	sheet	code 7	35.72	
lime	lump			705
	quick			880
linoleum	sheet	3.2 mm	4.50	
MDF	sheet	18 mm	13.80	
mortar	lime			1680
parquet	flooring	15 mm	7.00	
partitions	plastered brick	115 + 25 mm	250.00	
	plastered block	100 + 25 mm	190.00	
	p/b & skim on timber studs	100 + 25 mm	120.00	
patent glazing	alum. bars @ 600 mm c/c	single	19.00	
	alum. bars @ 600 mm c/c	double	35.00	
pea shingle				1500
perspex	corrugated sheets		4.90	
plaster	lightweight – 2 coat	13 mm	10.20	
	hardwall – 2 coat	13 mm	11.60	
	lath and plaster		29.30	
plasterboard	gyproc wallboard	9.5 mm	9.00	
	plaster skimcoat	3 mm	2.20	
plywood	sheet	6 mm	4.10	
polystyrene	expanded, sheet	50 mm	0.75	
PVC roofing	single ply membrane	2 mm	2.50	
quarry tiles	laid in mortar	12.5 mm	32.00	
roofing tiles	clay – plain	100 mm gauge	77.00	
	clay – single pantile	315 mm gauge	42.00	
	concrete – double roman	343 mm gauge	45.00	
	concrete – flat slate	355 mm gauge	51.00	
rubber stud flooring	tiles	4 mm	5.90	

Weights of materials – continued

Material	Description	Quantity of unit	kg/m²	kg/m³
sand	dry			1600
sarking	felt		1.30	
scalpings				2000
screed	cement/sand	50 mm	108.00	
shingle	coarse, graded, dry			1842
shingles	roof, untreated	95 mm gauge	8.09	
	tantalized	95 mm gauge	16.19	
slate	slab	25 mm	70.80	
slate roofing	best	4 mm	31.00	
	medium strong	5 mm	35.00	
	heavies	6 mm	40.00	
snow	fresh			96
	wet, compact			320
softboard	sheet	12.5 mm	14.45	
softwood	pitch pine, yew			670
	spruce			450
	western red cedar			390
softwood flooring	boards	22 mm	12.20	
soil	compact			2080
	loose			1440
stainless steel roofing	longstrip	0.4 mm	4.00	
steel	mild			7848
	sheet	1.3 mm	10.20	
stone	Bath			2100
	granite			2660
	marble			2720
	slate			2840
	York			2400
stone chippings				1760
tarmac		25 mm	53.70	
terrazzo	paving	16 mm	34.20	
thatch	including battens	300 mm	41.50	
timber	see hardwood softwood			
vinyl flooring	tiles	2 mm	4.00	
water				1000
weatherboarding	softwood	19 mm	7.30	
		25 mm	8.55	
woodwool	slabs	50 mm	36.60	
zinc	cast			6838
zinc roofing	longstrip	0.8 mm	5.70	

Newtons

The unit of force, the *newton*, is derived from the unit of mass through the relationship that force is equal to mass times the gravitational pull of 9.81 metres *per second per second* (9.81 m/s^2), in the direction of the force, e.g. 1 kilogram f = 9.81 newtons.

For approximate purposes 100 kgf = 1 kN.

Alternatively one newton is that force which, if applied to a mass of one kilogram, gives that mass an acceleration of one metre *per second per second* (1 m/s^2) in the direction of the force, so 1 N = 1 kg $\times$ 1 m/s^2.

When calculating the weight of materials for structures, the kilograms must be multiplied by 9.81 to get the equivalent figure in newtons (or 9.81 $\div$ 1000 for kN).

As a general rule, the following expressions are used:

superimposed loads	kN/m^2
mass loads	kg/m^2 or kg/m^3
stress	N/mm^2
bending moment	kNm
shear	kN

1 N/mm	=	1 kN/m
1 N/mm^2	=	1 $\times$ 10^3 kN/m^2
1 kNm	=	1 $\times$ 10^6 Nmm

Imposed loads

Imposed floor loads (for further information, see BS 6399 Part 1)

Floor type	Distributed load kN/m²*	Concentrated load kN*
Houses and blocks of flats not more than three storeys, no more than four self-contained units per floor	1.5	1.4
Bedrooms and dormitories except for those in single family dwelling units and in hotels and motels	1.5	1.8
Hotels bedrooms, hospital wards, toilet areas	2.0	1.8
Public, institutional and communal dining rooms, lounges, cafes and restaurants	2.0	2.7
Billiard rooms		
Operating theatres, X-ray rooms, utility rooms, reading rooms with no book storage	2.0	4.5
Offices for general use	2.5	2.7
Garages for vehicles under 2500 kg	2.5	9.0
Classrooms, chapels, banking halls	3.0	2.7
Hotel kitchens and laundries, laboratories	3.0	4.5
Offices with fixed computing equipment	3.5	4.5
Assembly buildings with fixed seating	4.0	3.6
Shop floors for retailing	4.0	3.6
Hotel bars	5.0	3.6
Assembly buildings without fixed seating, gymnasia, dance halls	5.0	3.6
Factories, workshops and similar buildings	5.0	4.5
Garages, parking and workshops for vehicles exceeding 2500 kg	To be determined for specific use	
Boiler rooms, plant rooms including weight of machinery	7.5	4.5
Bookstores, warehouses (per metre of storage height)	2.4	7.0
Stationery stores (per metre of storage height)	4.0	9.0

Imposed floor loads – continued

Floor type		Distributed load kN/m^2*	Concentrated load kN*
Corridors, hallways and aisles, etc. in institutional-type buildings (not subjected to crowds or wheeled vehicles), hostels, guest houses, residential clubs and communal areas in flats over three storeys. Foot traffic only		3.0	4.5
Stairs and landings as above		3.0	4.0
Corridors, hallways and aisles, etc. in all other buildings including hotels, motels and institutional buildings. Foot traffic only		4.0	4.5
Stairs and landings as above		4.0	4.0
Corridors, hallways and aisles, etc. in all other buildings including hotels, motels and institutional buildings. Foot traffic only		5.0	4.5
Balconies	Single family dwelling units and communal areas in blocks of flats with limited use (no greater than three storeys)	1.5	1.4
	Guest houses, residential clubs and communal areas in blocks of flats over three storeys	Same as rooms to which they have access, but with a minimum of 3.0	1.5/m run concentrated at the outer edge
	All others	Same as rooms to which they have access, but with a minimum of 4.0	1.5/m run concentrated at the outer edge

* Whichever produces the greater stress or deflection

Reduction in total distributed imposed floor load

Number of floors including roof carried by member	1	2	3	4	5–10	10+
Percentage reduction in total distributed load on all floors carried by member	0	10	20	30	40	50 max
Area supported m^2	40	80	120	160	200	250
Percentage reduction in total distributed imposed load	0	5	10	15	20	25 max

Imposed roof loads (for further information, see BS 6399 Part 3)

Roof type	Comments	Distributed load kN/m²*		Concentrated load kN*
All roofs	Where access is needed in addition to that needed for cleaning and repair	1.5	or	1.8
Flat roofs and sloping roofs up to 30°	Where no access is needed except for cleaning and repair	0.6	or	0.9
Roof slopes between 30° and 60° (α°) measured on plan	Where no access is needed except for cleaning and repair	0.6 (60 − α)/30	or	0.9
Roof slopes 60° or more	0	0		0.9

* Whichever produces the greater stress

Where access is needed for cleaning and repair, these loads assume spreader boards will be used during work on fragile roofs.

For buildings in areas of high snowfall, snow loading should be taken into consideration. The snow loading is a function of location, altitude and roof pitch. For buildings with parapets, valleys or changes in roof level, there can be local accumulation of snow from drifting. See BS 6399 Part 3 for further guidance.

Fire resistance

Minimum periods for elements of structure (minutes)

Building type		Basement storey		Ground and upper storeys			
		more than 10m deep	less than 10m deep	less than 5m high	less than 20m high	less than 30m high	more than 30m high
Flats and maisonettes		90	60	30[a]	60[c]	90[b]	120[b]
Houses		n/a	30[a]	30[a]	60[g]	n/a	n/a
Institutional[d], residential		90	60	30[a]	60	90	120[e]
Offices	without sprinklers	90	60	30[a]	60	90	X
	with sprinklers	60	60	30[a]	30[a]	60	120[e]
Shops & Commercial	without sprinklers	90	60	60	60	90	X
	with sprinklers	60	60	30[a]	60	60	120[e]
Assembly & Recreational	without sprinklers	90	60	60	60	90	X
	with sprinklers	60	60	30[a]	60	60	120[e]
Industrial	without sprinklers	120	90	60	90	120	X
	with sprinklers	90	60	30[a]	60	90	120[e]
Storage & other non-residential	without sprinklers	120	90	60	90	120	X
	with sprinklers	90	60	30[a]	60	90	120[e]
Car parks for light vehicles	open sided park	n/a	n/a	15[f]	15[f]	15[f]	60
	any other park	90	60	30[a]	60	90	120[e]

X = not permitted

a   Increased to 60 minutes for compartment walls separating buildings.

b   Reduced to 30 minutes for any floor within a maisonette, but not if that floor contributes to the support of the building.

c   As b above and, in the case of existing houses, of no more than three storeys being converted into flats. This may be reduced to 30 minutes providing the means of escape conform to section 2 of requirement B1.

d   Multi-storey hospitals should have a minimum 60 minutes standard.

e   Reduced to 90 minutes for elements not forming part of the structural frame.

f   As 'a' above and increased to 30 minutes for elements protecting the means of escape.

Source: *Building Regulations Approved Document B vol 2 – Table A2.*

Bending moments and beam formulae

Type of beam	Loading diagram	Maximum bending moment	Maximum shear	Maximum deflection d
Freely supported with central load		$\dfrac{WL}{4}$	$\dfrac{WL}{2}$	$dc = \dfrac{WL^3}{48EI}$
Freely supported with distributed load		$\dfrac{WL}{8}$	$\dfrac{W}{2}$	$dc = \dfrac{WL^3}{384EI}$
Freely supported with triangular load		$\dfrac{WL}{6}$	$\dfrac{W}{2}$	$dc = \dfrac{WL^3}{60EI}$
Fixed both ends with central load		$\dfrac{WL}{8}$	$\dfrac{W}{2}$	$dc = \dfrac{WL^3}{192EI}$
Fixed both ends with distributed load		$\dfrac{WL}{12}$	$\dfrac{W}{2}$	$dc = \dfrac{WL^3}{384EI}$
One end fixed, the other end freely supported		$\dfrac{WL}{8}$	$SA = \dfrac{5W}{8}$ $SB = \dfrac{3W}{8}$	$d = \dfrac{WL^3}{185EI}$ at $x = 0.42\,L$
Cantilever with end load		WL	W	$dB = \dfrac{WL^3}{3EI}$
Cantilever with distributed load		$\dfrac{WL}{12}$	W	$dB = \dfrac{WL^3}{8EI}$

W = total load
w = kN/m
L = length
E = modulus of elasticity
I = moment of inertia
S = shear

↓ = point load
▥ = distributed load
↑ = free support
⌇ = fixed support

Safe loads on subsoils (BS 8004: 1986)

Presumed allowable bearing values under static loading

Subsoil	Type	Bearing kN/m^2
Rocks	Strong igneous and gneissic rocks in sound condition	10 000
	Strong limestones and sandstones	4000
	Schists and slates	3000
	Strong shales, mudstones and siltstones	2000
Non-cohesive soils	Dense gravel, dense sand and gravel	>600
	Medium dense gravel, medium dense sand and gravel	<200 to 600
	Loose gravel, loose sand and gravel	<200
	Compact sand	>300
	Medium dense sand	100 to 200
	Loose sand	<100
Cohesive soils	Very stiff boulder clays, hard clays	300 to 600
	Stiff clays	150 to 300
	Firm clays	75 to 150
	Soft clays and silts	<75

Notes:
1 These values are for preliminary design only. Foundations always require site investigation first.
2 No values are given for very soft clays and silts; peat and organic soils; made-up or filled ground as presumably these would be thought unsuitable for any building.
3 Values for **Rocks** assume that foundations are carried down to unweathered rock.
4 Widths of foundations for **Non-cohesive soils** to be not less than one metre.
5 **Cohesive soils** are susceptible to long-term settlement.
6 Generally foundations should not be less than 1.0 to 1.3 m depth to allow for soil swell or shrink, frost and vegetation attack.

Timber (BS 5268: Part 2: 1996)

Grade stress and moduli of elasticity for various strength classes

Strength Class	Bending parallel to grain N/mm²	Tension parallel to grain N/mm²	Compression parallel to grain N/mm²	Compression* perpendicular to grain N/mm²		Shear parallel to grain N/mm²	Modulus of elasticity		Density average Kg/m³
							Mean N/mm²	minimum N/mm²	
C14	4.1	2.5	5.2	2.1	1.6	0.60	6800	4600	350
C16	5.3	3.2	6.8	2.2	1.7	0.67	8800	5800	370
C18	5.8	3.5	7.1	2.2	1.7	0.67	9100	6000	380
C22	6.8	4.1	7.5	2.3	1.7	0.71	9700	6500	410
C24	7.5	4.5	7.9	2.4	1.9	0.71	10800	7200	420
TR26	10.0	6.0	8.2	2.5	2.0	1.10	11000	7400	450
C27	10.0	6.0	8.2	2.5	2.0	1.10	12300	8200	450
C30	11.0	6.6	8.6	2.7	2.2	1.20	12300	8200	460
C35	12.0	7.2	8.7	2.9	2.4	1.30	13400	9000	480
C40	13.0	7.8	8.7	3.0	2.6	1.40	14500	10000	500
D30	9.0	5.4	8.1	2.8	2.2	1.40	9500	6000	640
D35	11.0	6.6	8.6	3.4	2.6	1.70	10000	6500	670
D40	12.5	7.5	12.6	3.9	3.0	2.00	10800	7500	700
D50	16.0	9.6	15.2	4.5	3.5	2.20	15000	12600	780
D60	18.0	10.8	18.0	5.2	4.0	2.40	18500	15600	840
D70	23.0	13.8	23.0	6.0	4.6	2.60	21000	18000	1080

Notes:

C14–C40 are for softwoods

C16 is considered to be sufficient for general use (former classification = SC3)

C24 is a good general quality timber (former classification = SC4)

TR26 is for manufactured softwood trusses

D30–40 are for hardwoods

* Where the specification prohibits wane at bearing areas, use the higher value

Rectangular timber beam formula (uniformly distributed load)

1 Obtain the total imposed and dead loading for the beam (W) in kN.
2 Select a strength class of timber to define bending stress (σ) in N/mm^2 and modulus of elasticity (E) in N/mm^2.
3 Choose breadth of beam (b) in mm.
4 Calculate the maximum bending moment (M) in kNm.

Check stress (σ):

$$M = \frac{WL}{8}$$

$$M = \sigma Z, \text{ and } Z = \frac{bd^2}{6}$$

$$\therefore \quad M = \sigma\frac{bd^2}{6} \text{ or } db^2 = \frac{6M}{\sigma}$$

hence $d = \sqrt{\dfrac{WL \times 6 \times 10^6}{8 \times b \times \sigma}}$

Check deflection (δ):

For spans up to 4.67 m, maximum deflection allowable is span × 0.003. Above 4.67 m deflection is limited to 14 mm for domestic floors.

For a single member, use E_{min}

$$\delta = L \times 0.003 = \frac{5WL^3}{384EI}, \text{ and } I = \frac{bd^3}{6}$$

hence $d = \sqrt{\dfrac{WL^2 \times 52.08 \times 10^3}{E \times b}}$

The depth of the section to use will be the greater of those calculated for stress or deflection.

Where:
b = breadth of beam, mm; d = depth of beam, mm; f = flexural stress, N/mm^2; L = clear span, m; M = bending moment, kNm; W = total load, kN; Z = section modulus, mm^3; I = second moment of area, mm^4; E = modulus of elasticity, N/mm^2

Timber floor joists

(For further information [such as spans for C24] see TRADA Span tables for solid timber members in floors, ceiling and roofs [excluding trussed rafter roofs] for dwellings).

Maximum clear spans for C16 grade softwood (m)

Dead load (kN/m²)	<0.25		0.25 to 0.50		0.50 to 1.25	
Joist centres (mm)	400	600	400	600	400	600
Joist size (b × d) (mm)	**Maximum Clear Span (m)**					
47 × 97	2.03	1.59	1.93	1.47	1.67	1.23
47 × 120	2.63	2.26	2.52	2.05	2.22	1.66
47 × 145	3.17	2.77	3.04	2.59	2.70	2.15
47 × 170	3.71	3.21	3.55	3.00	3.14	2.56
47 × 195	4.25	3.64	4.07	3.41	3.56	2.91
47 × 220	4.75	4.08	4.58	3.82	3.99	3.26
75 × 120	3.07	2.69	2.94	2.57	2.65	2.29
75 × 145	3.70	3.24	3.54	3.10	3.19	2.78
75 × 170	4.32	3.79	4.14	3.63	3.73	3.23
75 × 195	4.87	4.34	4.72	4.15	4.27	3.67
75 × 220	5.32	4.82	5.15	4.67	4.77	4.11

Dead loads exclude the self-weight of the joist.
The table allows for an imposed load of not more than 1.5 kN/m² and a concentrated load of 1.4 kN, but not for concentrated loads from trimmers, partitions, etc.
All joists beneath a bath should be doubled.

Floor decking (See NHBC Standards 6.4 –D14)

Joist centres (mm)	400	450	600
	Thickness of decking (mm)		
T & G softwood boarding	16	16	19
Chipboard	18	18	22
Plywood	12	12	16
Oriented strand board	15	15	18/19

Note: Oriented strand board should be laid with the stronger axis at right angles to the support.

Timber ceiling joists

(For further information [such as spans for C24] see TRADA Span tables for solid timber members in floors, ceiling and roofs [excluding trussed rafter roofs] for dwellings.)

Maximum clear spans for C16 grade softwood (m)

Dead load (kN/m²)	<0.25		0.25 to 0.50	
Joist centres (mm)	400	600	400	600
Joist sizes (b × d) (mm)	**Maximum Clear Span (m)**			
38 × 72	1.15	1.11	1.11	1.06
38 × 97	1.74	1.67	1.67	1.58
38 × 120	2.33	2.21	2.21	2.08
38 × 145	2.98	2.82	2.82	2.62
38 × 170	3.66	3.43	3.43	3.18
38 × 195	4.34	4.05	4.05	3.74
38 × 220	5.03	4.68	4.68	4.30
47 × 72	1.27	1.23	1.23	1.18
47 × 97	1.93	1.84	1.84	1.74
47 × 120	2.56	2.43	2.43	2.27
47 × 145	3.27	3.08	3.08	2.87
47 × 170	4.00	3.74	3.74	3.46
47 × 195	4.73	4.41	4.41	4.07
47 × 220	5.47	5.08	5.08	4.67

The table allows for an imposed load of not more than 0.25 kN/m² and a concentrated load of 0.9 kN.
No account has been taken for other loads such as water tanks or trimming around chimneys, hatches, etc.
Minimum bearing for ceiling joists should be 35 mm.

Engineered joists and beams

Engineered timber joists (TJI joists) allow for increased spans and reduced shrinkage in timber floor structures as well as more efficient use of material. Their higher cost means they compete with sawn timber only on larger spans and larger projects; typical savings in cross-section of section for a given joist depth as compared to sawn C24 softwood would be 20 to 30 per cent.

Parallam Beams (parallel strand lumber) have a vastly improved permissible stress and modulus of elasticity allowing of the order of 50 per cent increase in span on equivalent section of C24 softwood.

Prefabricated Timber Trusses

For simple rectangular roofs with flat ceilings at eaves level, a prefabricated roof is the easiest solution. Trusses are design and erected by a truss manufacture. The inner leaf of the cavity wall is used to support the trusses. Truss centres are generally at 600 and there is a nominal allowance for access into the ceiling void. The internal arrangement of timbers makes it hard to store items in the loft space. Access should be restricted to maintenance (such as dealing with cables, plumbing, etc). An allowance for water tanks is generally made.

More complicated shapes such as intersecting roofs can be achieved, as well as hip ends. Multiple trusses are used to support monopitch trusses forming the hips.

For further information see http://www.tra.org.uk (The Trussed Rafter Association).

Brickwork and blockwork (BS 5628: Part 1: 1992)

Slenderness ratio of load bearing brickwork and blockwork walls

The slenderness ratio involves the thickness and height and the conditions of support to the top and bottom of a wall, pier or column. It is defined as effective height ÷ effective thickness.

Effective height of walls

When the floor or roof spans at right angles to the wall with sufficient bearing and anchorage:

effective height = ¾ of actual height between centres of supports

For concrete floors having a bearing on walls, irrespective of the direction of span:

effective height = ¾ of actual height

For floors or roof spanning parallel with wall without bearing (but wall restrained to floor/roof plane with lateral restraint straps):

effective height = actual height

For walls with no lateral support at top:

effective height = 1½ times actual height

Effective thickness of walls

For solid walls:

effective thickness = actual thickness

For cavity walls:

effective thickness = 2/3 × (thickness of one leaf + thickness of the other) or thickness of outer or inner leaf, whichever is greatest.

The slenderness ratio should never exceed 27, except in cases of walls less than 90 mm thick where it should not exceed 20.

For more information see Building Regulation Approved Document A.

Concrete (BS 8500-1: 2002)

The grade of concrete required depends on several factors such as exposure, chemical attack and whether the concrete is reinforced. The cover to the reinforcement depends on the grade of concrete, exposure and potential chemical attack (from de-icing salts and ground water).

The following information is extracted from Table A.7 of BS 8500-1: 2002 (Guidance on the selection of designated and standardized prescribed concrete in housing and other applications). For concrete subjected to sulphates and hydrostatic head of ground water, refer to a Chartered Structural Engineer.

Application (concrete containing embedded metal should be treated as reinforced)	Designated concrete	Standardized prescribed concrete
Foundations		
Blinding and mass concrete fill	GEN1	ST2
Strip footings	GEN1	ST2
Mass concrete footings	GEN1	ST2
Trench fill foundations	GEN1	ST2
Fully buried reinforced foundations	RC30	N/A
General applications		
Kerb bedding and backing	GEN0	ST1
Drainage works to give immediate support	GEN1	ST2
Other drainage works	GEN1	ST2
Oversite below suspended slabs	GEN1	ST2
Floors		
House floors with no embedment metal		
– Permanent finish to be added, e.g. screed of floating floor	GEN1	ST2
– No permanent finish to be added e.g. carpeted	GEN2	ST3
Garage floors with no embedded metal	GEN3	ST4
Wearing surface: light foot and trolley traffic	RC30	ST4
Wearing surface: general industrial	RC40	N/A
Wearing surface: heavy industrial	RC50	N/A
Paving		
House drives and domestic parking	PAV1	N/A
Heavy-duty external paving with rubber tyre vehicles	PAV2	N/A

Steelwork

Universal beams – Safe distributed loads (kN) for grade 43 steel

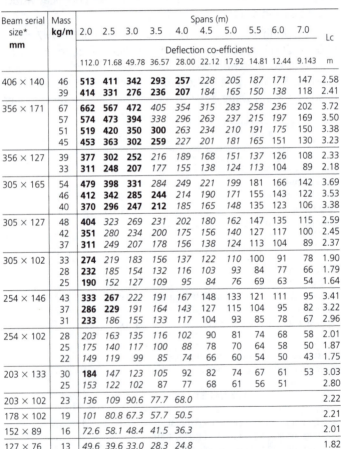

Beam serial size* mm	Mass kg/m	Spans (m)										Lc
		2.0	2.5	3.0	3.5	4.0	4.5	5.0	5.5	6.0	7.0	
		Deflection co-efficients										
		112.0	71.68	49.78	36.57	28.00	22.12	17.92	14.81	12.44	9.143	m
406 × 140	46	**513**	**411**	**342**	**293**	**257**	228	205	187	171	147	2.58
	39	**414**	**331**	**276**	**236**	**207**	184	165	150	138	118	2.41
356 × 171	67	**662**	**567**	**472**	405	354	315	283	258	236	202	3.72
	57	**574**	**473**	**394**	338	296	263	237	215	197	169	3.50
	51	**519**	**420**	**350**	**300**	263	234	210	191	175	150	3.38
	45	**453**	**363**	**302**	**259**	227	201	181	165	151	130	3.23
356 × 127	39	**377**	**302**	**252**	216	189	168	151	137	126	108	2.33
	33	**311**	**248**	**207**	177	155	138	124	113	104	89	2.18
305 × 165	54	**479**	**398**	**331**	284	249	221	199	181	166	142	3.69
	46	**412**	**342**	**285**	**244**	214	190	171	155	143	122	3.53
	40	**370**	**296**	**247**	**212**	185	165	148	135	123	106	3.38
305 × 127	48	**404**	323	269	231	202	180	162	147	135	115	2.59
	42	**351**	280	234	200	175	156	140	127	117	100	2.45
	37	**311**	249	207	178	156	138	124	113	104	89	2.37
305 × 102	33	**274**	219	183	156	137	122	110	100	91	78	1.90
	28	**232**	185	154	132	116	103	93	84	77	66	1.79
	25	**190**	152	127	109	95	84	76	69	63	54	1.64
254 × 146	43	**333**	**267**	**222**	191	167	148	133	121	111	95	3.41
	37	**286**	**229**	**191**	164	143	127	115	104	95	82	3.22
	31	**233**	186	155	133	117	104	93	85	78	67	2.96
254 × 102	28	203	163	135	116	102	90	81	74	68	58	2.01
	25	175	140	117	100	88	78	70	64	58	50	1.87
	22	149	119	99	85	74	66	60	54	50	43	1.75
203 × 133	30	**184**	147	123	105	92	82	74	67	61	53	3.03
	25	153	122	102	87	77	68	61	56	51		2.80
203 × 102	23	136	109	90.6	77.7	68.0						2.22
178 × 102	19	101	80.8	67.3	57.7	50.5						2.21
152 × 89	16	72.6	58.1	48.4	41.5	36.3						2.01
127 × 76	13	49.6	39.6	33.0	28.3	24.8						1.82

* Note that serial size is NOT actual size. Manufacture of beams of different weights of a given serial size involves moving the rollers in or out. The depth between the inside faces of the flanges remains constant, so the flange thickness and overall height vary.

Notes: See p. 125

Steel joists (RSJ) – Safe distributed loads (kN) for grade 43 steel

(Please note that these sections are not frequently rolled – check for availability.)

Joist nominal size **mm**	Mass **kg/m**	Spans (m)										Lc
		1.50	1.75	2.0	2.25	2.50	2.75	3.0	3.25	3.5	4.0	
		Deflection co-efficients										
		199	146	112	88.5	71.7	59.2	49.8	42.4	36.6	28.0	m
254 × 203	82				**518**	**500**	**454**	**416**	**304**	*357*	*312*	5.80
203 × 152	52	**362**	**356**	**311**	**277**	*249*	*226*	*207*	*191*	178	156	4.47
152 × 127	37	*210*	*180*	*158*	*140*	*126*	115	105	97	90	79	3.79
127 × 114	30	*136*	*116*	*102*	90	81	74	68	63	58	51	3.55
127 × 114	27	*131*	*112*	*98*	87	79	71	65	60	56	49	3.61
102 × 102	23	*84*	72	63	56	51	46	42	39	36	32	3.48
89 × 89	19	*61*	52	46	41	36	33	30	28	26	23	3.33
76 × 76	13	37	31	27	24	22	20	18	17	16	14	2.95

Notes:

These safe loads are designed in accordance with BS 449 (permissible stresses) and assume that the compression flange of the beam is laterally restrained if the span of the beam exceeds Lc. Sufficient lateral restraint can be achieved by positive mechanical fixing of floor joists to the flange (i.e. using cleats or straps). Skew nailing to timber plates or blocking into the web is generally not acceptable.

Loads printed in **bold** type may cause overloading of the unstiffened web, the capacity of which should be checked.

Loads printed in *italic* type do not cause overloading of the unstiffened web, and do not cause deflection exceeding span / 360.

Loads printed in ordinary type should be checked for deflection.

Source: British Constructional Steelwork Association Ltd

Steel hollow sections

Hot formed structural hollow sections (SHS) are manufactured to BS 4360: 1990 and BS 4848 Part 2: 1991.

The square and rectangular sections have tight corner radii which have higher geometric properties and therefore a higher load carrying capacity in compression than cold formed sections.

Cold formed hollow sections (CFHS) are manufactured to BS 6363: 1989.

The square and rectangular sections have larger corner radii which give lower geometric properties than hot formed sections of the same size and thickness. Cold formed hollow sections must NOT be substituted in a direct size-for-size basis for hot formed hollow sections without checking the design. Where structural properties are not critical, CFHS provide a cheaper solution.

SHS = structural hollow section
CHS = circular hollow section
RHS = rectangular hollow sections including square sections
CFHS = cold formed hollow section

Structural steel hollow sections
External sizes in mm

Hot formed			Cold formed		
circular	**square**	**rectangular**	**circular**	**square**	**rectangular**
26.9	40 × 40	50 × 30	26.9	25 × 25	50 × 25
42.4	50 × 50	60 × 40	33.7	30 × 30	50 × 30
48.3	60 × 60	80 × 40	42.4	40 × 40	60 × 30
60.3	70 × 70	90 × 50	48.3	50 × 50	60 × 40
76.1	80 × 80	100 × 50	60.3	60 × 60	70 × 40
88.9	90 × 90	100 × 60	76.1	70 × 70	70 × 50
114.3	100 × 100	120 × 60	88.9	80 × 80	80 × 40
139.7	120 × 120	120 × 80	114.3	90 × 90	80 × 60
168.3	140 × 140	150 × 100	139.7	100 × 100	90 × 50
193.7	150 × 150	160 × 80	168.3	120 × 120	100 × 40
219.1	160 × 160	200 × 100	193.7	140 × 140	100 × 50
244.5	180 × 180	200 × 120	219.1	150 × 150	100 × 60
273.0	200 × 200	200 × 150	244.5	160 × 160	100 × 80
323.9	250 × 250	250 × 100	273.0	180 × 180	120 × 40
406.4	300 × 300	250 × 150	323.9	200 × 200	120 × 60
457.0	350 × 350	300 × 100	355.6	250 × 250	120 × 80
508.0	400 × 400	300 × 200	406.4	300 × 300	140 × 80
		400 × 200	457.0		150 × 100
		450 × 250	508.0		160 × 80
		500 × 300			180 × 80
					180 × 100
					200 × 100
					200 × 120
					200 × 150
					250 × 150
					300 × 100
					300 × 200
					400 × 200

Seamless Hot formed hollow sections also available with thicker walls 457 to 771 mm Ø

Jumbo Hot formed square hollow and rectangular sections also available with thicker walls 350 to 750 mm square

Source: Corus: tubes and pipes

Lintels

There are many suppliers of lintels, both precast concrete and pressed metal. Precast lintels can be either composite or non-composite. Composite lintels rely on brickwork being built on top of the 65 deep lintels. Particularly for longer spans, this allows safer handling on site of lighter lintels. Such lintels MUST be propped until the brickwork over has cured. Similarly, all long span lintels should be propped until masonry over has cured.

Lintels are rarely, if ever, cast on site.

Lintel selector guides are available on the websites of the various manufacturers. You will need to know the thickness of the inner and outer leaves, the width of the cavity, clear span and loads to be carried.

The following is just a small example of what is available on the web. It is advisable to check the websites periodically as the products are revised:

Precast concrete lintels

Stowell Concrete Limited
(www.stowellconcrete.co.uk)

COMPOSITE lintel maximum uniformly distributed load for clear span kg/m (including self-weight of lintel)

Section w × h	No. of courses	0.60m	0.75m	0.90m	1.05m	1.20m	1.35m	1.50m	1.65m	1.80m	1.95m	2.10m	2.25m	2.40m	2.55m	2.70m	2.85m
100 × 65mm	2	2033	1407	1029	785	617	497	408	340	288	246	212	185	162	143	127	133
	5	2743	1900	1392	1062	836	674	554	463	392	336	291	254	223	197	175	156
	8	4166	2889	2118	1618	1275	1030	849	711	603	516	449	393	347	308	274	246
150 × 65mm	2	2168	1498	1094	833	653	524	430	357	301	257	221	191	166	146	129	–
	5	4002	2773	2030	1550	1219	983	809	676	572	490	424	370	325	288	245	–
	8	5837	4046	2967	2266	1785	1442	1188	994	844	725	628	549	484	429	383	–
220 × 65mm	2	2377	1639	1193	904	706	565	459	380	317	269	228	196	169	147	127	–
	5	5940	4115	3015	2300	1811	1460	1201	1004	851	729	631	560	484	428	381	–
	8	8195	5679	4161	3177	2501	2019	1661	1389	1178	1010	875	764	672	596	530	–

NON-COMPOSITE lintel maximum uniformly distributed load for clear span kg/m (including self-weight of lintel)

Section w × h	0.75m	0.90m	1.05m	1.20m	1.35m	1.50m	1.65m	1.80m	1.95m	2.10m	2.25m	2.40m	2.55m	2.70m	2.85m	3.00m	3.15m	3.30m	3.75m	4.05m
150 × 100mm	2381	1937	1282	1006	808	662	551	464	395	340	295	257	226	199	176	157	140	125	–	–
100 × 150mm	3590	2628	1880	1480	1191	976	816	691	638	511	458	390	344	302	272	244	219	198	–	–
140 × 150mm	–	–	3564	2806	2263	1862	1557	1319	1131	979	855	751	665	592	529	476	429	389	–	–
100 × 215mm	–	–	–	–	–	–	2952	2694	2413	2140	1882	1624	1402	1202	1004	856	723	664	517	423

Naylor precast concrete lintels
(www.naylorlintels.co.uk/lintelsselector.asp)

Hi-Spec Range Lintel: R6	
Section Properties	
Height	145 mm
Width	100 mm
M_S	5.564 kNm
M_U	9.609 kNm
$M_{U/1.5}$	6.406 kNm
Limiting M_R	5.564 kNm
Effective depth	95 mm
Self-weight	35 Kg/m

Load Table

Clear Span (mm)	Overall Length (mm)	Effective Span (mm)	Allowable Load (kN/m)			
			M_R	S_{R100}	S_{R150}	Limiting
700	900	795	70.07	50.74		50.74
900	1100	995	44.61	40.47		40.47
1000	1200	1095	36.77	36.74		36.74
1200	1500	1295	26.19		32.88	26.19
1500	1800	1595	17.14			17.14
1800	2100	1895	12.04			12.04
2100	2400	2195	8.89			8.89
2400	2700	2495	6.80			6.80
2700	3000	2795	5.34			5.34
3000	3300	3095	4.29			4.29
3200	3600	3295	3.75			3.75

Naylor precast concrete lintels – continued

Hi-Spec Range Lintel: R8	
Section Properties	
Height	215 mm
Width	140 mm
M_S	14.259 kNm
M_U	25.710 kNm
$M_{U/1.5}$	17.140 kNm
Limiting M_R	14.259 kNm
Effective depth	141.67 mm
Self-weight	72 Kg/m

Load Table

Clear Span (mm)	Overall Length (mm)	Effective Span (mm)	Allowable Load (kN/m)			
			M_R	S_{R100}	S_{R150}	Limiting
700	900	800	177.51	100.57		100.57
900	1100	1000	113.35	80.31		80.31
1000	1200	1100	93.55	72.95		72.95
1200	1500	1341	62.64		62.22	62.22
1500	1800	1641	41.60		50.72	41.60
1800	2100	1941	29.53			29.53
2100	2400	2241	21.97			21.97
2400	2700	2541	16.93			16.93
2700	3000	2841	13.40			13.40
3000	3300	3141	10.83			10.83
3200	3600	3341	9.49			9.49

Steel lintels for cavity walls

Lintels are made from galvanized steel with polyester powder corrosion-resisting coating. Single lintels are available with the steel bent into a 'top hat' shape using the cavity to give height to the lintel, but these form a thermal bridge across the cavity and may cause local condensation, so separate lintels for each leaf are advisable. To support masonry to the outer leaf, angle lintels are used, typically in conjunction with a separate box lintel to the inner leaf.

Bases of internal leaf lintels are slotted for plaster key.

Other profiles

Rebated combined lintels – for window/door frames set back in reveals.

Lintels for closed eaves – for windows tight under sloping roofs.

Lintels for walls with masonry outer skin and timber frame inside.

Lintels for masonry outer skin where inner skin is carried by concrete lintel.

Lintels for internal partitions and load bearing walls.

Special profiles for various styles of arches and cantilevered masonry corners.

If thermal bridging is an issue, each leaf could be supported on a box lintel. If the external leaf is facing brick, then an angle would be required.

Box 100

For internal openings, eaves or 100 block and tile hanging.

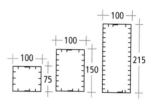

Manufactured length 150 mm increments	0600 1500	1650 1800	1950 2400	2550 2700	2850 3600	3750 4200	4350 4800
Height 'h'	75	150	150	150	215	215	215
Thickness 't'	2	1.6	2	2	2.5	2.5	2.5
Total allowable UDL (kN)	18	18	25	20	30	25	20

Box 140

For internal openings, eaves or 140/150 block and tile hanging.

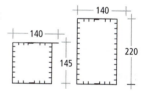

Manufactured length 150 mm increments	0600 1500	1650 1800	2250 2400	2550 2700	2850 3600	3750 4200	4350 4800
Height 'h'	145	145	145	145	220	220	220
Thickness 't'	1.6	2	2	2	2.5	2.5	2.5
Total allowable UDL (kN)	15	30	25	20	34	30	25

L10

For use with single 102 mm brickwork wall construction. Light duty loading condition.

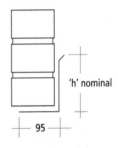

'h' nominal

95

Note: This lintel must be propped during construction.
To achieve loading figures indicated, lintel must be built-in with
brickwork/blockwork as shown. In addition, it must be suitably
restrained during construction. Heavier duty variants available.

Heavy duty and wider
masonry variants
available.

Manufactured length 150 mm increments	0600 1200	1350 1800	1950 2700	
Height 'h'	60	110	210	
Thickness 't'	3.0	3.0	28	
Total allowable UDL (kN)	14	8	10	

L11

For use with single leaf face brick or block wall.

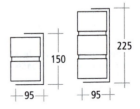

150

225

95   95

Note: This lintel must be propped during construction.
To achieve loading figures indicated, lintel must be built-in with
brickwork/blockwork as shown. In addition, it must be suitably
restrained during construction. Heavier duty variants available.

Heavy duty and wider
masonry variants
available.

Manufactured length 150 mm increments	0600 1800	1950 2400	2550 3000	
Height 'h'	150	225	225	
Thickness 't'	2.5	2.5	3.0	
Total allowable UDL (kN)	16	20	22	

Wind loads – simple calculation

BS 6262: 1982 CP describes a simple method of obtaining wind loads. This can be used for buildings less than 10 m above ground level and where the design wind speed is less than 52 m per second (m/s). This method should not be used for cliff-top buildings.

Find the basic wind speed from the map on p. 1. Multiply by a correction in Table 1 to get the design wind speed (m/s). Find the appropriate maximum wind loading from Table 2.

This should only be used for wind loads applied to glazing units and not the whole building. For more detailed wind calculations, refer to BS 6399: Part 2.

Table 1:   Correction factors for ground roughness and height above ground

Height above ground	Category 1	Category 2	Category 3	Category 4
3 m or less	0.83	0.72	0.64	0.56
5 m	0.88	0.79	0.70	0.60
10 m	1.00	0.93	0.78	0.67

Category 1   Open country with no obstructions. All coastal areas.
Category 2   Open country with scattered wind breaks.
Category 3   Country with many wind breaks, e.g. small towns, city outskirts.
Category 4   Surfaces with large and frequent obstructions, e.g. city centres.

Table 2:   Wind loading – probable maximum

Design wind speed m/s	Wind loading N/m^2	Design wind speed m/s	Wind loading N/m^2
28	670	42	1510
30	770	44	1660
32	880	46	1820
34	990	48	1920
36	1110	50	2150
38	1240	52	2320
40	1370		

Precast concrete floors

Precast concrete floors are used for ground floors over sloping or made-up ground where in-situ slabs may not be economic, and for upper floors where fire-resisting and sound insulating construction is needed, between flats for example. They can be used in a fully precast, 'dry' construction with a floating floor finish, or in a composite way with an in-situ structural topping or screed, which can improve structural performance and acoustic insulation. Crane handling of the beams is normally required so they are less used on smaller projects.

There are two main types of precast concrete floor: wideslab (sometimes known as hollowcore) and beam and block.

Bearing required is generally 75mm onto steelwork and 100mm onto masonry. Where shared bearing is required on a masonry wall, the wall should be 215mm thick (except for short span beam and block floors where staggered bearing might be possible).

Wideslab floors are precast slabs 1200mm wide with hollow cores (150 thick slab minimum). The depth of unit can vary from 100mm–450mm, depending on span and loading.

Beam and block floors are inverted T sections, 150–225 deep, with concrete blocks spanning between units. The blocks can span short or long direction (or alternate), depending on span and loading. All beams are sometimes required under partitions.

There are many manufacturers of precast concrete floors who provide a design and supply service. The following information is a small example of what is available on the internet. It is advisable to check the websites periodically as the products are revised.

Milbank Floors
(www.milbank-floors.co.uk)

The load/span tables show the maximum clear span for both domestic and other loading conditions, such as nursing homes, hotels and commercial developments. These tables are provided as a guide only. Please contact Milbank Floors for specific information.

Wideslab/Hollowcore

SECTION

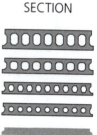

Prestressed Hollowcore Plank Load Span Table			Maximum span in metres. Spans below allow for characteristic service (live) loads + self weight + 1.5 kN/m² finishes and 1.5 kN/m² partitions							
Unit reference	Unit depth (mm)	Self weight (kN/m²)	Imposed live load kN/mm²							
			0.75	1.5	2.0	2.5	3.0	4.0	5.0	7.5
PS-250	250	3.46	10.0	9.53	9.25	8.96	8.74	8.30	7.93	7.14
PS-200	200	2.97	8.87	8.41	8.14	7.89	7.67	7.27	6.92	6.24
PS-150H	150	2.95	7.05	6.68	6.47	6.27	6.09	5.77	5.90	4.95
PS-150L	150	2.48	7.42	7.00	6.76	6.54	6.34	5.99	5.69	5.11
PS-100s	100	2.35	5.18	4.89	4.71	4.56	4.41	4.17	3.95	3.54

Beam and Block

150 mm deep T beam (based on 1/2 hour fire resistance) Medium density infill blocks 1350 kg/m² − 65 mm screed finish	** Type of block spacing	Self weight (kN/m²)	Spans below allow for characteristic service (live) load +self weight + 1.5 kN/m² finishes + 1.5 kN/m² partitions Imposed live load kN/mm²							
Beam centres*			0.75	1.5	2.0	2.5	3.0	4.0	5.0	7.5
			Maximum span in metres							
	W	1.76	4.07	3.82	3.67	3.54	3.42	3.21	3.04	2.54
	A	1.88	4.56	4.20	4.12	3.97	3.84	3.61	3.42	3.04
	N	2.09	5.27	4.95	4.77	4.61	4.46	4.20	3.98	3.55
	W	2.10	5.02	4.74	4.57	4.41	4.27	4.02	3.81	3.40
	A	2.27	5.46	5.16	4.98	4.81	4.66	4.39	4.17	3.73
	N	2.52	6.02	5.71	5.51	5.33	5.17	4.89	4.64	4.16
	N	2.76	6.37	6.05	5.85	5.66	5.50	5.20	4.95	4.44

** W = Wide (440 mm) A = Alternate (440 + 215 mm) N = Narrow (215 mm)

225 mm deep D Beam (based on 1 hour fire resistance) Medium density infill blocks 1350 kg/m² − 65 mm screed finish	* Type of block spacing	Self weight (kN/m²)	Spans below allow for characteristic service (live) load +self weight + 1.5 kN/m² finishes + 1.5 kN/m² partitions. Imposed live load kN/mm²							
Beam centres			0.75	1.5	2.0	2.5	3.0	4.0	5.0	7.5
			Maximum span in metres							
	W	2.36	6.31	5.94	5.73	5.54	5.37	5.07	4.81	4.30
	A	2.62	6.95	6.57	6.34	6.14	5.96	5.63	5.35	4.80
	N	3.08	7.84	7.39	7.20	6.98	6.78	6.43	6.12	5.52
	W	3.03	7.49	7.09	6.86	6.66	6.46	6.13	5.84	5.26
	A	3.35	8.00	7.60	7.36	7.15	9.95	6.60	6.29	5.68
	N	3.84	8.63	8.22	7.98	7.76	7.55	7.19	6.87	6.23
	N	4.22	8.95	8.54	8.30	8.08	7.88	7.51	7.19	6.54

** W = Wide (440 mm) A = Alternate (440 + 215 mm) N = Narrow (215 mm)

4
Services

Architects typically design services for small buildings, involving plumbers and electricians for detailed expertise on site; as services installations have become more sophisticated, so have the regulations controlling their installation in buildings. The number of specialist designers, suppliers and installers has increased to cover demands for detection and alarm systems for fire, security, air quality, etc.; audio and video systems; ambient energy systems, rainharvesting and grey water recycling systems; ventilation and air conditioning; more sophisticated lighting and control systems for all services either on site or remotely.

Particularly in new technologies, architects need to be wary of unofficially delegating design to subcontractors without formal design responsibility.

For larger buildings, whose services design typically involves mechanical and electrical consulting engineers, there has been a design reaction to this elaboration in increasing use of building management systems which, though improving integration, have had drawbacks in loss of personal control and user understanding.

While the need to improve energy efficiency has driven increasing complexity and sophistication in some areas, an alternative approach exemplified in passive design has been to aim for buildings less reliant on services, and for the remaining service systems to be more intelligible and controllable by users.

Drainage

Foul drains recommended minimum gradients

Peak flow l/s	Pipe size mm	Minimum gradient	Maximum capacity l/s
<1	75	1 : 40	4.1
<1	100	1 : 40	9.2
>1	75	1 : 80	2.8
>1	100	1 : 80*	6.3
>1	150	1 : 150†	15.0

* Minimum of 1 WC   † Minimum of 5 WCs

Land drains in normal soils – minimum gradients

Pipe Ø	Gradient	Pipe Ø	Gradient
50	1 : 500	150	1 : 2160
75	1 : 860	175	1 : 2680
100	1 : 1260	200	1 : 3200
125	1 : 1680	225	1 : 3720

Traps minimum sizes and seal depths

Appliance	Ø trap mm	Seal depth mm		Ø trap mm	Seal depth mm
washbasin	32	75	waste disposer	40	75
bidet	32	75	urinal	40	75
bath*	40	50	sink	40	75
shower*	40	50	washing machine*	40	75
syphonic WC	75	50	dishwasher*	40	75

* Where these fittings discharge directly into a gully the seal depth may be reduced to a minimum of 38 mm.

Hepworth waste valves used in lieu of traps avoid the risk of suction emptying the traps on long pipe runs.

Sources: *Building Regulations–Approved Document H*
Hepworth Building Products

Inspection chamber covers
Typical dimensions

Covers are manufactured in steel plate, galvanized steel and cast iron – overall sizes for cast iron will be larger. Covers may have single or double seals, plain or recessed tops, and be multiple leaf or continuous for ducting. Alternative features include chambered keyholes, handlift recesses and locking screws.

Most covers are available in the load classes shown below.

Typical clear opening mm	Overall frame mm
300 × 300	370 × 370
450 × 450	520 × 520
600 × 450	670 × 520
600 × 600	670 × 670
750 × 600	820 × 670
750 × 750	820 × 820
900 × 600	970 × 670
900 × 900	970 × 970
1000 × 1000	1070 × 1070

Load classes for inspection chamber covers

Class	Wheel load (slow moving traffic)	Typical application
A	5 kN	Pedestrian, cycle tracks
AA	15 kN	Private drives, car parking areas
AAA	25 kN	Restricted access roads
B	50 kN	Commercial delivery, refuse collection
C	65 kN	All roads but positioned within 0.5 m of kerb
D	108 kN	All roads restricted only by wheel loading

Source: St Gobain Pipelines

Single stack drainage system

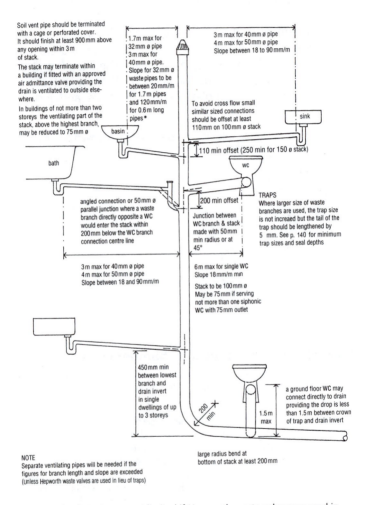

Soil vent pipe should be terminated with a cage or perforated cover. It should finish at least 900 mm above any opening within 3 m of stack.

The stack may terminate within a building if fitted with an approved air admittance valve providing the drain is ventilated to outside elsewhere.

In buildings of not more than two storeys the ventilating part of the stack, above the highest branch, may be reduced to 75 mm ø

1.7 m max for 32 mm ø pipe 3 m max for 40 mm ø pipe. Slope for 32 mm ø waste pipes to be between 20 mm/m for 1.7 m pipes and 120 mm/m for 0.6 m long pipes *

3 m max for 40 mm ø pipe 4 m max for 50 mm ø pipe Slope between 18 to 90 mm/m

To avoid cross flow small similar sized connections should be offset at least 110 mm on 100 mm ø stack

sink

basin

bath

110 min offset (250 min for 150 ø stack)

wc

angled connection or 50 mm ø parallel junction where a waste branch directly opposite a WC would enter the stack within 200 mm below the WC branch connection centre line

200 min offset

Junction between WC branch & stack made with 50 mm min radius or at 45°

TRAPS
Where larger size of waste branches are used, the trap size is not increaed but the tail of the trap should be lengthened by 5 mm. See p. 140 for minimum trap sizes and seal depths

3 m max for 40 mm ø pipe 4 m max for 50 mm ø pipe Slope between 18 and 90 mm/m

6 m max for single WC Slope 18 mm/m min

Stack to be 100 mm ø May be 75 mm if serving not more than one siphonic WC with 75 mm outlet

450 mm min between lowest branch and drain invert in single dwellings of up to 3 storeys

200 min

1.5 m max

a ground floor WC may connect directly to drain providing the drop is less than 1.5 m between crown of trap and drain invert

NOTE
Separate ventilating pipes will be needed if the figures for branch length and slope are exceeded (unless Hepworth waste valves are used in lieu of traps)

large radius bend at bottom of stack at least 200 mm

* Waste pipe lengths are not limited if Hepworth waste valves are used in lieu of traps

Sources: *Building Regulations–Approved Document H*
Hepworth Building Products

Rainwater disposal
Calculation of gutter and downpipe sizes

In the UK, the maximum rainfall intensity is generally taken as 75 mm per hour or 0.0208 litres per second (l/s). Note that this does not necessarily mean only high rainfall areas such as West Wales and Scotland: in surprisingly odd pockets like Norfolk and Oxford heavy downpours can exceed this figure.

To calculate the size of rainwater goods it is necessary to determine the *effective roof area* which, in the case of pitched roofs, is as follows:

Effective
roof area = $(H \div 2 + W) \times L = m^2$
Where H = vertical rise between
eaves and ridge
W = plan width of slope
L = length of roof

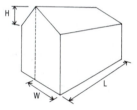

To determine the maximum flow multiply the effective area by 0.0208.

Typical maximum flow capacities

Gutter mm	Downpipe mm	Outlet at one end of roof				Outlet at centre of roof			
		Level gutter m²	l/s	Gutter to fall m²	l/s	Level gutter m²	l/s	Gutter to fall m²	l/s
75 half round	51 Ø	15	0.33	19	0.40	25	0.54	30	0.64
110 half round	69 Ø	46	0.96	61	1.27	92	1.91	122	2.54
116 square	62 sq	53	1.10	72	1.50	113	2.36	149	3.11t

Refer to manufacturers' catalogues for actual flow capacities, as profiles of gutters can vary.

Rule of thumb

100–112 mm gutter with 68 mm Ø downpipe placed at centre of gutter will drain 110 m² effective roof area; placed at end of gutter will drain 55 m² effective roof area. Gutter will drain more if laid to slight (1: 60) fall.

Sustainable Urban Drainage Systems (SUDS)

SUDS applies sustainability to surface water management to minimize the impacts from development on the quantity and quality of run-off, and maximize amenity and biodiversity opportunities.

The key drivers for implementation of SUDS are:

1 Section H of the Building Regulations requires priority to disposal of surface water by infiltration.
2 The Code for Sustainable Homes (CSH) makes it MANDATORY to ensure both run-off rate and volume do not increase for the developed site. If this is not practicable, discharge to controlled limits may be considered.
3 BREEAM also credits use of attenuation to manage flood risk.
4 Statutory water authorities control discharge of surface water into sewers and where infiltration is impractical attenuation (site storage) will be required.
5 Discharge to a water course is determined by the Environment Agency who requires a SUDS-based approach, often expressed in planning conditions.

The Environment Agency publication, 'Preliminary Rainfall Management for Developments' gives methodology for estimation of greenfield run-off rates and storage requirements. Larger scale developments will almost certainly require computer analysis.

The criteria to establish storage requirements vary between authorities but all compare critical rainfall events with infiltration or permitted discharge rates. Infiltration is determined by site tests, permitted discharge by calculation or by the practicalities of flow control. Water authorities typically use 30-year storm return periods and require that storage be contained within the system. The Environment Agency will require consideration of the 100-year return period with climate change uplift.

Requirements for long-term storage apply to larger sites or where the green field run-off is very low, e.g. chalk soil, as design storage volume and the time required to fully discharge both increase. Long-term storage is separated from the primary drainage system and either infiltrates or is allowed to discharge at very low rates (2 litres per second per hectare). For small sites long-term storage is rarely an issue as permeable paving can be substituted.

All these matters require discussion and agreement on a case by case basis.

SUDS schemes work by maximizing infiltration and provide interception storage and treatment by encouraging flow across soft landscaping, or through permeable paving. Interception storage scores additional CSH credits. SUDS features provide storage in swales basins or ponds and on small sites gap graded aggregate or 'milk crate' void formers under permeable paving can fulfil this function.

Design of SUDS requires engineering calculation with landscape architecture to ensure amenity and biodiversity are provided. Safety has to be considered and restrictions on depth of water, gradation of slopes and (where appropriate) use of fencing have to be considered holistically to address risk in any given environment. Design must also address maintenance and this is key to the question of adoption. The forthcoming Flood and Water Management Bill will make adoption of SUDS schemes mandatory even on private developments.

Sources:

R&D Technical Report W5-074, EA/DEFRA, 2005, www.defra.gov.uk/environment/flooding/documents/research/sc030219.pdf

The SUDS Manual, CIRIA C697 2007

Permeable Pavements, Interpave www.paving.org.uk

Water supply regulations

The Water Supply (Water Fittings) Regulations 1999 supersede the Water Supply Byelaws. Their aim is to prevent: waste, misuse, undue consumption, contamination or false measurement of water supplied by a *Water Undertaker* (WU). The regulations should be read in conjunction with the WRAS Guide, which includes detailed information of sizes, flow rates, valves, etc. Below is a VERY BROAD and BRIEF interpretation of the regulations.

Application of the regulations

The regulations apply only to fittings supplied with water by a WU. They do not apply to water fittings for non-domestic or non-food production purposes providing the water is metered; the supply is for less than 1 month (3 months with written consent) and no water can return through a meter to a mains pipe. They do not apply to fittings installed before 1 July 99.

Notification

Water undertakers must be notified of the following:
Erecting any building, except a pond or swimming pool of less than 10 000 litres capacity
Altering any water system in non-residential premises
Changing the use of a property
Building over or within 2 m of a public sewer. A CCTV survey may be necessary
Installing:

- A bath with a capacity greater than 230 litres
- A bidet with ascending spray or flexible hose
- A single shower unit with multi-head arrangement
- A pump or booster drawing more than 12 litres/min
- A water softener with a waste or needing water for regeneration or cleaning
- A reduced pressure zone valve or any mechanical device which presents serious health risks
- A garden watering system other than hand-held hose
- External pipes higher than 730 mm or lower than 1350 mm
- An automatically filled pond or swimming pool with a capacity of more than 10 000 litres.

Contractor's certificate

Contractors approved by the WU must issue certificates to clients stating that the work complies with the regulations. For items of *Notification* (see above) copies of these certificates must be sent to the WU. Contravention of the regulations may incur a fine not exceeding £1000 (in 2000 AD).

Fluid categories

Water is described in five fluid categories ranging from 'wholesome' water supplied by a WU to water representing serious health hazards. These categories are used, amongst other things, to define which type of *backflow prevention* (see below) is required.

Contamination and corrosion

Water for domestic use or food purposes must not be contaminated by materials such as lead and bitumen. Water fittings must not be installed in contaminated environments such as sewers and cesspits.

Quality and testing

Water fittings should comply with British Standards or European equivalent and must withstand an operating pressure of not less than 1.5 times the maximum operating pressure. All water systems must be tested, flushed and, if necessary, disinfected before use.

Location

Water fittings must not be installed in cavity walls, embedded in walls or solid floors, or below suspended or solid ground floors unless encased in an accessible duct. External pipes underground must not be joined by adhesives nor laid less than 750 mm deep or more than 1350 mm deep unless written consent is obtained.

Protection against freezing

All water fittings outside buildings or located within buildings but outside the thermal envelope should be insulated against freezing. In very cold conditions, in unheated premises, water should be drained down before the onset of freezing or alternative devices installed to activate heating systems.

Backflow prevention

Except where expanded water from hot water systems is permitted to flow backwards, water installations must have adequate devices for preventing backflow as follows:

- To prevent backflow between separate premises
- Connection of grey or rainwater to a 'wholesome' water pipe
- Bidets with flexible hoses, spray handsets, under-rim water inlets or ascending sprays
- WC cisterns with pressure flushing valves
- WCs adapted as bidets
- Baths with submerged inlets (e.g. jacuzzis)
- Non-domestic washing machines and dishwashers
- Sprinkler systems, fire hose reels and fire hydrants
- Garden hoses and watering systems.

Cold water services

Every dwelling, including those in multi-storey dwellings should have separate *stop valves* for mains entry pipes inside each premises.

Drain taps must be provided to completely drain water from all pipes within a building.

All domestic premises must have at least one tap for *drinking water* supplied directly from the mains.

Cold water cisterns

Cold water cisterns for dwellings are no longer mandatory providing there is adequate *water flow rate* and *mains pressure in the street.* Check this with the WU before designing new installation.

Cisterns must be fitted with *float valves* and *servicing valves. Overflow/warning* pipes, with vermin and insect-proof screens, must be fitted to discharge conspicuously to outside. Where cisterns are joined together, care must be taken to avoid one cistern overflowing into another and that water is fully circulated between cisterns and not short-circuited. Cisterns should be *insulated* and be fitted with light and insect-proof *lids.* 330 mm minimum unobstructed space must be provided above the cistern for inspection and maintenance.

Hot water services

Temperature control devices and *relief valves* must be fitted to unvented water heaters. *Expansion valves* must be fitted to unvented hot water systems larger than 5 litres. Primary circuit vent pipes should not discharge over domestic cisterns nor to a secondary system. Secondary circuit vent pipes should not discharge over feed and expansion cisterns connected to a primary circuit. Ideally, hot water should be stored at 60°C and discharged at 50°C (43°C for shower mixers). Long lengths of hot water pipes should be *insulated* to conserve energy.

Garden water supplies

Double check valves (DCVs) must be fitted to hose union taps in new houses. Hose union taps in existing houses should be replaced with hose union taps which incorporate DCVs. Watering systems must be fitted with DCVs as well as *pipe interrupters with atmosphere vent and moving element* at the hose connecting point or a minimum of 300 mm above the highest point of delivering outlet.

Pools and fountains filled with water supplied by a WU must have an *impervious lining.*

WCs and Urinals

Single flush cisterns to WCs should not exceed 6 litres capacity. Manual *pressure flushing* valves to WC cisterns must receive at least 1.2 litres/second flow at the appliance. WC cisterns installed before July 99 must be replaced with the same size cistern. Existing single flush cisterns may not be replaced by dual-flush cisterns.

Automatic *urinal flushing cisterns* should not exceed 10 litres capacity for a single urinal and 7.5 litres/hour per bowl, stall or 700 mm width of slab.

Urinal pressure valves should deliver no more than 1.5 litres per flush.

Low water consumption WC pans and cisterns are available down to 4 litres. Passive Infra-red (PIR) flush controls are available to minimize wastage in urinals. Waterless urinals are available but require a careful cleaning regime.

Sources: Water Supply (Water Fittings) Regulations 1999 The WRAS Water Regulations Guide

Water storage
Plastic cold water cisterns
Rectangular

Litres	galls	size l × w × h mm	weight kg*
18	4	442 × 296 × 305	0.9
68	15	630 × 448 × 420	3.2
91	20	665 × 490 × 510	4.2
114	25	700 × 540 × 532	5.0
182	40	940 × 610 × 590	7.3
227	50	1155 × 635 × 600	9.0

Circular

Litres	galls	size Ø @ top × h mm	weight kg*
114	25	695 × 510	3.5
182	40	795 × 590	4.4
227	50	860 × 620	4.8
273	60	940 × 620	5.8
455	100	1060 × 750	10.4
591	130	1060 × 920	14.5

* Empty weight – one litre of water weighs one kilogram so full weight of cistern equals litre capacity in kilograms plus empty weight.

Source: Titan Environmental Ltd

Water hardness
☐ soft to moderately soft
▨ hard to moderately soft
■ hard to very hard

Hard water supplies lead to lime-scale formation in and around appliances; this leads to substantial reductions in efficiency, particularly in boilers and hot water cylinders. Scale formation can be reduced by fitting scale reducers to incoming cold mains. These work by magnetism, electronic charge or chemical treatment to reduce the amount of hard scale formed and clear scale deposits, retaining the calcium carbonate in suspension; they are low in cost and appear to have no health effects.

Water softeners remove the calcium carbonate from the water, rendering it 'soft'; they should be fitted near drinking water taps – typically at kitchen sinks. They require recharging with salt at regular intervals and are substantially more expensive to install and maintain than conditioners.

In hard water areas, it is advisable to fit conditioners or softeners to all buildings with hot water systems.

Hot water usage

Typical average consumption – litres

bath	60 per bath
shower	2.5 per minute
power shower	10–40 per minute
handwashing	2 per person
hairdressing	10 per shampoo
cleaning	10 per dwelling per day
kitchen sink	5 per meal

Cold water fill appliances

dishwasher	13 per cycle
washing machine	45–70 per cycle

Hot water storage

Typical storage requirements @ 65°C – litres per person

house or flat	30
office	5
factory	5
day school	5

boarding school	25
hospital	30
sports centre	35
luxury hotel	45

Domestic indirect copper hot water cylinders

BS ref.	Unlagged Height A mm	Unlagged Diameter B mm	Capacity litres	Heat Surface m^2
0	1600	300	96	0.42
1	900	350	80	0.31
–	600	400	62	0.26
2	900	400	96	0.42
3	1050	400	114	0.50
4	675	450	84	0.37
5	750	450	95	0.48
6	825	450	106	0.53
7	900	450	117	0.61
8	1050	450	140	0.70
9	1200	450	162	0.79
9E	1500	450	206	0.96
10	1200	500	190	0.88
11	1500	500	245	1.10
12	1200	600	280	1.18
13	1500	600	360	1.57
14	1800	600	440	1.97

50 mm or 100 mm CFC-free urethane foam lagging insulation will be added to increase the diameter of the cylinder.

Building Regulations require hot water cylinders to have factory-applied insulation designed to restrict heat losses to 1 watt per litre or less.

In soft water areas, copper cylinders should be specified with an aluminium protector rod which is fixed inside the dome by the manufacturers. This encourages the formation of a protective film on the copper and will lengthen the life of the cylinder which may otherwise be subject to pitting.

Source: Range Cylinders Ltd

Unvented mains pressure cylinders

Mains pressure cylinders

For buildings with good mains pressure and appropriately sized water main pipework, mains pressure hot water supply offers significant advantages including equal pressure hot and cold supplies, adequate pressure at all locations for showers, location of the cylinder anywhere and elimination of cold water storage tanks; existing systems of pipework need to be checked for mains pressure.

Appropriate mains pressure cylinders are widely available in stainless steel and enamelled mild steel, pre-insulated, with single or double coils for boiler and solar applications, though in fewer sizes than copper tank-fed cylinders.

Cylinders for solar water heating

Hot water cylinders installed with solar water systems should be as large as practicable so as to maximize the efficiency of the system; although the solar coil in the base of the cylinder will heat the whole cylinder, the boiler coil in the upper part will heat only the upper part, so, when there is no further preheating from the solar system, at night for example, once the solar hot water is used, the boiler can heat only half the cylinder capacity.

Thermal stores

Whereas conventional hot water cylinders store the hot water that is used, thermal stores store the primary water as a heat storage 'battery' which provides for hot water usually via an internal pipe coil near the top of the store; heating outputs are typically around the middle or upper third of the store and inputs, often from several heat sources such as boilers, woodstoves, etc., are towards the base, with the solar thermal input usually the lowest. Typically, thermal stores are larger than hot water cylinders, often of several hundred litre capacity for a house; with substantial insulation, they are bulky as well as heavy, so provision needs to be made early on in design. They are especially efficient for intermittent inputs, so work well with solar, wind and biomass energy.

U-values

To understand the use of U-values it is necessary to distinguish between the thermal measurement expressions below:

Thermal conductivity (K-value)

The heat (W) transmitted through unit area (m^2) of a material of unit thickness (m) for unit temperature difference (K) between inside and outside environments, expressed as W/mK (or W/m °C).

Thermal resistivity (R-value)

The reciprocal of thermal conductivity, i.e. mK/W (or m °C/W). It measures how well a material resists the flow of heat by conduction.

Thermal resistance (R-value)

This means how well a *particular thickness* of material resists the passage of heat by conduction, calculated from the R-value in units of m^2K/W (or m^2 °C/W).

Thermal transmittance (U-value)

The reciprocal of thermal resistance, i.e. W/m^2K (or W/m^2 °C). This measures the amount of heat transmitted per unit area of a particular thickness per unit temperature difference between inside and outside environments.

U-value calculation formula:

$$U = \frac{1}{R_{SI} + R_{SO} + R_A + R_1 + R_2 + R_3 \ldots}$$

where R_{SI} = thermal resistance of internal surface
R_{SO} = thermal resistance of external surface
R_A = thermal resistance of air spaces within construction
R_1, R_2, R_3, etc. = thermal resistance of successive components

$$R = \frac{1}{K\text{-value}} \times \frac{\text{thickness of material mm}}{1000}$$

Summary of U-values:

Standard U-values for new construction elements
(figures account for repeating thermal bridges)

Exposed element	W/m² K			
	L1A	L1B	L2A	L2B
Pitched roof (between 11°–70°) with insulation between rafters	0.20	0.18	0.25	0.18
Pitched roof with insulation between joists	0.20	0.16	0.25	0.16
Flat roof (0°–10°) or roof with integral insulation	0.20	0.18	0.25	0.18
Walls, including basement walls	0.30	0.28	0.35	0.28
Party walls	0.20	N/A	N/A	N/A
Floors, including ground floors and basement floors	0.25	0.22	0.25	0.22
Swimming pool basin	0.25	0.25	0.25	0.25
Window, roof window, rooflight	2.0	1.6	2.2	1.8
All doors (except high usage entrance doors*)	2.0	1.8	2.2/*3.5	1.8/*3.5
Vehicle access and similar large doors	N/A	N/A	1.5	1.5

Note the differences between LA and LB; the new lower U-values in existing buildings are there to make up for some shortfall in the existing, unaltered building.

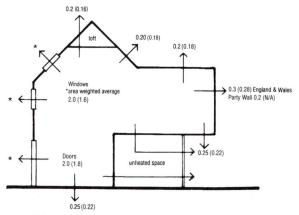

The first figure is LIA; second figure in brackets LIB.

Upgrading retained thermal elements

(If the retained element is worse than the threshold, it should be improved to the minimum value or better)

Exposed element	W/m^2 K		
	Threshold		**Minimum**
Cavity walls from	0.70	to	0.55
Other walls from	0.70	to	0.30
Floors from	0.70	to	0.25
Pitched roofs, ceiling insul	0.35	to	0.16
Pitched roofs, rafter insul	0.35	to	0.18
Flat roofs/integral insul	0.35	to	0.18

Source: Building Regulations–Approved Documents L1 & L2 2010

R-values

Surface resistance R-values normal exposure		m²K/W		Air space R-values 25 mm exposure	m²K/W R_A
	Rsɪ inside surface	Rso outside surface		in cavity wall	0.18
				loft space under sarking	0.18
				between metal cladding & lining	0.16
roof/ceiling	0.10	0.04		in cold flat roof	0.16
wall	0.12	0.06		loft space under metal cladding	0.14
				between roofing tiles & felt	0.12
floor	0.14	0.04		behind tile hanging	0.12

K-values

Thermal conductivity of typical building materials

Material		kg/m³	W/mK	Material		kg/m³	W/mK
asphalt	19 mm	1700	0.50	mortar	normal	1750	0.80
blocks	lightweight	1200	0.38	phenolic foam	board	30	0.020
	med. weight	1400	0.51	plaster	gypsum	1280	0.46
	heavyweight	2300	1.63		sand/cement	1570	0.53
bricks	exposed	1700	0.84		vermiculite	640	0.19
	protected	1700	0.62	plasterboard	gypsum	950	0.16
calcium silicate	board	875	0.17	polystyrene	expanded	25	0.032
cellulose	loose fill	32	0.038				–0.040
			–0.040	polyurethane	board	30	0.025
chipboard		800	0.15				–0.028
concrete	aerated slab	500	0.16	rendering	external	1300	0.50
	lightweight	1200	0.38	roofing tiles	clay	1900	0.85
	dense	2100	1.40		concrete	2100	1.10
felt/bitumen	3 layers	960	0.50	screed		1200	0.41
fibreboard		300	0.06	sheep's wool	slabs	19	0.040
fibreglass	quilt	25	0.033	stone	reconstructed	1750	1.30
			–0.04		sandstone	2000	1.30
flax	slabs	40	0.038		limestone	2180	1.50
			–0.040		granite	2600	2.30
glass	sheet	2500	1.05	stone chippings		1800	0.96
hardboard	standard	900	0.13	timber	softwood	650	0.14
hemp	slabs	40	0.40	vermiculite	loose	100	0.063
hempcrete	200 mm spray render	225	0.25	woodwool	slabs	600	0.11
mineral wool	quilt	12	0.033				
			–0.04				
	slab	25	0.035				

Conservation of fuel and power

The *requirement* of Building Regulations Part L 2010 is that reasonable provision shall be made for the conservation of heat and power by limiting heat gains and losses through the building fabric and services, by providing energy efficient services and controls, and by providing the building's owner with sufficient information for efficient operation and maintenance.

The regulations are split into L1A for new dwellings, L1B for existing dwellings and L2A & L2B for new and existing non-dwellings.

For new dwellings, compliance has to be demonstrated by SAP calculations comparing Dwelling Emission Rate (DER) against a Target Emission Rate (TER), at both design stage and once the building is completed. The DER must show a minimum of a 25 per cent improvement over the TER. The dwelling must also achieve minimum standards of thermal efficiency in both the construction element U-values and airtightness; the risk of overheating in summer must be avoided by careful design of ventilation, glazing orientation and shading; and the construction should be designed to meet minimum standards to avoid significant thermal bridging.

A strategic approach should be adopted whereby the aim is to reduce energy demands overall, meet the remaining energy demand with high efficiency systems that are well controlled, and then consider the use of renewable energy to offset the energy demand; a renewable energy system should not be used as a basis for a poorly insulated building.

Works to existing buildings, e.g. Extensions, will need to comply as for a new build, and the area of windows, doors and rooflights should not exceed 25 per cent of the total floor area. For a material Changes of Use, and Renovation, i.e. a conversion, a 'reasonable upgrade' is required that is technically, functionally and economically feasible and can be demonstrated by improving the existing construction elements to minimum standards whose simple payback is no more than 15 years, and improving the building services.

In addition to demonstrating the improvements above it may be necessary to show Heat Loss calculations either for the whole building or a new extension, or area weighted U-value calculations to adequately show compliance.

Non-dwellings are subject to similar regulation as above, except that: the method of compliance for Part L2A differs; the Building Emission Rate (BER) replaces the DER; and SBEM, not SAP, is used to model the comparison to the TER. Here, a flat minimum of 25 per cent is not applicable; instead the building's performance improvement is based on the building Use Class, and its basic glazing type – Top lit, Side Lit or None lit.

For the Building Services it is important that the guidance in the Domestic Building Services Compliance Guide or the Non Domestic Building Services Compliance Guide is referred to for minimum performance criteria. It would be beneficial to have an appreciation of the effect of using different fuels for heating; this is due to the fuel factors that are applied in the energy calculations. It is a relative figure, however, for gas it is 0.198 and for electricity it is 0.517, therefore using mains electricity for heating would see an increase in the DER.

In both L1B and L2B there is guidance as to how to apply the regulations to historic buildings, those of special architectural interest, and those that are Listed or in Conservation Areas.

Heat losses

As a rough guide, building heat losses will be between 20 to 50 W/m^3.

For normal conditions and temperatures 30 W/m^3 is average. Higher figures for tall, single storey buildings or large areas of glazing, lower figures for well-insulated buildings with minimal exposure, e.g. a building with 400 m^3 of heated space may require between 8 and 20 kW depending on conditions.

Recommended indoor temperatures

	°C
Warehousing; factory – heavy work	13
General stores	15
Factory – light work; circulation space	16
Bedroom; classroom; shop; church	18
Assembly hall; hospital ward	18
Offices; factory – sedentary work	19
Dining room; canteen; museum; art gallery	20
Laboratory; library; law court	20
Living room; bed-sitting room	21
Sports changing room; operating theatre	21
Bathroom; swimming pool changing room	22
Hotel bedroom	22
Indoor swimming pool	26

Source: *Series A Design Data CIBSE*

Air permeability

Air permeability for buildings has a maximum level of $10 \, m^3/(h.m^2)$ measured at 50 pascals. This is determined by the air pressure test conducted on completion of the construction. Each building type will need to be tested; however, on multi building sites a minimum of 3 of every building type should be tested. For those untested buildings a confidence factor of 0.20 or 25 per cent, whichever is greater, will be added to the test figure when applied to those untested buildings. This means that air permeability design figures will need to be set at a maximum of 8 for any buildings that will not be tested, to be certain that if the actual test figure of 8 is achieved, when the confidence factor is added, the untested buildings still result in a maximum compliance level of 10.

Non-repeating thermal bridges

Non-repeating thermal bridges occur at joins between insulated elements in the building, e.g. walls and floors, and are represented as a linear psi value in W/m. In the SAP calculation, all linear psi values are added together and divided by the total building fabric area to give a total linear transmittance 'y' value in W/m^2.

Accredited or Enhanced Details, if used, are a proven method of designing for minimum non-repeating thermal bridges. These have had the psi values calculated by an accredited person and are also proven in their buildability, and can be given a total 'y' value of 0.08 or 0.04. If an architect chooses to design their own details and psi value, these are not proven in their buildability and will be subject to a confidence factor of 0.02 or 25 per cent, whichever is the greater, applied to the calculated 'y' value.

Non-repeating thermal bridges can have a significant effect on the heat losses of the building; careful detailing and on-site checking of the construction are important to ensure these are kept to a minimum.

Heat loss calculation

The heat loss from a building is the addition of all the individual *fabric heat losses* of the doors, windows, walls, floor and ceilings, plus any *ventilation loss*.

Fabric heat loss arises when heat is transferred from the warm interior to the cold exterior through the external surfaces of the building. This occurs by a combination of conduction, convection and radiation.

Fabric heat loss calculation, expressed as Total Watts:

Total W = Sum of (Element area m^2 × U-value of fabric) × (inside °C – outside °C)
Each element must be calculated separately and then added together.

For inside temperatures see list of *Recommended indoor temperatures* on p. 160. For outside temperature – 1°C is the figure normally used in the UK.

Ventilation loss occurs when the warm air inside the building leaves and is replaced by cool air from outside; it is the heat lost through cracks, service openings and gaps in doors and windows for example.

With an average level of draught-proofing the following air changes per hour are assumed:

> living rooms, bed-sitting rooms = 1.5
> bedrooms   = 1
> kitchens and bathrooms   = 2
> halls and stairways   = 2
> rooms with open flue **add**   = 11

Ventilation heat loss calculation, expressed as Total Watts.

Total W = 1/3 × number of air changes per hour × volume m^3 × (inside °C – outside °C)

Source: *The Green Building Bible Vol. 2, Fourth Edition*

Central heating and hot water systems

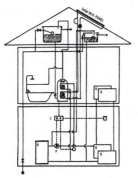

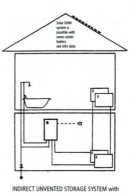

CONVENTIONAL CENTRAL HEATING and HOT WATER INSTALLATION
This system uses storage cisterns, usally located in the roof space to provide pressure for the hot water storage system, which consists of an indirect cyclinder being fed from the boiler. Cold water may also be distributed around the house from the main storage cistern. Solar water heating can be added straightforwardly to this system by substituting a larger twin coil hot water cylinder and a solar thermal collector.

INDIRECT UNVENTED STORAGE SYSTEM with SEALED PRIMARY
This system stores hot water at mains pressure and provides space heating and water cyclinder may be located anywhere. Solar hot water can be simply added by substituting a larger twin coil mains pressure cyclinder and a solar thermal collector.

- ● = Service main
- ▶◀ = Stopcock
- Ⓐ = Motorised valve
- ⚓ = Pump
- B = Boiler
- R = Radiator
- C = Controls
- T = Thermosat

Sp = solar panel   TCC = Twin coil alternative cyclinder for solar

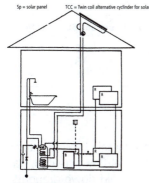

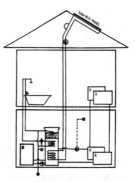

UNVENTED SYTEM with INSTANTANEOUS COMBINATION BOILER
This system is most suitable for small houses and flats where space is at a premium. As there is no hot water storage cylinder, the flow of hot water will be somewhat reduced but this is usually only noticed when running a bath or simultaneously using several taps. Some combination boilers are designed to suit preheated water, but many are not; space will be required for a solar preheat cylinder.

PRIMARY HEAT STORE with DIRECT VENTED PRIMARY
Here the hot water is stored at low pressure in a tank which is fed by a small feed tank over it. Mains water is fed into a high capacity coil where it is heated at mains pressure and blended with cold to stabilize the temperature. The system may be heated by a boiler or an immersion heater. With a boiler the recovery time is very fast. The flow rate is slightly less than an unvented storage system. Combining solar water heating with a thermal store simply requires an additional coil in the base of the store.

Source: Ideal Standard Ltd (revised for solar)

Heating and hot water systems

When specifying heating and hot water systems reference should be made to either the Domestic Building Services Compliance Guide or the Non Domestic Building Services Compliance Guide for the minimum efficiencies the equipment must achieve, although in reality these minimum efficiencies will need to be improved upon to achieve compliance. The Guides provide information for new and replacement systems.

The Guides also provide details of the minimum controls packages that are appropriate for each heating type; for example, for a domestic gas condensing boiler with hot water cylinder, the following provision would be appropriate:
Boiler interlock
Time and Temperature Controls including programmers, room thermostats and TRVs
Load or weather compensation
Insulated hot water cylinder with thermostat
Insulated pipework

Type of condensing boiler	Minimum SEDBUK% rating
Mains natural gas	88
LPG	88
Oil	88

Radiators

Radiators – despite their name – work largely by convection, and ideally need to be located to suit the airflows created, traditionally under windows to counteract cold down-draughts, though this is less critical with double glazing and draught stripping. Standard radiators are made as pressed steel panels and some higher performance radiators are made in aluminium; thermostatic control – usually by TRVs – for each radiator is advisable for energy efficiency.

Typical panel radiators – steel

Heights: 300, 450, 600, 700 mm
Lengths: 400 to 3000 in 100 mm increments

Type	Thickness	Approx Output*
Single panel without convector	47 mm	1500 W/m^2
Single panel with convector	47 mm	2200 W/m^2
Double panel with convector	77 mm	3300 W/m^2
Double panel with double convector	100 mm	4100 W/m^2

* m^2 measured on elevation

Typical column radiators – steel

Heights: 185, 260, 300, 350, 400, 450, 500, 550, 600, 750, 900, 1000, 1100, 1200, 1500, 1800, 2000, 2200, 2500, 2800, 3000 mm

Type	Thickness	Approx Output*
Two columns wide	62 mm	2150 W/m^2
Three columns wide	100 mm	3000 W/m^2
Four columns wide	136 mm	3700 W/m^2
Five columns wide	173 mm	4600 W/m^2
Six columns wide	210 mm	5400 W/m^2

* m^2 measured on elevation

Sources: Caradon Ideal Ltd, Zehnder Ltd

Underfloor heating

This is the most widely used large-scale radiant heating system which has the efficiency benefit of promoting a temperature gradient to match human comfort, i.e. 'warm feet and cool head', and avoids the build-up of hot air at ceiling level, particularly in high spaces. With comfort achievable at lower temperatures, fuel savings of 20 per cent or more as compared with a radiator system are common.

Floors are typically heated by oxygen-barriered polythene hot water pipes embedded in screed or set into insulation below timber floors. With pipes at 150 mm centres, heat outputs of around 120 W per sqm of a tiled or similar floor finish can be expected from a water temperature of 45°C. The low water temperature allows for the most efficient use of condensing boilers or alternative heat sources such as ground source heat pumps or solar thermal stores.

Electric underfloor heating has similar design advantages but typically high running costs and the environmental disadvantages of high primary energy use as with any electrical heating.

Ventilation

Means of ventilation

Required by the Building Regulations for rooms without full mechanical ventilation

	Rapid ventilation (e.g. opening window)	Background ventilation	Minimum fan extract rates or PSV*
Domestic buildings			
Habitable room	1/20th floor area	8000 mm²	no requirement
Kitchen	opening window (unsized) **or** fan with 15 mins overrun timer	4000 mm²	30 l/s (108 m³/h) adjacent to hob **or** 60 l/s (216 m³/h) elsewhere **or** PSV
Utility room	opening window (unsized) **or** fan with 15 mins overrun timer	4000 mm²	30 l/s (108 m³/h) **or** PSV
Bathroom (with or without WC)	opening window (unsized) **or** fan with 15 mins overrun timer	4000 mm²	15 l/s (54 m³/h) **or** PSV
Sanitary accommodation (separate from bathroom)	1/20th floor area **or** fan @ 6 l/s (21.6 m³/h)	4000 mm²	no requirement (but see rapid ventilation)

Means of ventilation – continued

	Rapid ventilation (e.g. opening window)	Background ventilation	Minimum fan extract rates or PSV*
Non-domestic buildings			
Occupiable room	1/20th floor area	$<10\,m^2$ = 4000 mm^2 $>10\,m^2$ = 4000 mm^2 + 400 mm^2 per m^2 of extra floor area	no requirement
Kitchen (domestic type, i.e. not a commercial kitchen)	opening window (unsized)	4000 mm^2	30 l/s (108 m^3/h) adjacent to hob **or** 60 l/s (216 m^3/h) elsewhere
Bathrooms (including shower rooms)	opening window (unsized)	4000 mm^2 per bath/ shower	15 l/s (54 m^3/h) per bath/shower
Sanitary accommodation (and/or washing facilities)	1/20th floor area **or** fan @ 6 l/s (21.6 m^3/h) per WC **or** 3 air changes/h	4000 mm^2 per WC	no requirement (but see rapid ventilation
Common spaces (where large numbers of people gather)	1/50th floor area **or** fan 1 l/s (3.6 m^3/h) per m^2	no requirement	no requirement (but see rapid ventilation)
Rest rooms (where smoking permitted)	1/20th floor area	$<10\,m^2$ = 4000 mm^2 $>10\,m^2$ = 4000 mm^2 + 400 mm^2 per m^2 of extra floor area	16 l/s (57.6 m^3/h) per person

* PSV = passive stack ventilation
See notes on next page

Means of ventilation
Notes to tables on pages 166 and 167

Rapid ventilation openings should have some part at least 1.75 m above floor level. Methods of **background ventilation** are typically adjustable trickle ventilators or airbricks with hit-and-miss louvres located at least 1.75 m above floor level.

PSV means passive stack ventilation operated manually and/ or automatically by sensor or controller in accordance with BRE Information Paper 13/94 or a BBA Certificate.

Passive stack systems are usually adequate for domestic-sized WCs, bathrooms and kitchens; since they have no fans or motors they consume no energy and require no maintenance apart from cleaning. Duct sizes are typically 125 mm diameter or equivalent rectangular section. They need to rise vertically at least 2 m and preferably 3 m above inlets and can include only limited bends; they need to discharge via special terminals at or near roof ridges.

An **open flued appliance** may be considered to provide ventilation if it has a free flue area of at least 125 mm diameter and is permanently open, i.e. no damper.

However if an open flued appliance is within the same room as an extract fan this may cause spillage of flue gases so:

Where a **gas appliance** and a fan are located in a kitchen the *maximum* extract rate should be 20 l/s (72 m^3/h).

An extract fan should *not* be provided in the same room as a **solid fuel appliance**.

Kitchens, utility rooms, bathrooms and WCs which do not have openable windows should be provided with an *air inlet*, e.g. a 10 mm gap under the door.

Kitchen extract ventilation 'adjacent to hob' means within 300 mm of centreline of hob and should be either a cooker hood or a fan with a humidistat.

Utility rooms which are accessible only from outside the building need not conform with the ventilation requirements of the Building Regulations.

Adjacent rooms may be considered as one room if there is a permanent opening(s) of at least 1/20th of the combined floor areas, in the dividing wall.

Where a non-habitable space such as a **conservatory** adjoins a habitable room, the habitable room may be ventilated with opening(s) of at least 1/20th of the combined floor areas in both the dividing wall and the wall to the outside, both openings to have at least 8000 mm^2 background ventilation. The opening(s) to the dividing wall may be closable.

Source: *Building Regulations Approved Document F1 2006*

Heat reclaim vent systems

HRV systems can be particularly appropriate for new, low energy, 'airtight' buildings and those with multiple extract needs or where passive systems are not feasible.

Typically, multiple bathrooms, WCs, kitchens, etc. within a single occupancy have linked extracts powered by a single low speed (boostable) fan through a heat exchanger to preheat incoming replacement air that is delivered to circulation areas or main spaces, achieving heat reclaim efficencies around 70 per cent. In summer, airflow is diverted away from the heat exchanger. For a small house or flat, the central fan unit is typically the size of a small kitchen wall cupboard; flat or round section ducts can be located in floor, loft or partition voids.

For very low energy buildings without space heating systems, heating coils fed from a water heating appliance can be incorporated in HRV systems to give a warm air back-up.

Extractor fans

Sizing of fans

The size of a fan should take into account the size of the room and not necessarily be the minimum required by the Building Regulations.

It therefore makes sense to calculate the size of fan needed by using the desired number of air changes per hour and relating them to the room size.

Suggested air changes per hour for typical situations

Domestic		Non-domestic	
Living rooms	3–6	Cafés and restaurants	10–12
Bedrooms	2–4	Cinemas and theatres	6–10
Bathrooms	6–8	Dance halls	12–15
WCs	6–8	Factories and workshops	6–10
Kitchens	10–15	Commercial kitchens	20–30
Utility rooms	10–15	Offices	4–6
Halls and passages	3–5	Public toilets	6–8

To calculate the extract performance needed for a fan, multiply the volume of a room (m^3) by the number of air changes per hour required (ACH):

e.g. Domestic kitchen $4\,m \times 5\,m \times 2.5\,m = 50\,m^3$
air changes required $= 12$
$50 \times 12 = \mathbf{600\,m^3/h}$

one m^3/h	$= 0.777\,l/s$
one l/s	$= 3.6\,m^3/h$

To reduce energy consumption, it is desirable to restrict ventilation rates and use 'extraction at source' as far as possible, ideally controlled according to demand. Given effectively controlled ventilation, air changes in domestic living spaces and bedrooms can be reduced to below 1 – below 0.6 for passivhaus standards – and maintain good air quality. For carefully built or refurbished buildings achieving high standards of airtightness, background ventilation systems including heat recovery can transfer up to 90 per cent of the heat from exhaust air to incoming air.

Siting of fans

- Site fans as far away as practicable from the main source of air replacement, which is usually the room door.
- Site fans where there is reasonable access for cleaning and maintenance.
- Fans in bathrooms must be sited out of reach of a person using a fixed bath or shower and must be kept well away from all sources of spray.
- Insulate ducts passing through unheated roof spaces to minimize condensation.
- Slope horizontal ducts slightly away from fan.
- Vertical ducts, and ducts in roof spaces, should be fitted with a condensate trap with a small drainpipe to outside.
- See pp. 166–168 for Building Regulation requirements and siting of extractor fans.

Types of fans

Axial fans are designed to move air over short distances, as through walls or windows.

Centrifugal fans are designed to move air over long distances and perform well against resistance built up over long lengths of ducts.

Sources: Vent-Axia Ltd and Xpelair Ltd

Electrical installation

Safety is paramount when electrical installation works are being carried out. Depending on the work being carried out, one or more of the following regulations need to be complied with:

- BS7671:2008, also known as the IEE Wiring Regulations, 17th edition
- Building Regulation Part L
- Building Regulation Part M
- Building Regulation Part P

Electricity

Electricity is sold by the *unit*.
One unit is consumed at the rate of one kilowatt for one hour (kWh).

Comparative costs of domestic appliances

Most appliances have energy efficiency ratings between A and G; A being the most efficient.

Appliance	Time per unit	
3 kW radiant heater	20 minutes	
2 kW convector heater	30 minutes	
iron	2 hours	
vacuum cleaner	2 hours	
colour TV	6 hours	
100 watt lamp	10 hours	
60 watt lamp	16 hours	
20 watt mini fluorescent	50 hours	
Tall larder refrigerator	63 hours	
Typical usage of larger appliances		kWh
chest freezer	per week	5–8
dishwasher	one full load	1
cooker	per week for family of four	23
hot water cylinder	per week for family of four	85

Fuses – rating for 230 volt AC appliances

Rating	Colour	Appliance wattage
2 amp	black	250 to 450
3 amp	red	460 to 750
5 amp	black	760 to 1250
13 amp	brown	1260 to 3000

To find the correct amp rating of a socket for an appliance, divide the watts of the appliance by the volts, i.e. watts ÷ 230 = amps.

Guidelines to allocating (socket) outlets in domestic rooms

The table below should be used as a guide and is not mandatory. Where quantities of outlets are recommended they should be considered a minimum.

Room	Socket Outlets
Entrance lobby	1 No. 2-gang switched socket outlet
Hall / landing	1 No. 2-gang switched socket outlet
Storage cupboard	switched fused spurs for equipment such as TV amplifiers, electric hot water heaters, etc.
Lounge	4 No. 2-gang switched socket outlets
Kitchen	1 No. 45 Amp cooker switch + outlet plate
	4 No. 2-gang switched socket outlets
	1 No. grid switch plate c/w switches controlling unswitched socket outlets for appliances such as extract hood, washer dryer, fridge freezer, dishwasher, extract fan, etc.
Kitchen utility	Outlets for appliances
	2 No. 2-gang switched socket outlets
Bedrooms	3 No. 2-gang switched socket outlets
Bathrooms	Switched fused connection unit for towel rail (depending on development)
	1 No. shaver socket
Garage	2 No. 2-gang switched socket outlets

It should be noted that socket outlets alone do not make a complete electrical installation. Consideration will also need to be given to the following, on a room by room basis:

- Lighting (numbers of points, type of lighting)
- Lighting switching
- Television outlets
- BT outlets
- Room thermostat(s) for heating
- Smoke detectors
- Access control (depending on development)
- Positioning of the consumer unit.

Electrical installation graphic symbols

SUPPLY and DISTRIBUTION

electricity meter	
transformer	
distribution board	
isolator	
terminal to earth	
fuse	
circuit breaker	
lightning protection	
cable / conduit on diagrams	
cable / conduit on plans	

POWER

socket outlet	
switched socket outlet	
twin socket outlet	
socket outlet with pilot lamp	
connection unit	
switched connection unit	
connection unit with cable outlet	
connection unit with pilot lamp	
connection unit, four gang	
shaver socket	
cooker control unit with two pole switch	

COMMUNICATIONS SOCKETS

FM radio	
television	
private service television	
closed circuit television	
telephone	
telex	
modem	
fax	

SWITCHES

	one pole switch
	one pole switch, two gang
	two, three, four pole switches
	two way switch
	intermediate switch
	switch with pilot lamp
	pull cord switch
	switch, time operated
	switch, period operated
	switch, temperature operated
	dimmer switch
	push button switch
	push switch, illuminated
	push on/push off switch

LUMINAIRES

	luminaire
	enclosed luminaire
	reflector
	spotlight open, enclosed
	flood open, enclosed
	linear open, enclosed
	emergency/safety open, enclosed
	emergency/safety self contained
	linear emergency/safety open, enclosed
	luminaire on wall open, enclosed
	luminaire on pole open, enclosed
	luminaire on suspension cable
	luminaire with built-in pull cord

Source: BS 1192: Part 5: 2007

Electric circuits in the home

Typical domestic electrical layout

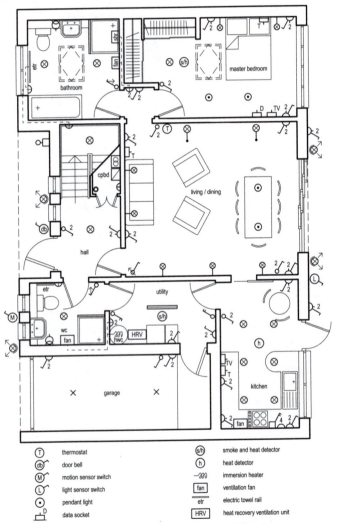

T	thermostat	s/h	smoke and heat detector
db	door bell	h	heat detector
M	motion sensor switch	⟶⟋⟍⟍	immersion heater
L	light sensor switch	fan	ventilation fan
⊙	pendant light	etr	electric towel rail
D	data socket	HRV	heat recovery ventilation unit

as different symbols are often used, an explanatory key is usually included with the drawings

Lighting

Part L

All lighting installations need to incorporate an element of energy efficient lamps in order to comply with Building Regulation Part L. Below is a summary of conditions to ensure compliance:

Part L1A

- Fixed energy efficient light fittings shall be not less than the greater of one per 25 m² of dwelling floor area or part thereof or one per four fixed lighting fittings
- Fixed external lighting shall use efficient lamps such that the lamp capacity does not exceed 150 watts per light fitting and that the lighting automatically switches off when there is enough daylight and when it is not required at night.

Part L1B. Same requirements as Part L1A subject to the following work being carried out:

- A dwelling is extended
- A new dwelling is created from a material change of use
- An existing lighting system is being replaced as part of the re-wiring works.

Part L2A

General lighting efficacy in office, industrial and storage areas in all building types:

- Reasonable provision would be to provide lighting with an average initial efficacy of not less than 45 luminaire-lumens/circuit-watt as averaged over the whole area of these types of space in the building.

General lighting efficacy in all other types of space:

- For lighting systems serving other types of space, it may be appropriate to provide luminaires for which photometric data is not available and/or are lower powered and use less efficient lamps. For such spaces, the requirement would be met if the installed lighting has an average initial (100 hour) lamp plus ballast efficacy of not less than 50 lamp lumens per circuit-watt.

- Display lighting: Reasonable provision for display lighting would be to demonstrate that the installed display lighting has an average initial (100 hour) efficacy of not less than 15 lamp-lumens per circuit-watt. In calculating this efficacy, the power consumed by any transformers or ballasts should be taken into account.

Part L2B. Same requirements as Part L2A but only applicable to those areas affected by building works.

Lighting glossary

colour rendering The ability of a light source to render colours naturally without distorting the hues seen under a full radiator (similar to daylight) in which all the wavelengths of the visible spectrum are present.

Colour Rendering Index (CRI) An index based on eight standard test colours where the unit is *Ra*. Ra100 is the maximum value. Ra85 and above is considered appropriate for everyday comfort. The index can also be arranged in values of 1 to 4 according to DIN 3035.

compact fluorescent Small-scale fluorescent lamps, often with integral gear, for long life, low energy use in small fittings.

Correlated Colour Temperature (CCT) The colour appearance determined from its colour temperature given in degrees Kelvin. The lower the figure the warmer the light. Less than 3300 K is warm (red); 3300–5300 K intermediate and more than 5300 K cold (blue). The human eye cannot differentiate between individual spectral colours of a light source; it can only perceive a mixture of colours.

dichroic mirror lamp A small lamp with a built-in spiral, often faceted, mirror reflector. The mirror is made to reflect only certain colours of light and transmit heat radiation so as to produce a cool beam of light. The facets help to reduce striations in the beam, producing softer focusing with blurred edges to the beam.

discharge lamp A light source from an electrical discharge passing through a glass containing vapour or gas.

efficacy The ratio of initial lumens divided by lamp watts (lm/W). Typical efficacy for a GLS lamp is 8–18 rising to 100–180 for a low pressure sodium lamp.

emergency lighting Low output battery-powered lighting for escape purposes when mains power fails.

flood (F) A lamp designed with a wide beam.

fluorescent tube A discharge tubular lamp, generally fitted with argon and low pressure mercury vapour. It has a phosphor coating on the inside giving off light (fluorescing) when excited by an electric arc through the vapour.

GLS General Lighting Service: standard *tungsten filament* pear shaped lamps.

halogen lamp An incandescent lamp filled with low pressure vapour of iodine or bromine. Sometimes referred to as *tungsten-halogen*.

HID High-Intensity Discharge lamps, i.e. *metal-halide*, *mercury* and *sodium* lamps.

illuminance The amount of light falling on a surface. The unit is *lux*, which is one lumen per square metre (lm/m^2).

incandescent lamp A tungsten filament enclosed in a glass envelope either under vacuum or filled with inert gas so that it can be electrically heated without burning out. Incandescent means luminous or glowing with heat; as a result can be an inefficient light source emphasizing reds, yellows and greens while subduing blues.

initial lumens The light output of a lamp measured after one hour for incandescent lamps and 100 hours for fluorescent and discharge lamps. Lumens quoted in manufacturers' catalogues are 'initial' lumens.

LED LEDs are 'solid state' emitters of coloured light made from similar materials (semiconductors) to those used to manufacture electronic integrated circuits. They produce light by a very different method to incandescent, fluorescent or discharge lamps and do not require heat or high voltages to operate. An LED 'die', which typically measures just 0.25×0.25 mm, is encapsulated into a solid resin to produce an individual LED component with connecting leads.

Light-Loss Factor (LLF) The loss in light output from a luminaire due to dirt on the lamp or fitting. Now more normally referred to as *maintenance factor*.

Light Output Ratio (LOR) The ratio of the total light emitted by a luminaire to the total output of the lamp(s) it contains – which is always less than unity.

lumen (lm) The unit of *luminous flux* used to measure the amount of light given off by a light source.

luminaire A light fitting.

luminance   The brightness of a surface in a given direction, measured in *candelas* per square metre (cd/m^2).

luminous flux   The flow of light energy from a source, or reflected from a surface, standardized for the human eye and measured in *lumens*. It is used to calculate *illuminance*.

lux   The unit of *illuminance* measured in lumens per square metre (lm/m^2). Bright sunlight is 100000 lux; full moon is 1 lux.

maintained illuminance   The minimum light level over an area immediately prior to cleaning/re-lamping.

maintenance factor   The proportion of initial light output from an installation after some specified time.

metal halide lamps   High pressure mercury discharge lamps with additives which can vary the light appearance from warm to cool.

Rated Average Life (RAL)   The time by which 50 per cent of lamps installed can be expected to have failed.

sodium lamp (SON)   A highly efficient lamp with a warm yellow light, used mainly for street and flood lighting. It has poor colour rendering, with the low pressure (SOX) types making all colours except yellow appear brown or black.

spot (S)   A lamp producing a narrow beam of light as opposed to the medium/wide beam of a *flood*.

tri-phosphor lamp   A *fluorescent* lamp with good colour rendering.

tungsten-filament lamp   An *incandescent* lamp.

tungsten-halogen lamp   A *halogen* lamp.

Lighting: levels and colours

Comparative light levels	lux
Bright sunlight	100 000
Worktop near window	3 000
Full moon on clear night	1

Recommended lighting levels	lux
Houses/Flats/Bedsits	
Entrance lobbies	200
Lounges	150
Kitchen	150–300
Bathrooms	150
WCs	100
Communal Areas	
Main entrances	200
Corridors	20–100
Staircases	100
Lounges	100–300
TV lounges	50
Quiet/rest rooms	100
Dining rooms	150
Laundries	300
Stores	100

Colour temperatures	K
Blue sky	10 000
Uniform overcast sky	7 000
Average natural daylight	6 500
HP mercury cool white lamp	4 000
Fluorescent warm white lamp	3 000
Halogen filament lamp	3 000
GLS tungsten filament	2 700
HP sodium lamp	2 050

CIE Colour Rendering Index

Ra		Group
100	Where accurate colour matching is required, e.g. printing inspection	1A
90	Where good colour rendering is required, e.g. shops	1B
80	Where moderate colour rendering is acceptable	2
60	Where colour rendering is of little significance but marked distortion unacceptable	3
40	Where colour rendering is of no importance	4

Lamps

Listed on the following pages is a survey of the main types of lamps available.

Excluded are the many variations of certain types and those which may be used for more specialized situations such as infra-red, UV stop, horticultural, black light, etc. Also excluded are the high output, low sodium lights used mainly for road lighting. The list is therefore not comprehensive and manufacturers' catalogues should be consulted for more information.

Lumens quoted are for *Initial lumens*. The lowest values have been given, which are for pearl or opal versions of a lamp or the 'warmer' colour temperature fluorescent tubes.

Sources: G.E. Lighting Ltd, Osram Ltd, Philips Lighting Ltd, Concord Sylvania

Incandescent lamps

Incandescent lamps soon redundant for energy reasons.

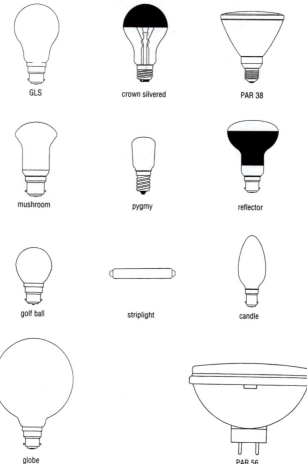

GLS

crown silvered

PAR 38

mushroom

pygmy

reflector

golf ball

striplight

candle

globe

PAR 56

Halogen lamps

dichroic 35 mm & 50 mm

PAR 30

metal reflector

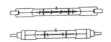

linear halogen

BTT halogen

single ended capsule

globe halogen

tubular halogen

Fluorescent lamps and tubes

single U tube

2D

self ballasted

double U tube

compact
fluorescent globe

circular

7 mm sub-miniature

16 mm miniature

26 mm standard tube

38 mm standard tube

triple U tube

double U tube
(for GLS replacement)

Lamp comparison

	GLS incandescent lamp		FBT double U compact fluorescent lamp		
	Lumens	**Watts**	**Watts**	**Lumens**	
	410	40	7	460	
	700	60	11	600	
	930	75	15	900	
	1350	100	20	1200	

High-intensity discharge lamps

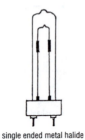

single ended metal halide

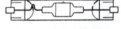

double ended metal halide

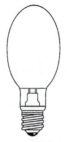

mercury elliptical

mercury reflector

HP sodium elliptical

HP sodium tubular

Sound

Acoustic insulation

Soundproofing of construction requires three conditions to be fulfilled:

1 Airtight construction to prevent sound transmission in air.
2 Heavyweight construction to reduce low frequency sound transmission.
3 Lightweight insulation to reduce high frequency sound transmission.

Better quality or more primitive methods of traditional construction tended to achieve good acoustic insulation between most buildings, through substantial masonry walls, but tended to have poor insulation between storeys due to air leaky timber floors; with heavy lath and plaster ceilings, sound transfer is much reduced.

Modern construction usually aims to minimize weight and thickness for economic reasons; for smaller buildings this usually means precast concrete or multi-layer timber floors and either double skin/double thickness masonry, or else double-leaf timber frame party walls.

In timber construction, air gaps or 'floating layers' are critical to reducing transmission while in masonry construction, which is more reliant on weight, similar performance is achieved by building either double skin or double thickness walls. In both types of construction, workmanship has to be careful and thorough to achieve effective acoustic insulation.

Building Regulations Part E includes 'Robust Standard Details' for party walls and party floors that have been field tested; new construction requires either use of such details or field testing.

Noise levels

The level of hearing is expressed in decibels from 0 dB, the threshold of hearing, to 140 dB, the threshold of pain.

Ears respond to sound frequencies or pitch from around 20 Hz bass to 20 kHz treble. Most people are more sensitive to high rather than low frequencies, but old age reduces the perception of higher frequencies.

Recommended maximum dBA*

- Hospital and general wards   55
- Small consulting rooms   50
- Large offices   45–50
- Private offices   40–45
- Living rooms   40–45
- Small classrooms   40
- Large lecture rooms   35
- Bedrooms   30–40
- Music studios   30

* **dBA** are decibels weighted to simulate the response of our ears as opposed to plain **dB** which do not depend directly on human reaction.

Source: BS 8233: 1999

Sound levels

	dB range
	140
• Threshold of pain	130
• Pneumatic drill	120
• Loud car horn @ 1 m	110
• Pop group @ 20 m	100
• Inside tube train	90
• Inside bus	80
• Average kerbside traffic	70
• Conversational speech	60
• Typical office	50
• Family living room	40
• Library	30
• Bedroom at night	20
• Broadcasting studio	10
• Threshold of hearing	0

Source: Pilkington United Kingdom Ltd

Sound transmission loss of some typical building elements

Material	dB
One layer 9.5 mm plasterboard	25
Cupboards used as partitions	25–35
6 mm single glazing	29
75 mm timber studs with 12.5 mm plasterboard both sides	36
115 mm brickwork plastered one side	43
75 mm clinker concrete block plastered both sides	44
6 mm double glazing with 100 mm air gap	44
100 mm timber studs with 12.5 mm plasterboard both sides & quilt in cavity	46
115 mm brickwork plastered both sides	47
230 mm brickwork plastered one side	48
230 mm brickwork plastered both sides	55

Building Regulations Part E; 2000 effective since 2003. The latest revisions to the Building Regulations require pre completion testing for sound insulation for residential conversions and new buildings. The use of robust details in new houses and flats will be accepted as an alternative to testing.

5
Building Elements

Stairs

Building Regulations requirements

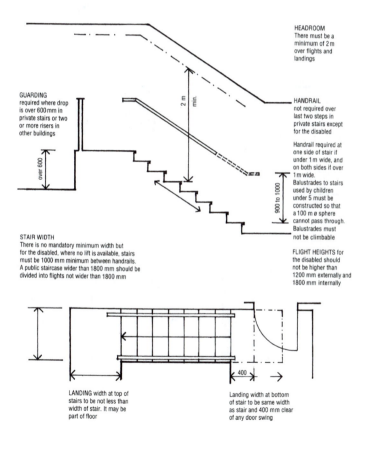

HEADROOM
There must be a minimum of 2 m over flights and landings

GUARDING
required where drop is over 600 mm in private stairs or two or more risers in other buildings

over 600

2 m min.

HANDRAIL
not required over last two steps in private stairs except for the disabled

Handrail required at one side of stair if under 1 m wide, and on both sides if over 1 m wide. Balustrades to stairs used by children under 5 must be constructed so that a 100 m ø sphere cannot pass through. Balustrades must not be climbable

900 to 1000

STAIR WIDTH
There is no mandatory minimum width but for the disabled, where no lift is available, stairs must be 1000 mm minimum between handrails. A public staircase wider than 1800 mm should be divided into flights not wider than 1800 mm

FLIGHT HEIGHTS for the disabled should not be higher than 1200 mm externally and 1800 mm internally

400

LANDING width at top of stairs to be not less than width of stair. It may be part of floor

Landing width at bottom of stair to be same width as stair and 400 mm clear of any door swing

Building Regulations requirements – continued

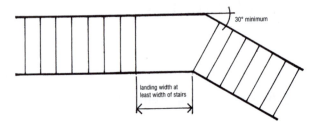

30° minimum

landing width at
least width of stairs

LONG FLIGHTS
Stairs with more than 36 risers in consecutive flights should make at least one change of direction of not
less than 30°. No more than 16 risers in any flight of stairs serving areas used as a shop or for assembly

TAPERED TREADS measurement of going

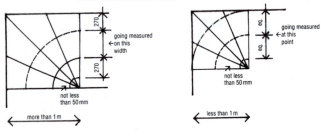

270

going measured
←on this
width

270

not less
than 50 mm

more than 1 m

going measured
←at this
point

not less
than 50 mm

less than 1 m

ALTERNATING TREADS
may be permitted for
loft conversions where
there is no room for a
proper staircase. They
may only access one
room and must have
handrails both sides
and non-slip surface
to treads

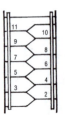

LOFT CONVERSIONS
Headroom may be
reduced if height at
centre of stair is at
least 1900 mm and not
less than 1800 mm at
side of stair

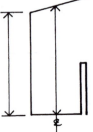

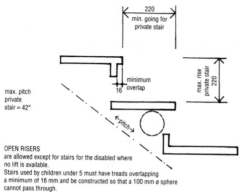

OPEN RISERS
are allowed except for stairs for the disabled where
no lift is available.
Stairs used by children under 5 must have treads overlapping
a minimum of 16 mm and be constructed so that a 100 mm ø sphere
cannot pass through.

SOURCES:
Building Regulations Approved Documents
K   Stairs, ramps and guards
M   Access for disabled people
B   Fire safety
N   Glazing (for glass balustrades)
BS 6180: 1982 for strength of balustrades
Spiral and helical stairs should be in
accordance with BS 5395: Part 2: 1984

RISE and GOING	max. rise	min. going
Private stair	220	220
External stair for the disabled	150	280
Internal stair for the disabled	170	250
Institutional & Assembly stair	180	280
Assembly building < 100 m²	180	250
Other stair	190	250

normal ratio: twice the rise plus going
(2R + G) should be between 550 mm and 700 mm

Gradients

%	Slope	Application
5%	1:20	maximum uphill gradient preferred by cyclists maximum outdoor slope for pedestrians
6.5%	1:15.4	maximum downhill gradient preferred by cyclists
5.0%	1:20	maximum wheelchair ramp for a maximum length of 10 m and rise of 500 mm
6.7%	1:15	maximum wheelchair ramp for a maximum length of 5 m and rise of 333 mm
8.3%	1:12	maximum wheelchair ramp for a maximum length of 2 m and rise of 166 mm
8.5%	1:11.8	maximum indoor slope for pedestrians
10%	1:10	maximum ramp for lorry loading bays and most car parking garages
12%	1:8.3	any road steeper than this will be impassable in snow without snow tyres or chains maximum for dropped pavement kerbs of less than 1 m long
15%	1:6.7	absolute maximum for multi-storey car parks

Fireplaces

Building Regulation requirements
Fireplace recesses

minimum dimensions of solid non-combustible material

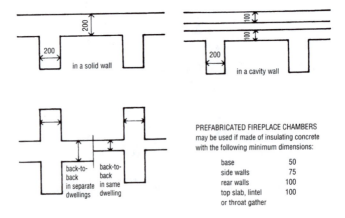

in a solid wall

in a cavity wall

back-to-back in separate dwellings | back-to-back in same dwelling

PREFABRICATED FIREPLACE CHAMBERS
may be used if made of insulating concrete
with the following minimum dimensions:

base	50
side walls	75
rear walls	100
top slab, lintel or throat gather	100

Constructional hearths

minimum dimensions

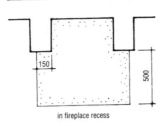

in fireplace recess

CONSTRUCTIONAL HEARTHS are required for an open
fire, a gas flue where the flame is less than 186 mm
above floor finish, a solid fuel or oil burning appliance
where the temperature of the floor may exceed 100°C. If
below this temperature then appliance may sit on a non-
combustible board or tiles – both at least 12 mm thick.

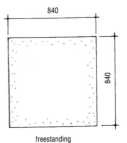

freestanding

Hearths must be at least 125 mm thick of
solid non-combustible material which
may include the thickness of any non-
combustible decorative surface.

Superimposed hearths

Minimum dimensions from the face of an appliance

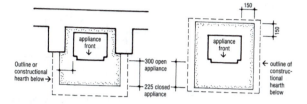

Superimposed hearths are optional. They must be made of solid non-combustible material and be placed over a constructional hearth as shown on p. 196. An appliance must be located on a hearth (whether a constructional or superimposed hearth) with the minimum dimensions as shown in the drawings above. The edge of this area of hearth must be clearly marked such as by a change of level.

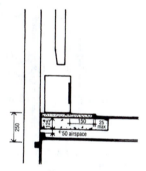

Minimum distances allowed between COMBUSTIBLE material and hearth. A combustible floor finish may only extend 25 mm under a superimposed hearth.

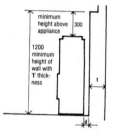

WALLS ADJACENT TO HEARTHS which are not part of a fireplace recess must have the following thickness and be of solid non-combustible material:

	t
HEARTH abutting a wall where **d** is 0–50	200
where **d** is 51–300	75
HEARTH not abutting a wall where hearth edge < 150	75

SOURCE:
This is a summary of some of the requirements from The Building Regulations Approved Document J 2002

Chimneys and flues

Building Regulations requirements

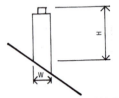

HEIGHT OF CHIMNEY (H) which includes terminal should not exceed 4½ times the smallest width dimension (W) (Bld. Regs. Doc A)

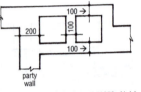

party wall

MINIMUM WALL THICKNESSES of brick and block chimneys excluding any liner
100 mm between one flue and another
100 mm between flue and outside air
100 mm between flue and another part of the same building
200 mm between flue and another compartment or building

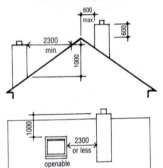

Pitched roofs

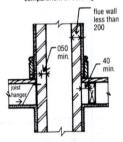

COMBUSTIBLE MATERIAL should be separated from masonry chimneys by at least 200 mm from flue OR 40 mm from the outer face of the chimney unless it is a floorboard, skirting, dado, picture rail, mantelshelf or architrave. Metal fixings in contact with combustible materials should be at least 50 mm away from flue.

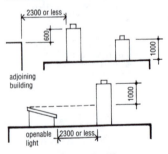

Flat roofs with a pitch of less than 10°

CHIMNEY FLUE OUTLETS minimum height above roof

COMBUSTION AIR will be required for the correct operation of all flueless and open flued appliances and some room sealed models, and to ensure that the products of combustion are carried to the outside air.

These requirements are summarized from The Building Regulations Approved Document J 2002

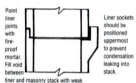

Flues in chimneys should be vertical where possible. Maximum permitted offset is 45° to the vertical. Provision must be made to sweep flues. For sizes of flues see Table 2.2 in the Building Regs.

FLUE OFFSETS

FLUE PIPES should be used only to connect an appliance to a chimney. They should not pass through a roof space, internal wall or floor except to pass directly into a masonry chimney. Horizontal connections to the back of an appliance should not be longer than 150 mm. Flue pipes should have the same diameter or cross-sectional area as that of the appliance outlet.

Flue pipes may be made of:
Cast iron to BS 41
Mild steel at least 3 mm thick
Stainless steel at least 1 mm thick
Vitreous enamelled steel to BS 6999

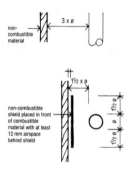

Point liner joints with fire-proof mortar. Fill void between liner and masonry stack with weak mortar or insulating concrete.

Liner sockets should be positioned uppermost to prevent condensation leaking into stack.

Brick and block chimneys should be lined unless made of refractory material.

FLUE LINERS

BALANCED FLUES (room sealed) are mandatory for gas appliances fitted in bathrooms, shower rooms and gas fires or heaters of more than 14 kW (gross) in bedrooms. For positioning of balanced flues, see the numerous dimensional limitations as shown in diagram 3.4 of the Building Regs.

FLUES FOR GAS BOILERS – all new gas and oil boilers are required to be high efficiency condensing models under Building Regulations Part L. The majority of these will have fan assisted balanced flues with a concentric flue pipe where combustion air is delivered via the outer pipe and flue gases are discharged via the inner pipe; fan assistance allows these pipes to run horizontally for up to 10 metres or to include a number of bends. Alternatively, inlet and outlet pipes can be separated and, due to the very low flue temperatures, can be formed in plastic waste pipes. Condensing boilers often cause significant plumes of water vapour at their flue outlets, which needs to be considered in flue location alongside the limits in the Building Regulations diagram J 3.4.

Flueless instantaneous gas water heaters should not be installed in rooms less than 5 m³.

FACTORY-MADE insulated chimneys should conform to BS 4543 and be fitted to BS 7566.

SOURCE:
These requirements are summarized from The Building Regulations Approved Document J 2002.

non-combustible material   3 x ø

non-combustible shield placed in front of combustible material with at least 12 mm airspace behind shield   1½ x ø   ½ ø   1½ ø   ø   1½ ø

UNINSULATED FLUEPIPE — minimum distances away from combustible material

Flues for wood/biomass burning appliances as for solid fuel. Particular care is needed to allow for liners installed to cope with tars draining down flues; insulated flues tend to perform better with less condensate; existing traditional masonry chimneys are prone to tar leakage and staining. The use of thermal stores in conjunction with biomass can minimize these problems by allowing intermittent hot burns.

Doors

Standard doors are still manufactured primarily in imperial sizes. The manufacturers claim that this is because of demands by the building trade. There is also a need for replacement doors in older properties and the apparently odd size 2'8" × 6'8" is still produced for this reason. There is more demand for metric sizes for large-scale building projects but the choice is still limited. Unless a large quantity of doors is ordered, standard sized doors are still significantly cheaper than specials.

Because of the need to accommodate wheelchair users, wider doors are now more in demand. A new standard size of 864 × 1981 is produced by some manufacturers. An 800 mm clear opening is considered the absolute minimum for a wheelchair user. Sixty mm should be deducted from the actual door width to arrive at the clear opening size. This dimension takes into account the thickness of the door and hinges standing open at one side and the rebate or stop on the other side.

Typical sizes of single leaf standard doors (metric)

	926 × 2040	826 × 2040	807 × 2000	726 × 2040	626 × 2040	526 × 2040	Thickness (mm)
Exterior							
Solid panelled			*				44
Glazed panelled			*				44
Flush		*	*				44
Steel faced			*				44
Framed and ledged			*				44
Ledged and braced			*				36
Interior							
Solid panelled				*			35
Glazed panelled		*	*	*			40
Flush	*	*		*	*	*	40
Moulded panelled	*	*		*	*	*	35 and 40
Fire							
½ hour	*	*	*	*	*	*	44
1 hour		*		*			54
Structural openings	1010	910	890	810	710	610	

Typical sizes of single leaf standard doors (imperial)

	838 × 1981 2'9" × 6'6"	813 × 2032 2'8" × 6'8"	762 × 1981 2'6" × 6'6"	686 × 1981 2'3" × 6'6"	610 × 1981 2'0" × 6'6"	Thickness (mm)
Exterior						
solid panelled	*	*	*			44
glazed panelled	*	*	*			54
Flush	*	*	*	*	*	44
steel faced	*		*			44
framed and ledged	*	*	*	*	*	44
ledged and braced	*	*	*	*	*	36
Interior						
solid panelled	*		*	*	*	35 & 40
glazed panelled	*	*	*	*	*	35 & 40
Flush	*	*	*	*	*	35 & 40
moulded panelled	*	*	*	*	*	35 & 40
Fire						
1/2 hour	*	*	*	*	*	44
1 hour	*	*	*	*		54

Other types of doors

Fire doors

Fire doors are available in most standard sizes in flush doors, and some are also available in internal moulded panelled doors. Half-hour and one-hour fire doors are only rated FD 30(S) and FD 60(S) when used with appropriate door frames which are fitted with intumescent strip (combined with smoke seal). The intumescent strips and smoke seals may also be fitted to the top and along edges of the fire door. Existing panelled doors, particularly in Listed Buildings, can be upgraded to give 30 and 60 minutes' fire protection, using intumescent papers and paints.

Source: Envirograph

French doors

Two-leaf glazed doors, opening out, are manufactured in hardwood and softwood in the following typical sizes:

Metric: 1106 wide × 1994 mm high; 1200, 1500 and 1800 wide × 2100 mm high

Imperial: 1168 wide × 1981 mm high (3'10" × 6'6") and 914 wide × 1981 mm high (3'0" × 6'6").

Sliding and sliding folding glazed doors

These are available in hardwood, softwood, softwood with external aluminium cladding, uPVC and aluminium in hardwood frames in the following metric nominal opening sizes typically:

2 leaf:	1200, 1500, 1800, 2100, 2400 wide × 2100 mm high	OX and XO
3 leaf:	2400 to 4000 wide in 200 mm increments × 2100 mm high	OXO
4 leaf:	3400 to 5000 wide in 200 mm increments × 2100 mm high	OXXO

Opening configurations are often labelled:

O = fixed panel and X = sliding panel when viewed from outside.

Some manufacturers offer all panels sliding.

Many manufacturers will make bespoke sizes to suit the height and width of openings dependent on the weight of the leaves.

Garage doors

Garage doors are manufactured in hardwood, softwood, plywood, steel and GRP. Doors can be hinged, or up and over, and can be electrically opened. The following typical sizes exclude the frame which is recommended to be a minimum of ex 75 mm timber.

	W mm	h mm
Single:	1981 × 1981	(6'6" × 6'6")
	1981 × 2134	(6'6" × 7'0")
	2134 × 1981	(7'0" × 6'6")
	2134 × 2134	(7'0" × 7'0")
	2286 × 1981	(7'6" × 6'6")
	2286 × 2134	(7'6" × 7'0")
	2438 × 1981	(8'0" × 6'6")
	2438 × 2134	(8'0" × 7'0")
Double:	4267 × 1981	(14'0" × 6'6")
	4267 × 2134	(14'0" × 7'0")
	other double doors available in widths up to 4878 (16'0")	

Door handing

The traditional way of describing the configuration of a door is by the 'hand' – see **1**. There is also the ISO coding method **2** which describes a door's action as clockwise or anticlockwise. Despite its name it is not international and not widely used. Different components for a door sometimes conflict as, for instance, a door which requires a right-hand rebated mortice lock may need a left-hand overhead door closer. When in doubt, the specifier should draw a diagram.

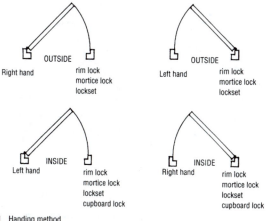

1 Handing method
   The definition of an OUTSIDE FACE of a door is:
   the external side of a door in an external wall;
   the corridor side of a room door;
   the side of a communicating door on which the hinge knuckles are not seen when the door is closed;
   the space between them in the case of twin doors;
   the room side of a cupboard, wardrobe or closet.

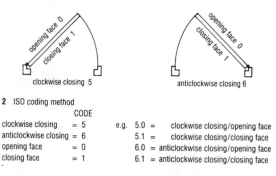

2 ISO coding method

	CODE	
clockwise closing	= 5	e.g. 5.0 = clockwise closing/opening face
anticlockwise closing	= 6	5.1 = clockwise closing/closing face
opening face	= 0	6.0 = anticlockwise closing/opening face
closing face	= 1	6.1 = anticlockwise closing/closing face

Direction of CLOSING and DOOR FACE are given to identify the door configuration as examples above.

Traditional wooden doors – definitions and typical sections

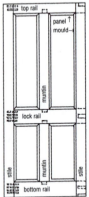

The rails are fixed to the full height styles with haunched tenons & wedged.

Muntins are tenoned to rails

Dowels, as shown on LHS, can also be used for a stronger joint which withstands well uneven shrinkage.

All frame sections are grooved at least 9 mm to house the panels.

Stiles are normally ex 100 × 50 or 125 × 50

Bottom & lock rails are deeper, typically ex 200 × 50

Panels should be min. 6 mm ply for internal doors and min. 9 mm ply for external doors

Four–panelled door

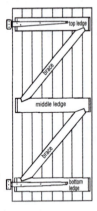

Door made up of ex 150 × 32 ledges and ex 100 × 32 braces with ex 25 mm t+g 'V' jointed boarding not more than ex 125 mm wide.

Ledges are screwed to the boards and the boards are nailed to the ledges.

Door hung with steel Tee hinges or with stronger wrought iron strap hinges and fastened with a suffolk latch.

Ledged & braced boarded door

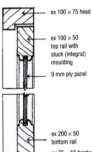

ex 100 × 75 head

ex 100 × 50 top rail with stuck (integral) moulding

9 mm ply panel

ex 200 × 50 bottom rail

ex 75 × 50 hardwood weather mould best morticed into door

Rebate in door frame for ms weather bar

ex 125 × 50 hardwood cill carried under side frames with min. 9° slope

External door frame
for inward opening door

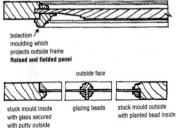

bolection moulding which projects outside frame
Raised and fielded panel

outside face

stuck mould inside with glass secured with putty outside
Glazed door

glazing beads

stuck mould outside with planted bead inside

architraves master joint between plaster & lining and provide stop-end for skirting

Door frame
ex 100 × 75 with rebate for door stop. Can be erected before walls or built into opening

Door lining
ex 32 mm with width to suit wall
Linings are thinner than door frames and for internal doors only. They have planted stops and are fitted to finished opening

Windows

Standard windows listed below are manufactured in softwood, softwood with aluminium cladding, hardwood, thermally broken aluminium and steel, and in PVC in a wide range of sizes and types. The sizes are approximate. Standard sized windows are less significant on smaller projects and most windows are made to order from standard sections or purpose-made. Very low energy windows to meet Passivhaus standards – whole window U-values < 0.8 W/m^{2}K – are typically made with laminated frames and sashes including insulation material.

Side hung casements

This is by far the most common type of standard window. They are available as single sashes or in twos, threes and fours. There are numerous combinations of fully-opening side hung sashes, one or more fixed lights and smaller top hung vents, with or without glazing bars. Side hung sashes can be fitted with concealed friction stays fixed over the top and under the bottom of sashes, in lieu of conventional hinges, for easier cleaning from inside.

Widths: 630, 915, 1200, 1770 and 2340 mm.
Heights: 750, 900, 1050, 1200 and 1350 mm.

Bay windows

Square, splayed at 45° semi-circular and shallow curved bay windows are available using combinations of fixed lights, side and top hung casements and double hung sashes to suit structural opening widths of approximately 1200 to 3500 mm with projections as little as 130 mm for shallow curved bays and up to 1000 mm for semi-circular bays.

Top hung casements

Top hung sashes generally without glazing bars.

Widths: 630, 915 and 1200 mm singles;
             1770 mm single with fixed side light.

Heights: 450, 600, 750, 900, 1050 and 1200 mm.

Also vertical configurations with central horizontal transom and top hung opening sash to top half mimicking traditional double hung sashes.

Widths: 480, 630, 915, 1200 mm singles;
1700 and 2340 mm doubles.

Heights: 750, 900, 1050, 1200, 1350, 1500 and 1650 mm.

Fixed lights
A range of fixed light windows sometimes referred to as *direct glazed*.

Widths:	300, 485, 630 and 1200 mm.
Heights:	450, 600, 750, 900, 1050, 1200 and 1350 mm.
Circular:	600 mm Ø 'Bullseye'.
Semi-circular:	630, 915 and 1200 mm Ø fanlights with or without two 60° glazing bars.

Double hung sashes
Softwood double hung sashes with spiral balances, some fitted with a tilting mechanism allowing for easier cleaning from the inside. With and without glazing bars.

Widths: 410, 630, 860, 1080 mm singles;
1700 and 1860 mm combinations.
Heights: 1050, 1350 and 1650 mm.

Traditional double hung sashes hung on lead weights in boxes can be made to any size.

H-windows
High performance softwood windows with complex hinge mechanism allowing partial projection for ventilation and complete reversal for cleaning. Available also as a side hung escape window.

Widths: 450, 600, 900, 1200, 1350, 1500 and 1800 mm.
Heights: 600, 900, 1050, 1200, 1350, 1500 and 1600 mm.

Sources: JELD-WEN UK, Premdor

Tilt and turn windows
These are the most widely available European high performance windows, particularly in the very low energy ranges, to

Passivhaus standards, etc; they have two opening configurations: bottom hung inwards tilt for relatively secure ventilation, and side hung inwards turn for cleaning or escape.

Energy ratings

The BFRC Scheme is the UK's national system for rating the energy efficiency of windows and is recognized within the Building Regulations as a method to show compliance for replacement windows installation.

1 The rating level – A, B, C, etc...
2 The energy rating, e.g. $-3kW/m^2K$ in this example the product will lose 3 kilowatt hours per square metre per year.
3 The window U-value, e.g. $1.4W/m^2K$.
4 The effective heat loss due to air penetration as L, e.g. $0.01 W/m^2K$.
5 The solar heat gain, e.g. $g = 0.43$.

Source: British Fenestration Rating Council www.bfrc.org

Glazing

Most windows have rebates suitable for double-glazing units (as required under Building Regulations) up to a thickness of 28mm for high performance, although slim double-glazed units are available with overall thicknesses of 10–12mm for use specifically in historic buildings. Double-glazed units are available with a choice of plain, obscured, annealed, laminated or toughened glass. To meet Building Regulations Part L, double glazing has to include a low-e coating applied to the outer face of the inner pane. Hard coatings are more robust for handling, but soft coatings are more efficient thermally. Inert gas filling, such as argon, krypton or xenon, and the use of non-metallic insulating spacers to the perimeter, maximize thermal performance, with triple glazing the next step to bring whole window U-values down to below 0.8, as appropriate for CSH Level 5 or 6 and Passivhaus standards, for example. 2 + 1 triple-glazed units can incorporate blinds to assist with solar control and glare.

Leaded lights are windows made up of small panes of glass, either regular or patterned as in stained glass, which are set in lead cames – 'H' section glazing bars.

Protection
The Building Regulations require that all glazing below 800 mm above floor level in windows and below 1500 mm above floor level in doors and sidelights, and sidelights which are within 300 mm of a door, should be fitted with safety glass. See p. 218. Small panes should have a maximum width of 250 mm and an area not exceeding 0.5 m^2 and should be glazed with glass a minimum 6 mm thick. See diagrams on p. 209.

Weather stripping
Weather stripping should always be provided as standard to all opening lights to minimize air leakage.

Finishes
Timber windows are normally supplied primed for painting or with a base coat for staining. Options may include complete painting or staining with guarantees available up to 10 years.

Ventilation
Most windows are now fitted with ventilators in the head-frame providing either 4000 mm^2 in the narrower windows or 8000 mm^2 controllable secure ventilation to suit current Building Regulations in the wider windows.

Fittings
Fasteners, peg stays, hinges, etc. all supplied with the windows in aluminium, chrome, stainless steel, gold spray, lacquered brass, brown, white or other colour finishes, at extra cost.

Swept heads
Elliptical curves for the tops of panes available factory-fitted or supplied loose. Curved shapes not usually available in aluminium clad timber windows.

Traditional wooden windows – definitions and typical sections

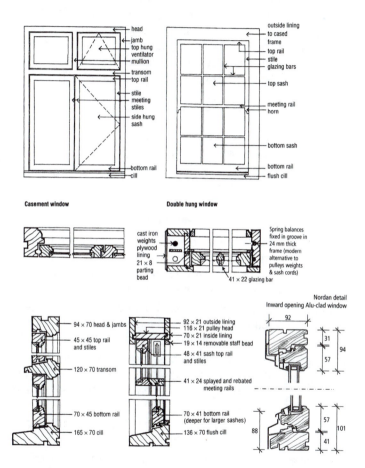

Casement window

- head
- jamb
- top hung ventilator
- mullion
- transom
- top rail
- stile
- meeting stiles
- side hung sash
- bottom rail
- cill

Double hung window

- outside lining to cased frame
- top rail
- stile
- glazing bars
- top sash
- meeting rail
- horn
- bottom sash
- bottom rail
- flush cill

cast iron weights
plywood lining
21 × 8 parting bead

Spring balances fixed in groove in 24 mm thick frame (modern alternative to pulleys weights & sash cords)

41 × 22 glazing bar

Nordan detail
Inward opening Alu-clad window

92

31
94
57

57
101
88
41

- 94 × 70 head & jambs
- 45 × 45 top rail and stiles
- 120 × 70 transom
- 70 × 45 bottom rail
- 165 × 70 cill

- 92 × 21 outside lining
- 116 × 21 pulley head
- 70 × 21 inside lining
- 19 × 14 removable staff bead
- 48 × 41 sash top rail and stiles
- 41 × 24 splayed and rebated meeting rails
- 70 × 41 bottom rail (deeper for larger sashes)
- 136 × 70 flush cill

Roof windows

Horizontally-pivoted roof windows

Designed for roof pitches between 15° and 90°. Lacquered pine or polyurethane-coated frames, double glazed with a choice of glass: clear, obscured, toughened, laminated and low-e coated. Glass cavities are gas filled with optional coatings to achieve U-values of 1.7 down to 1.0, or 0.5 if triple glazed W/m²K:

Standard sizes, overall frame w × h mm

550 × 700				1140 × 700	
550 × 780*					
550 × 980*+	660 × 980	780 × 980*+	940 × 980		1340 × 980
	660 × 1180*	780 × 1180*	940 × 1180	1140 × 1180*+	
		780 × 1400*	940 × 1400	1140 × 1400	1340 × 1400
		780 × 1600	940 × 1600*	1140 × 1600	1340 × 1600
		780 × 1800			

* = ex stock
+ = can be combined with tilted insulated kerb for flat roofs

Finishes:	Externally – grey aluminium as standard, other metals available. Internally – lacquered or white painted timber frames; polyurethane frames finished white.
Fittings:	Control bar at head operates window and ventilation flap; friction hinges; barrel bolt for locking in two positions; security bolts.
Flashings:	Available to suit most roofing materials. If required they can enable windows to be fitted side-by-side or one-above-the-other and in groups. An insulation collar and vapour barrier maximizes energy efficiency.
Accessories:	External awning blinds (essential to control heat gain from south facing rooflights); roller shutters. Internal insect screens; interior linings. Roller, black-out, pleated or venetian blinds. Cord, rod and electronic controls for operating sashes, blinds, etc.

Break-glass points.

Smoke ventilation system to automatically open window in the event of fire.

Pre-installed electric system to operate high level skylights via an infra-red remote control.

Top hung roof windows

Designed for low roof pitches where a pivoted window might interfere with headroom. Suitable for pitches between 15° and 55° (and up to 77° with special springs). Can be rotated 180° for cleaning. Some versions are available for an escape/access door. Sizes similar to pivoted windows.

Additional fixed light windows

These may be fitted directly above or below a roof window, within the same plane, to extend the view and increase daylight.

Balcony system

A top hung roof window opens out horizontally and is combined with a bottom hung lower sash fixed in the same plane. The lower sash opens out to a vertical position and railings automatically unfold to close the sides and create a small balcony.

Roof terrace system

This system combines a top hung roof window with a vertical side hung opening out sash fixed below with no intermediate transome, allowing access to a balcony or terrace.

Additional vertical windows

Where floor level is below the eaves and more light and view is required, bottom hung or tilt-and-turn windows may be fixed in the vertical plane directly below roof windows fixed in the sloping roof above.

Conservation Area roof windows

Horizontal pivot windows with a central vertical glazing bar, recessed installation and black aluminium external finish suitable for Listed Buildings and Conservation Areas.

Sizes:	550 × 980*	660 × 1180	780 × 1400

* A version of this window is available as a side hung escape/access roof window.

Source: Velux Company Ltd

Rooflights

Individual rooflights are typically square, rectangular or round on plan and come as flat glass sheets, domes or pyramids. Plastic rooflights to be suitable for any space except a protected stairway must be rated TP(a) rigid.

Typical sizes nominal clear roof openings
Square: 600, 900, 1200, 1500, 1800 mm.
Rectangular: 600 × 900, 600 × 1200, 900 × 1200,
                1200 × 1500, 1200 × 1800,
                1200 × 2000 mm.
Round: 600, 750, 900, 1050, 1200, 1350, 1500,
                1800 mm Ø.

Materials

Toughened/ laminated glass: double or triple glazed. Fire rating: Class 0. Can be walked on

Polycarbonate: Clear, opal and tinted. Almost unbreakable, good light transmission, single, double or triple skins
Fire rating: TP(a) Class 1
Average U-values: single skin $5.3\,W/m^2K$
                   double skin $2.8\,W/m^2K$
                   triple skin $1.9\,W/m^2K$

PVC: Clear, opal and tinted. Cheaper than polycarbonate but will discolour in time. Single and double skins
Fire rating: TP(a) Class 1
U-values: single skin $5.05\,W/m^2K$
             double skin $3.04\,W/m^2K$

Curbs

Curbs are generally supplied with rooflights, but they may also be fitted directly to builder's timber or concrete curbs. Curbs typically have 30° sloping sides, are made of aluminium or GRP and stand up 150–300 mm above roof deck. They can also be supplied as a composite insulated panel with vertical sides.

They may be uninsulated, insulated or topped with various forms of ventilators, normally fixed or adjustable louvres, hand or electrically operated.

Access hatch: Hinged rooflight, manually or electrically operated, typically 900 mm sq.

Smoke vent: Hinged rooflight linked by electron magnets to smoke/heat detecting systems.

Optional extras: Bird and insect mesh for vents in curbs. Burglar bars – hinged grille fixed to curb or in-situ upstand.

Sources: Cox Building Products, Duplus Domes Ltd, Ubbink (UK) Ltd, Sunsquare Ltd

Patent glazing A system of puttyless glazing normally used for roofs but can also be used for curtain walling. The glazing bars, usually aluminium, can be several metres long and are normally spaced at 600 mm centres. The bars have concealed channels to drain the moisture out at the eaves of the roof or the bottom of the wall glazing. Double glazed with sealed units or single glazed over external spaces.

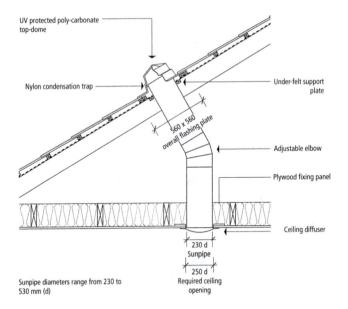

UV protected poly-carbonate top-dome

Nylon condensation trap

Under-felt support plate

560 x 560 overall flashing plate

Adjustable elbow

Plywood fixing panel

Ceiling diffuser

230 d
Sunpipe

250 d
Required ceiling opening

Sunpipe diameters range from 230 to 530 mm (d)

Sunpipes

A mirror-coated tube which transfers daylight from a diamond faceted dome, or flush square rooflight, at roof level to an internal space. It can suit any roof profile and bend to suit the geometry. Diameters range from 230–530 mm and can be combined with solar powered ventilation.

Source: Monodraught Sunpipe

Security fittings

Security against intruders is becoming ever more sophisticated with new electronic technology. However, it is important to ensure the physical protection of buildings and particularly to have a secure perimeter. 'Secured by Design' focuses on crime prevention at the design, layout and construction stages of homes and commercial premises and promotes the use of security standards for a wide range of applications and products.

External doors

External doors must be sufficiently strong and properly installed to resist shoulder charges and kicking. Doorframes should have minimum 18 mm rebates and be firmly fixed to openings at 600 mm centres. Doors should have a minimum thickness of 44 mm with stiles at least 119 mm wide to accommodate locks. Panels should not be less than 9 mm thick. Flush doors should be of solid core construction. Meeting styles of double doors should be rebated.

Door ironmongery

Front doors should be fitted with a *high security cylinder lock* for use when the building is occupied, with an additional five- or seven-lever *mortice deadlock* to BS 3621. Back and side doors should be fitted with a similar deadlock with two *security bolts* at the top and bottom. Deadlocks should have *boxed striking plates* to prevent jemmy attack and *hardened steel rollers* to resist hacksawing. Doors should be hung on three (1½ pairs) metal broad *butt hinges*. Outward opening doors should have *hinge bolts* to prevent doors being levered open on the hinge side. Position *letter plates* at least 400 mm from any lock. Fit *door viewers* and *door chains* to any door likely to be opened to strangers. Chains should be fixed with 30 mm long screws to prevent being forced open. Entrance doors should be lit so that callers can be seen at night. Burglars are wary of breaking glass, so glass doors are not necessarily vulnerable providing the glass is fixed from the inside. However, sliding glass doors are particularly vulnerable. The main mortice lock bolt should be supplemented by a pair of key-operated locking bolts fixed at the top and bottom. *Anti-lift devices* should be fitted in the gap between the door panel and frame to prevent the outer door being lifted off the runners.

Windows
Rear windows are most at risk, as are windows accessible from balconies or flat roofs. Sliding windows should be designed so that it is impossible to remove sashes or glass from the outside. External hinge pins and pivots should be secured by burring over. Avoid rooflights which have domes fixed with clips that can be broken from outside. Where escape from fire is not required, fix *metal bars* or *grilles* below rooflights.

Window ironmongery
All ground floor, basement and any upper floor vulnerable windows should be fitted with two *security bolts* to each casement sash and to the meeting rails of double hung sashes. Upper floor sashes should have at least one security bolt. For greater safety choose locks with a *differ key* rather than those with a common key, which experienced intruders will own. Many window handles include locks as standard.

Other physical devices
Collapsible grilles, sliding shutters and, where appropriate, *blast and bullet-proof screens* and *ram stop bollards*.

Safes for domestic use can be as small as 'two brick' *wall safes* or *floor safes* let into floors. Larger floor safes weigh from 370 kg to 2300 kg and must be anchored to floors. Locks may be key, combination or electronic.

Electronic devices include the following:

- Access control –   voice/video, keypad, card reading entry, phone systems
- Intruder detection –   intruder alarms, CCTV surveillance, security lighting
- Fire protection –   smoke and heat detection, fire alarms, 'break glass' switches, automatic linking to fire stations.

Sources: *A Guide to the Security of Homes*
Home Security and Safety
Banham Patent Locks Ltd
Chubb Physical Security Products
www.securedbydesign.com

Protection for glazing indoors and windows Based on Building Regulations Approved Document N

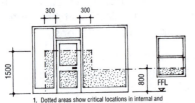

1. Dotted areas show critical locations in internal and external glazing in doors, side panels, screens and windows.

There are certain areas of glazing which can prove hazardous, particularly to children.

1. Shows the extent of these areas which should be glazed with safety glass or safety plastic to BS 6206:1981.

2. Alternatively glass in these areas should be in small panes **OR**

3. If glazed with standard annealed glass these areas should be protected inside and out with a permanent screen.

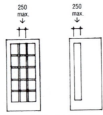

2. If annealed glass is used, it should be in small panes not larger than 0.5 m² with a maximum width of 250 mm. The glass should be at least 6 mm thick.

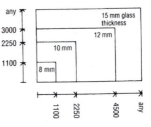

4. Annealed glass thickness/ dimension limits. Some annealed glass is considered suitable for use in public buildings for showrooms, offices, etc. and will conform providing it does not exceed the thickness/dimension limitations shown above.

Large areas of glass in non-domestic buildings should 'manifest' themselves with a line of pattern, logo, etc. at 1500 mm above FFL, unless the presence of the glass is made obvious by the use of mullions, transoms, wide frames, large handles or something similar.

3. If annealed glass is used for low level glazing then it must be protected inside and out with permanent screens. These should be at least 800 mm high, unclimbable, i.e. not horizontal rails, and designed so as to prevent a 75 mm ø sphere touching the glazing.

6
Materials

Brickwork and blockwork

Brick sizes

The work (actual) size of the standard brick is

$$215 \times 102.5 \times 65\,mm$$

For the co-ordinating size, which includes the width of one mortar joint, add 10 mm, i.e.

$$225 \times 112.5 \times 75\,mm$$

Metric modular sizes:

$$190 \times 90 \times 65\,mm$$

Other less available brick sizes:

$$215 \times 102.5 \times 50\,mm$$
$$215 \times 102.5 \times 73\,mm$$
$$215 \times 102.5 \times 80\,mm$$

Weights of bricks

	kg/m^3
Blue	2405
Engineering	2165
Sand cement	2085
Fire brick	1890
London stock	1845
Sand lime	1845
Flettons	1795
Red facings	1765

Compressive strengths and percentage water absorption

Brick	N/mm²	water absorption % by mass
Engineering Class A	>70	<4.5
Engineering Class B	>50	<7.0
Flettons	14–25	15–25
London stocks	3–18	20–40
Hand moulded facings	7–60	10–30

Frost resistance and soluble-salt content of bricks

Designation	Frost resistance	Soluble-salt content
FL	frost resistant	low salt content
FN	frost resistant	normal salt content
ML	moderate frost resistance	low salt content
MN	moderate frost resistance	normal salt content
OL	not frost resistant	low salt content
ON	not frost resistant	normal salt content

Spacing of wall ties

65–90 mm leaf thickness   = 450 horizontally/450 mm vertically
Over 90 mm leaf thickness = 900 horizontally/450 mm vertically
For wider cavities spacing may decrease

Cavity wall ties

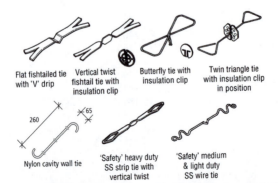

Flat fishtailed tie with 'V' drip

Vertical twist fishtail tie with insulation clip

Butterfly tie with insulation clip

Twin triangle tie with insulation clip in position

Nylon cavity wall tie

'Safety' heavy duty SS strip tie with vertical twist

'Safety' medium & light duty SS wire tie

Cavity wall ties are made in stainless steel (wire diameters from 2.5–4.5 mm) or reinforced plastic for reduced thermal bridging, which can be equivalent to 50 mm of cavity insulation. Lengths are from 150–300 mm depending on wall thickness and cavity width. Extra-long ties are available for insulated cavities up to 250 mm wide.

Traditional fishtailed ties are now largely superseded because of their sharp edges by SS 'safety' ties as less wire is used in their manufacture. Most ties can be fitted with clips to retain partial cavity insulation boards. Outer leaf moisture drips from central twists and kinks.

Block sizes

The standard block face dimensions are:
440 × 215 mm and 440 × 140 mm, with thicknesses of 75, 90, 100, 140, 150, 190, 200 and 215 mm.

Health & safety restrictions on site manual lifting limit block weights to no more than 20 kg, which restricts the use of dense solid blocks in standard formats to 100 mm thickness, or requires their substitution by lightweight aggregate or hollow blocks; hollow dense blocks up to 190 mm thick are within the 20 kg limit.

SOLID
440 × 100 × 215 h (most used size)
Load bearing and good for external fair-faced work

HOLLOW
Voids open at both ends
Can be used for vertical reinforcement

CELLULAR
Voids closed at one end
Voids normally laid uppermost
Lighter and therefore easier to lay
Slightly cheaper than solid blocks

THERMAL
Lightweight concrete blocks to give lower U-values

SOUND ABSORBING
Slots in one face connect to voids filled with mineral wool
Unplastered & fair faced. Useful for sports halls, sound studios, etc.

CONCRETE BLOCKS are generally available in four main grades:
Architectural: 'The Best'; precision made and consistent in colour for fair-faced work
Fair faced: Good quality for unplastered or painted walls
Paint quality: Suitable for a direct paint finish
Standard: Cheapest and suitable for plastering and rendering

Typical foundation block sizes are:
$440 \times 215\,mm$ and $440 \times 140\,mm$, with thicknesses of 224, 275, 305 and 355 mm. Unless these are mechanically handled, lightweight blocks are used.

Compressive strength:
Blocks range from 2.8 to $7.0\,N/mm^2$ depending on composition. $4.0\,N/mm^2$ is average.

There is a wide range of medium and lightweight blocks available from most block manufacturers; the most effective thermal insulating blocks are made from aerated concrete and can achieve conductivities as low as 0.11, which can make a significant contribution to wall insulation.

Several aerated concrete block makers have ranges of thin joint 'glued' masonry which speeds construction, improves accuracy and thermal performance.

The airflow resistance of concrete blocks varies according to their manufacture: aggregate blocks with open-textured faces and low fines content can be seriously leaky and cause significant heat loss, particularly if finished with dry lining rather than wet plaster.

For environmental reasons, unfired clay blocks and bricks alongside hemp-lime and similar materials are available for less structurally demanding conditions.

Paving slabs

Concrete paving slabs: sizes up to 600×600, and thicknesses from 38–50 mm.

Setts: mixed sizes 200×100, $100 \times 100 \times 40$–80 mm

Stone: mixed sizes from 300×300–600×900, thickness 15–40 mm, often sold in packs to cover approx. $15\,m^2$.

Permeable paving is specified to allow water to drain through and be collected as part of Sustainable Urban Drainage Systems.

Geotextile membranes should be used below paving to prevent weed growth and minimize the use of chemical weed killers.

Brickwork bonds

ENGLISH BOND
A strong bond which is easy to lay but is somewhat monotonous in appearance.

FLEMISH BOND
This bond with its even, readily understood pattern is generally considered more attractive than English bond.

ENGLISH GARDEN WALL BOND
This bond reduces the numbers of headers making it easier to build both faces of the wall as fair faced.

FLEMISH GARDEN WALL BOND
This requires a fairly large area of wall for the pattern to be appreciated. Careful laying is needed to keep the perpends true, especially if the headers are a different colour from the stretchers.

BOND STRENGTH
In any bond, it is important that the perpends (vertical joints) should not be less than one quarter of the brick length from those in the adjacent course.

STRETCHER BOND
Sometimes called *running* bond, this is the bond for half brick walls.

Mortar mixes for brickwork and blockwork

Grade desig- nation	Cement : lime : sand	Masonry cement : sand	Cement : sand with plasticiser	Compressive strengths N/mm² preliminary site	
I	1 : ¼ : 3	–	–	16.0	11.0
II	1 : ½ : 4 to 4½	1 : 2 ½ to 3½	1 : 3 to 4	6.5	4.5
III	1 : 1 : 5 to 6	1 : 4 to 5	1 : 5 to 6	3.6	2.5
IV	1 : 2 : 8 to 9	1 : 5 ½ to 6½	1 : 7 to 8	1.5	1.0

Notes:
1 Mortar designation I is strongest, IV is weakest.
2 The weaker the mix the more it can accommodate movement.
3 Where sand volume varies, use the larger quantity for well-graded sands and the smaller quantity for coarse or uniformly fine sands.
4 Grade I and II for high strength bricks and blocks in walls subject to high loading or walls subject to high exposure such as retaining walls, below DPC, parapets, copings and free standing walls.
5 Grade III and IV for walls between DPC and eaves not subject to severe exposure.

Pure lime mortars, using lime putty or hydraulic lime without cement, are widely used for historic building work and for new work where expansion joints are to be avoided; for weaker bricks and stones, lime mortars offer a longer life and better weather resistance.

Joints

Flush
Maximum bearing area
Useful for coarse textured bricks
Evens out run-off and absorption;
best for long life and weather resistance

Bucket handle
More visual joint emphasis than flush and almost as strong and weather resistant

Struck or weathered
Gives a shadow line to joint. If correctly made is strong and weather resistant

Recessed
This can allow rain to penetrate and should be confined to frost-resistant bricks and sheltered situations.

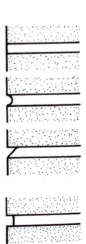

Special bricks

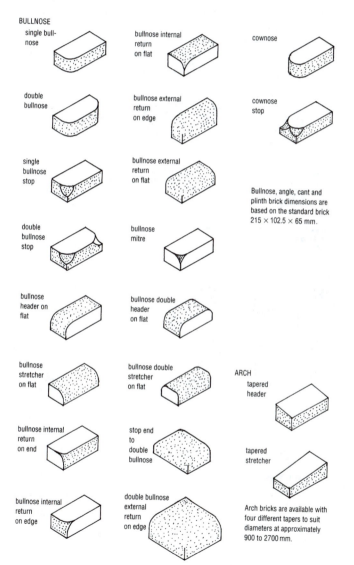

BULLNOSE

single bull-
nose

bullnose internal
return
on flat

cownose

double
bullnose

bullnose external
return
on edge

cownose
stop

single
bullnose
stop

bullnose external
return
on flat

Bullnose, angle, cant and
plinth brick dimensions are
based on the standard brick
215 × 102.5 × 65 mm.

double
bullnose
stop

bullnose
mitre

bullnose
header on
flat

bullnose double
header
on flat

bullnose
stretcher
on flat

bullnose double
stretcher
on flat

ARCH

tapered
header

bullnose internal
return
on end

stop end
to
double
bullnose

tapered
stretcher

bullnose internal
return
on edge

double bullnose
external
return
on edge

Arch bricks are available with
four different tapers to suit
diameters at approximately
900 to 2700 mm.

Special bricks – continued

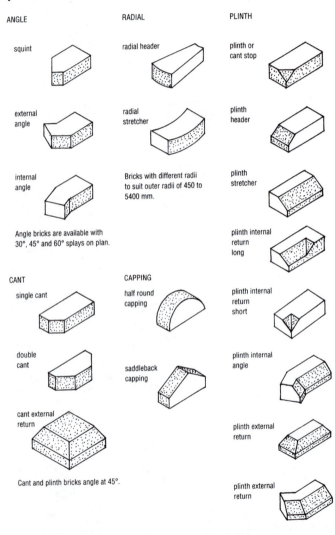

ANGLE

squint

external angle

internal angle

Angle bricks are available with 30°, 45° and 60° splays on plan.

RADIAL

radial header

radial stretcher

Bricks with different radii to suit outer radii of 450 to 5400 mm.

PLINTH

plinth or cant stop

plinth header

plinth stretcher

plinth internal return long

plinth internal return short

plinth internal angle

plinth external return

plinth external return

CANT

single cant

double cant

cant external return

Cant and plinth bricks angle at 45°.

CAPPING

half round capping

saddleback capping

Dotted shading indicates faced surfaces as standard.

Source: Ibstock Brick Ltd

Brick paving patterns

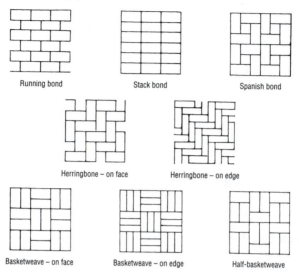

Running bond

Stack bond

Spanish bond

Herringbone – on face

Herringbone – on edge

Basketweave – on face

Basketweave – on edge

Half-basketweave

Clayware – definitions

earthenware Pottery made from brick earth; softer than stoneware. Exposed surfaces are often glazed.

firebrick Bricks made from any clay which is difficult to fuse and generally has a high quartz content. Used for fire backs and boiler liners for temperatures up to 1600°C.

stoneware Highly *vitrified clayware* used for sanitary fittings and drainpipes.

vitreous china A strong high-grade ceramic ware made from white clays and finely ground minerals. All exposed surfaces are coated with an impervious non-crazing vitreous glaze. Used for sanitary ware, it is easy to clean but brittle compared with *glazed stoneware*.

vitrified clayware Clay which is hard-burnt to about 1100°C and therefore vitrified throughout. It has low water absorption, and can be used unglazed for floor tiles, drainpipes, etc. Can be fair cut with an angle grinder.

Concrete – some types and treatments

aerated concrete A lightweight concrete with no coarse aggregates, made of cement, lime, sand and chemical admixtures which cause bubbles to make a cellular consistency. It has low strength but good insulation properties. It is easily cut and nailable. There are many grades, some unsuitable below ground. Water absorption will impair its thermal performance.

bush hammering Tooling concrete or stone with a compressed air hammer to remove 1 to 6 mm of the outer skin to reveal a surface texture that improves its appearance.

glass-reinforced concrete (GRC) Precast concrete, reinforced with glass fibre to make thin panels with improved strength and impact resistance.

granolithic finish A thin topping of cement, granite chippings and sand laid over a concrete slab, preferably as a monolithic screed to provide a good wearing surface. Can be made non-slip by sprinkling carborundum powder over the surface before final trowelling.

polymer-impregnated concrete Concrete made with a polymer to improve the strength by filling all the voids normally left in conventional concrete. Water absorption is thus reduced and the concrete has greater dimensional stability.

refractory concrete Concrete made with high alumina cement and refractory aggregate, such as broken firebrick, to withstand very high temperatures.

Stonework

Building stone comes from three rock types:
- **Igneous** rocks formed from cooled molten rock, e.g. granite
- **Metamorphic** rocks formed from the re-crystallization of previous rocks after heat and pressure, e.g. slate and marble
- **Sedimentary** rocks formed from ancient sediments deposited on sea or river beds and then compacted or naturally cemented, e.g. limestone or sandstone.

Typical building stones

Stone	County	Colour	Dry weight kg/m^3	Compressive strength kN/m^2
Granites				
Cornish	Cornwall	silvery grey	2610	113 685
Peterhead	Grampian	bright red	2803	129 558
Rubislaw	Grampian	bluish-grey	2500	138 352
Sandstones				
Bramley Fell	W Yorks.	grey to buff	2178	42 900
Darley Dale	Derbys.	light grey	2322	55 448
Forest of Dean	Glos.	grey to blue	2435	67 522
Kerridge	Derbys.	buff	2450	62 205
Runcorn red	Cheshire	red & mottled	2082	27 242
Limestones				
Ancaster	Lincs.	cream to brown	2515	23 380
Bath	Wilts/ Somerset	lt. brown to cream	2082	24 024
Clipsham	Leics.	pale cream to buff	2322	29 172
Mansfield	Notts.	creamy yellow	2242	49 550
Portland	Dorset	lt. brown to white	2210	30 780

Mortar mixes for stonework

Typical mix			Application
cement	: lime : sand	1 : 3 : 12	dense stones (granite, etc.), not limestones
putty/hydraulic	: lime : sand	2 : 5	most building stones
cement	: lime : sand	1 : 2 : 9	exposed details, not limestones
cement	: lime : sand	1 : 1 : 6	most sandstones

Joints	mm thickness
internal marble cladding	1.5
external cladding	2 to 3
slate cladding	3
large slabs	4.5
polished granites	4.5
fine ashlar	6 maximum
rubble walls	12 to 18

Sources: *Building Construction, Stone in Building*

Dampness in buildings

Typical causes

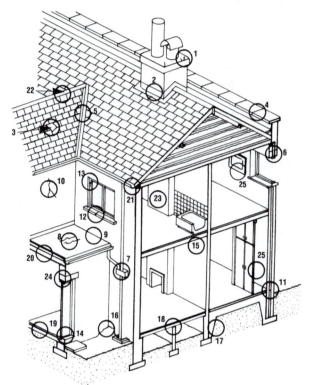

WATER PENETRATION
1 Defective haunching to chimney top
2 Defective chimney flashing
3 Slipped or cracked slates
4 Lack of DPC under parapet coping
5 Defective flashing to valley gutter
6 Lack of cavity tray over window head
7 Cracked RWP and blocked hopper
8 Cracked asphalt to flat roof
9 No asphalt upstand at junction of flat roof to wall
10 Cracked rendering
11 Mortar droppings on cavity ties transmitting water to inner skin
12 Cracked window sill
13 Defective paint and putty to window frame
14 Lack of door threshold letting in driving rain
15 Damp patch on wall from defective sealant round bath edge above

RISING DAMP
16 Earth bridging damp-proof course
17 No vertical tanking to earth retaining wall
18 No DPC under timber joists on sleeper wall
19 Faulty DPM under floor

CONDENSATION
20 No vapour barrier in flat roof causing interstitial condensation
21 Blocked eaves ventilation to roof space
22 Lack of ridge ventilator to ventilate roof space
23 Lack of air brick to blocked up flue
24 Cold spot condensation showing inside solid concrete lintel
25 Damp low down on external walls in unventilated cupboards and behind pictures

Source: *Dampness in Buildings*

Damp proofing

Damp-proof courses (DPCs)

DPCs provide an impermeable barrier to the passage of moisture from below, from above or horizontally. They can be flexible, semi-rigid or rigid. Rigid DPCs are only suitable for rising damp. Soft metal DPCs are expensive but safest for intricate situations. Cavity trays are needed above elements that bridge cavities to direct water to outside and at ground floor level where radon is present. DPCs should be bedded *both* sides in mortar. Seal DPCs to floor membranes. Upper and vertical DPCs should always lap over lower or horizontal ones. DPCs must not project into cavities where they may collect mortar and bridge the cavity.

Type	Material	Minimum thickness mm	Joint	Application	Remarks
Flexible polymer based	polyethylene	0.46	100 mm min. lap and sealed	H at base of walls, under cills, vertical jambs	appropriates lateral movement; tough, easy to seal, expensive, can be punctured
	bitumen polymer	1.5	100 mm min. lap and sealed	H at base of walls, stepped; CT; V at jambs	
Flexible bitumen based	bitumen/hessian base	3.8	100 mm min. lap and sealed	H at base of walls, under copings, cills; CT, V at jambs	hessian may decay, but OK if bitumen not disturbed. If cold, warm DPC before use, may extrude under high loads or temperatures
	bitumen/hessian base/lead	4.4	100 mm min. lap and sealed	H at base of walls, under copings, cills; CT, V at jambs	lead lamination gives extra tensile strength
Semi-rigid	mastic asphalt	12.0	none	H under copings	grit should be added for key, liable to expand
	lead	1.8	100 mm min., welted against damp from above	H under copings, chimney stacks	corrodes in contact with mortar, protect by coating both sides with bitumen
	copper	0.25	100 mm min., welted against damp from above	H under copings, chimney stacks	good against corrosion, difficult to work, may stain masonry green
Rigid	slate	two courses 4.0	laid to break joint	H at base of free-standing and retaining walls	very durable, bed in 1 : 3 sand cement
	brick to BS 3921	two courses 150	laid to break joint	H at base of free-standing and retaining walls	good for free-standing walls

H = horizontal; V = vertical; CT = cavity tray.

Damp-proof membranes (DPMs) and ground gas protection

DPMs are sheet or liquid membranes designed to resist damp caused by capillary action. They do not have to perform as well as tanking membranes, which must resist water pressure. DPMs may be positioned under site slabs providing the hardcore is smoothed with 25 mm minimum rolled sand or preferably 25 mm smooth blinding concrete. This position is more vulnerable to damage than placing them over smooth finished site slabs. In this position the membrane prevents bonding between slab and screed, so a thick screed is needed, ideally at least 63 mm.

DPMs must be carried up to lap or join DPCs in walls. Brush-applied membranes are better than sheets in this respect.

Ground gas protection against radon, methane, carbon dioxide and hydrocarbons is provided by sheet membranes and cavity barriers as required by Building Control.

Care must be taken not to penetrate membranes when laying. Any pipe ducts must be in position before screeds are poured, as any subsequent chasing could well damage the DPM.

Type	Description
Low density polyethylene film (LDPE)	Min 0.3 mm thick. Cheapest DPM, protects against methane and radon gas. No good against any water pressure. Joints must be rigorously taped. Easy to penetrate on site. Often made of recycled material
Cold-applied bitumen solutions; coal tar; pitch/rubber or bitumen rubber emulsions	Ideally three coats. Must be carefully applied to avoid thin patches and pinholes
LDPE plus bitumen sheet	Not as easily displaced as LPDE film and easier to overlap. Small perforations less likely, as will 'self heal'
High density polyethylene (HDPE) with bitumen to both faces	High performance PE core is coated both sides with bitumen, with upper surface bonded to this PE film. Underside has film which is released before laying
Drained cavity membranes	Below ground walls and floors are lined with studded polyethylene and polypropylene membranes allowing water to be controlled and diverted away from the structure draining via channels to external drainage
Self-adhesive sheet membranes	HDPE used with tanking primers for improved adhesion are resistant to puncture and tearing
Cementitious coatings	These can be used externally and internally, and in conjunction with drained cavity membranes

Sources: Visqueen Building Products

Plaster and render

External rendering

Rendering mortars are essentially the same as those for laying masonry, but should be made with clean, sharp, washed, plastering sand.

Where possible, use the same mix for undercoats as for finishing coats, otherwise the undercoat should be stronger than the finishing coat.

Strong backgrounds, such as concrete or engineering brick, may need an initial keying coat or spatter dash such as 1 : 1½ or 1 : 3 cement : sand thrown on and not trowelled.

For severe exposures, two undercoats are preferable.

On metal lathing, two undercoats are invariably needed. It is particularly important to reduce the chances of rendering cracking and increase the possibility of moisture evaporating through it to the exterior; these factors are crucial for the rendering of existing buildings that may have poor DPCs or none.

Since strong cement mixes increase shrinkage cracking and prevent evaporation, they should be avoided. Traditional buildings should be rendered using hydraulic or putty lime without cement; render for modern buildings should preferably be carried out with weak cement : hydrated lime : sand mixes for improved flexibility, or with proprietary render mixes. Undercoats can have polypropylene or glass fibres included in the mix to minimize cracking.

Rendering mixes for different backgrounds and exposures

Use	Background	Severe	Moderate	Sheltered
First and subsequent undercoats	dense, strong	II	II	II
	moderately strong, porous	III	III	III
	moderately weak, porous	III	IV	IV
	metal lathing	I / II	I / II	I / II
Final coats	dense, strong	III	III	III
	moderately strong, porous	III	IV	IV
	moderately weak, porous	III	IV	IV
	metal lathing	III	III	III

Plaster and render glossary

aggregate Sand particles or crushed stone that form the bulk of a mortar or render.

binder A component that hardens to bind aggregates together; normally lime and Portland cement.

browning Undercoat plaster made from *gypsum* and *sand*. It replaced lime and sand 'coarse stuff'. Now generally superseded by pre-mixed *lightweight plasters*.

cement Usually Portland cement, so called because it resembles Portland stone when set. It is a mixture of chalk and clay burnt in a kiln. When mixed with water it hardens in a process known as hydration.

dash External rendering thrown onto a wall by hand or applicator.

dry dash Coarse aggregate thrown onto a wet *render* coat, giving an exposed aggregate finish.

dry hydrated lime Ordinary (non-hydraulic) lime produced as a dry powder by adding just enough water to slake the quicklime (adding more water produces *lime putty*). Hydrated lime is typically used in cement : lime : sand mixes to improve workability and flexibility.

gypsum A solid white mined mineral, the main constituent of which is calcium sulphate, used as a *binder* in gypsum plaster.

gypsum plaster Plaster made of gypsum with lightweight aggregates and a *retarder*. It is unsuitable for external work or damp areas. It is used as a smooth finishing coat.

hemihydrate plaster A plaster made by gently heating gypsum to drive off most of its chemically combined water to become half-hydrated. In its pure form it is plaster of Paris, but with the addition of *retarders*, such as keratin, it becomes the basic material for all gypsum plaster, and is known as retarded hemihydrate plaster.

hydrated lime *Quicklime* slaked with water.

hydraulic lime Lime that can set in the absence of air under water. It is made by burning lime with up to 22 per cent clay. It is widely available in bagged powdered form and conveniently similar in handling to cement for masons unused to lime putties.

Keene's cement Hard-burnt anhydrous (water-free) gypsum mixed with alum to form a plaster, which can be trowelled to a smooth, intensely hard finish.

lightweight plaster Plaster with lightweight aggregates such as expanded perlite combined with *retarded hemihydrate plaster*. It has low shrinkage and is thermally insulating.

lime Chalk or limestone burnt in a kiln to 825°C or more.

lime putty *Hydrated lime* soaked to give it plasticity. Used for lime plasters, renders, mortars, grouts and limewash.

mortar A mixture of sand, cement and water, used primarily for bedding and pointing brickwork, laying floor tiles, and as undercoats to plaster and final coats of external walls.

non-hydraulic lime High calcium lime made by slaking relatively pure limestone. Mortars and renders made from this lime set slowly and are relatively soft, but accommodate normal building movement well and have high levels of vapour permeability and porosity.

pebble dash A dry dash finish in which clean washed pebbles are pushed into wet render and left exposed.

plaster Usually gypsum plaster for interiors, or cement render for exterior work.

pozzolana A natural volcanic silica dust originally from Pozzuoli, Italy. When mixed with lime it sets hard, even under water, making Roman cement. The term *pozzolanic additive* now includes other aggregates, such as pulverized fuel ash (PFA) and brick dust, which have similar hydraulic properties.

quicklime *Lime* before it has been slaked. It reacts strongly with water to produce *hydrated lime*.

rendering *Mortar* undercoats and finishing coats for external walls and to receive tiling in wet areas.

retarder Added to cement, plaster or mortar to slow down the initial rate of setting by inhibiting hydration.

spatter dash Cement and sand in a very wet mix, sometimes with a binding agent, flicked on in small blobs with an applicator. Used to create a key for backgrounds with poor suction.

stucco Smooth rendering, originally lime and sand but now cement lime mortar. Often with decorative mouldings shaped to imitate rusticated masonry or column embellishments.

Tyrolean finish A spattered textured render achieved by being thrown against a wall with a hand-operated applicator.

Sources: *The Penguin Dictionary of Building*
Illustrated Dictionary of Building

Pre-mixed plasters

Pre-mixed plasters are made from gypsum, which is a natural mineral deposit – calcium sulphate dihydrate. They should conform to BS EN 13279-1:2008 BS EN 13279-2:2004 *Specification for gypsum binders and gypsum plasters*.

Pre-mixed plasters should not be used in continuously damp or humid places, nor should they be used where the temperature exceeds 43°C. Gypsum plasters are unsuitable for external work because gypsum is partially soluble in water. Gypsum plasters can be badly affected by damp: lime- or cement-based plasters may perform better in such situations.

British Gypsum 'Thistle' plasters are in three categories:

Undercoat plasters

Thistle Dri-Coat	A cement-based undercoat plaster for old walls, where plaster has been removed and a chemical DPC inserted.

Thistle Browning	An undercoat plaster for solid backgrounds of moderate suction with an adequate mechanical key.
Thistle Bonding Coat	An undercoat plaster for low suction backgrounds such as plasterboard, concrete or other surfaces treated with a PVAC agent.
Thistle Hardwall	An undercoat plaster with high impact resistance and quicker drying surface. May be applied by hand or machine.
Thistle Tough Coat	For most masonry backgrounds. Can be spray applied, higher coverage.
Normal thickness:	11 mm to walls, up to 8 mm to ceilings plus 2 mm of finish plaster.

One coat plasters

Thistle Universal	One coat plaster suitable for most backgrounds with a smooth white finish. May be applied by hand.
Thistle Projection	For spray application to most backgrounds.
Normal thickness:	13 mm to walls, up to 10 mm to ceilings.

Finish plasters

Thistle Multi-Finish	A versatile final coat plaster for a wide range of backgrounds.
Thistle Board Finish	A final coat plaster for plasterboards, Dri Coat.
Normal thickness:	2 mm.

Source: British Gypsum Ltd

Metals

Metals commonly used in the construction industry

Name	Symbol	Atomic number*	Description
Aluminium	Al	13	Lightweight, fairly strong metal normally used as an alloy for castings, sheet or extrusions
Brass	–	–	An alloy containing zinc and more than 50% copper. Easily formed, strong and corrosion resistant
Bronze	–	–	An alloy of copper and tin, sometimes combined with other elements. Hard and corrosion resistant
Copper	Cu	29	A durable, malleable metal, easy to form but hardens quickly when worked and needs annealing. Good electrical and thermal conductivity
Iron	Fe	26	A heavy metal, the fourth most abundant element on the earth's crust. Almost always alloyed with other elements
Lead	Pb	82	The heaviest of the heavy metals, dull blue-grey, easily fusible, soft, malleable and very durable
Stainless steel	–	–	An alloy of steel and up to 20% chromium and 10% nickel. Corrosion resistant but more difficult to fashion than carbon steel
Steel	–	–	An alloy of iron and a small, carefully controlled proportion of carbon, normally less than 1%
Tin	Sn	50	A metal nearly approaching silver in whiteness and lustre, highly malleable and taking a high polish. Used to form alloys such as bronze, pewter, etc.
Titanium	Ti	22	Relatively light, strong transitional metal found in beach sands. As strong as steel but 45% lighter, and twice as strong as aluminium but 60% heavier
Zinc	Zn	30	A hard, brittle, bluish white metal, malleable and ductile between 95° and 120°C obtained from various ores. Corrodes 25 times more slowly than steel

*A ratio of the average mass of atoms in a given sample to one-twelfth the mass of a carbon 12 atom.

Bi-metal compatibility

Contact between dissimilar metals should be avoided where possible.

Where contact cannot be avoided and moisture may be present, metals should be separated as shown in the table below.

	Stainless steel	Mild steel	Copper/bronze	Cast iron	Aluminium
Stainless steel	✔	✗	✔	✗	✗
Mild steel	✗	✔	✗	✔	✗
Copper/bronze	✔	✗	✔	✗	✗
Cast iron	✗	✔	✗	✔	✗
Aluminium	✗	✗	✗	✗	✔

✔ = may be in contact; ✔ = may be in contact in dry conditions; ✗ = should not be used in contact.

Metals – some commonly used industrial techniques

aluminium extrusions Aluminium sections made by pushing aluminium through a series of dies until the required intricate shapes are obtained.

brazing A simple, inexpensive way of joining two pieces of hot metal with a film of copper-zinc alloy, a hard solder also referred to as the *filler*. Brazed steel joints are less strong than welded joints.

cast iron An alloy of iron and carbon containing more than 1.7 per cent carbon (normally 2.4–4 per cent). Components are made by casting from remelted pig (ingot) iron with cast iron and steel scrap. It has a low melting point and flows well, and is useful for more intricate shapes than steel or wrought iron.

forging (smithing) The act of hammering metal into shape when it is red-hot, traditionally on an anvil. Formerly referred to iron, but now includes steel, light alloys and non-ferrous metals worked with power hammers, drop stamps and hydraulic forging machines.

shot blasting Cleaning metal surfaces by projecting steel shot with a jet of compressed air. Used as a preparation for painting or metal coating.

sweating Uniting metal parts by holding them together while molten solder flows between them, as in a capillary joint, which is a spigot and socket joint in metal tubing.

tempering Reducing the brittleness of steel by heating and slow cooling (annealing).

welding Joining pieces of metal made plastic or liquid by heat and/or pressure. A filler metal whose melting temperature is the same as that of the metal to be jointed may also be used. Arc welding fuses metals together with an electric arc, often with a consumable metal electrode.

wrought iron Iron with a very low carbon content (0.02–0.03 per cent). It is very malleable and cannot be hardened by tempering. It is soft, rusts less than steel but is more expensive, so it has largely been replaced by mild steel. Used for chains, hooks, bars and decorative ironwork.

Metal finishes

anodizing A protective durable film of oxide formed by dipping an aluminium alloy object into a bath of chromic or sulphuric acid through which an electric current is passed. The film may be coloured with dyes.

chromium plating The electrolytic deposition of chromium onto other metals to produce a very hard, bright finish. When applied to iron or steel, chromium adheres best if a layer of nickel or copper is first deposited.

galvanizing A coating for steel which is quite durable and gives good protection against corrosion in moderate conditions. Components are hot dipped in molten zinc or coated with zinc electrolytically.

powder coating Polyester, polyurethane, acrylic and epoxy plastics sprayed and heat-cured onto metals such as aluminium or galvanized steel for a 50–100-micron thick film. Finished components can also be hot dipped in polyethylene or nylon for a 200–300-micron thick film.

sherardizing A protective coating of zinc on small items such as nuts and bolts, which are rolled for 10 hours in a drum containing sand and zinc dust heated to 380°C. The coating is thin but the zinc diffuses into the steel to form a zinc alloy. It does not peel off, distorts less and is more durable than galvanizing.

stove enamelling Drying of durable enamel paints by heat, normally over 65°C, either in a convection oven or by radiant heat lamps.

vitreous enamelling A glazed surface finish produced by applying powdered glass, dry or suspended in water, which is fused onto metal. This is a true enamel – not enamel paint.

Sources: *The Penguin Dictionary of Building*
Illustrated Dictionary of Building

Insulation

Thermal insulation

Next to a vacuum, trapped air or inert gas is the most effective way to trap heat, so all insulants work in this way from the most natural, like sheep's wool, to the most technologically sophisticated oil-based materials like phenolic foam.

Construction insulants have to perform in different circumstances – wet and dry for example – so different materials are appropriate.

Some 'insulants' also function in other ways such as aerated concrete blockwork walls; others such as multi-foils, combine air-trapping technology with reflectance to resist heat transfer – though some of the multi-foil manufacturers' performance claims have been shown to be exaggerated.

The relative performance of insulants is measured either by their conductivity ('K-value') – the lower the better – or by their resistivity ('R-value') – the higher the better. In the UK, K-values and their relatives, U-values (thermal transmittance, see p. 155), are used, whereas in the US, R-values (resistivity) and R-values (thermal resistance of particular thicknesses of a material) are the norm.

Table of insulation materials

CHARACTERISTICS AS INSULANTS

Insulants	K-value	Vapour permeability	Moisture tolerance	Rigidity	For masonry walls	For timber frames/ roofs	Structural use	Origin	Embodied energy	CO_2 impact	Relative cost
Aerated Concrete	0.16	medium	High	high	wall blocks	no	yes	mineral	high	high	medium
Hemp & Limecrete	0.07	high	medium	medium	infill	infill	semi-structural	plant & mineral	medium	very low	high
Softwood	0.14	medium	Low	high	no	yes	yes	plant	low	very low	medium
Woodwool slabs	0.11	high	medium	high	no	yes	yes	plant & mineral	medium	low	medium
Vermiculite granules	0.065	high	good/LiV*	none	no	yes	no	mineral	high	medium	low
Multi-foils	0.035/CbS*	low	High/LiV*	none	protected cavity insul.	yes	no	oil	very high	high	very high
Glass wool	0.033–0.04	high	Med/LiV*	none	cavity insul.	yes	no	mineral	high	high	low

Table of insulation materials – continued

Material											
Mineral wool	0.033–0.04	high	Med/LiV*	varies	cavity insul.	yes	no	mineral	high	high	low
Sheep's wool	0.035	high	High	none	no?	yes	no	animal	low	low	high
Cellulose fibre	0.038	high	Very poor	none	no	yes	no	plant & recycled	low	low	low to medium
Expanded polystyrene	0.032–0.04	low	Med/LiV*	low	cavity insul.	yes	no	oil	high	high	low
Extruded polystyrene	.028–0.036	none	High	medium	cavity insul.	yes	no	oil	high	high	medium
Polyeure-thane foams	.022–0.028	none	High	medium	protected cavity insul.	yes	no	oil	high	high	medium to high
Isocyanurate foams	.022–0.028	none	medium	medium	protected cavity insul.	yes	no	oil	high	high	high
Phenolic	0.02	none	high	medium	protected cavity insul.	yes	no	oil	high	high	high

Notes: LiV: Loss in insulating value when wet; quilts permanently if saturated; batts and slabs recover when dried out.
CbS: Assumes cavities both sides: including these, typical 30 mm thick multi-foils occupy approx 60 mm and perform as well as 60 mm mineral fibre.
Protected: These insulants not yet marketed for full fill cavity insulation, so require cavity, membrane or polystyrene cavity board protection.

Although there are substantial differences in insulating performance between, say, phenolic foam (k : 0.02) and sheep's wool (k: 0.039), other factors such as vapour permeability and moisture control in relation to adjacent materials make comparison more complex.

In many situations, especially in existing buildings, the space or cost implications of using more environmentally benign insulants such as recycled cellulose fibre or sheep's wool may be prohibitive and the long-term environmental value of using a much higher performance, oil-based insulant with high embodied energy may be worthwhile.

Although cavity wall insulation is a relatively low cost and reliable means of substantially improving insulation of cavity-walled buildings, the small size – usually 50 to 70 mm – of the existing cavities and the limited choice and insulation value of reliable cavity wall insulants – blown mineral fibre and blown polystyrene beads – mean that most installations still do not achieve current building regulations.

For higher performance, internal or external insulation – for example with 125 mm of phenolic foam board – can bring U-values right down to Passivhaus standards below 0.15.

Each installation is disruptive and expensive with internal insulation requiring refitting of internal joinery, plaster details and services on outside walls, as well as perimeter floor dismantling to allow insulation between joists.

External insulation has the benefit of leaving interiors undisturbed and potentially still occupied but requires full height access scaffolding, as well as refitting of rainwater goods, roof eaves details, window sills, etc; it is also subject to weather delays. Its benefit in comparison to internal insulation is that the thermal mass of existing masonry walls remains within the building's thermal envelope.

In new buildings, materials such as hemp–lime concrete or aerated concrete, which combine thermal insulation, acoustic insulation, thermal mass and structural function, may prove ideal, whereas for thermal dry lining to an existing building, minimizing thickness – with maximum insulation – may be the overriding criteria for selection.

Insulation and condensation

One of the most critical details for successfully insulating buildings, beyond the selection of the insulant itself, is the control of water vapour from human activities within the building, i.e. breathing, sweating, washing, cooking, etc. As buildings have been better sealed to save energy, this has become even more crucial.

Since extract facilities, whether passive or fan-powered, cannot be relied upon to be either wholly effective or correctly controlled, it is important that there is a rising 'gradient of permeability' towards the building's outside skin so that the building can 'breathe' without causing – or at least without trapping – condensation at its cold exterior.

The worst examples of this problem occur with an impermeable outer skin such as flat roofing or sheet metal cladding and the best examples of its avoidance are in fully permeable traditional lime-mortared masonry or earth walling, or in open-vented timber cladding to framed structures.

There are two ways to deal with the problem (for the least permeable outer skins as in flat roofing, both are needed). The first is to ventilate an air space between the insulation and the external skin so that the vapour and condensation has a chance to evaporate; the second is to introduce a 'vapour check' – most commonly sheet polythene but sometimes integral with lining materials – on the warm side of the insulation to reduce the amount of vapour reaching the cold surface. It is important that the vapour check is not expected to be perfect: although 'vapour barriers' are theoretically possible, they require careful design and thorough and conscientious workmanship on site, which cannot realistically be expected in most circumstances.

Roofing

Tiles, slates and shingles

Typical minimum pitches

Bituminous shingles	17°
Cedar shingles	14°
Cedar shakes	20°
Clay tiles – plain	35°
Clay tiles – interlocking	15°
Concrete tiles – plain	35°
Concrete tiles – interlocking	15°
Fibre cement slates	20°
Natural slates	22.5°
Stone slates – sandstone and limestone	30°

Note: In areas of high winds and driving rain, these minimum pitches may not be advisable.

Lower pitches may be possible with hook fixings and correct underlays.

Roofing slates

Type	Size mm	No./m²	Batten gauge	No./m²	Batten gauge	No./m²	Batten gauge
		50 mm lap		**75 mm lap**		**100 mm lap**	
Princesses	610 × 355	10.06	280	10.55	267	11.05	255
Duchesses	610 × 305	11.71	280	12.28	267	12.86	255
Small Duchesses	560 × 305	12.86	255	13.55	242	14.26	230
Marchionesses	560 × 280	14.01	255	14.76	242	15.53	230
Wide Countesses	510 × 305	14.26	230	15.11	217	15.99	205
Countesses	510 × 255	17.05	230	18.07	217	19.13	205
Wide Viscountesses	460 × 255	19.13	205	20.42	192	21.79	180
Viscountesses	460 × 230	21.21	205	22.64	192	24.15	180
Wide ladies	405 × 255	22.16	177	23.77	165	25.80	152
Ladies	405 × 205	27.56	177	29.56	165	32.09	152

Grade	Thickness	Weight
Best	4 mm	31 kg/m²
Medium Strong	5 mm	35 kg/m²
Heavies	6 mm	40 kg/m²

Slates are now more commonly available in metric sizes and 6, 7, 8 and 10 mm thicknesses.

Source: Alfred McAlpine Slate Ltd

Roofing tiles

	Clay PLAIN	Clay interlocking SINGLE PANTILE	Concrete interlocking DOUBLE ROMAN	Concrete interlocking DOUBLE PANTILE	Concrete interlocking FLAT SLATE
Size *mm*	265 × 165	380 × 260	418 × 330	420 × 330	430 × 380
Pitch min	35°	22.5°	17.5°	22.5°	17.5°
Pitch max	90°	90°	90°	44°	44°
Headlap min	65 mm	65 mm	75 mm	75 mm	75 mm
Gauge max	100 mm	315 mm	343 mm	345 mm	355 mm
Cover width	165 mm	203 mm	300 mm	296 mm	343 mm
Coverage	60/m^2	15.6/m^2	9.7/m^2	9.8/m^2	8.2/m^2
Weight @ max gauge	77 kg/m^2	42 kg/m^2	45 kg/m^2	46 kg/m^2	51 kg/m^2
Weight per 1000	1.27 tonnes	2.69 tonnes	4.69 tonnes	4.7 tonnes	6.24 tonnes

Coverage relates to tiles laid at the maximum gauge. The number of tiles will increase as gauge decreases.

Weights are approximate and relate to tiles laid at maximum gauge. Weights will increase as gauge decreases.

Sarkings

Sarkings are weatherproof membranes laid over rafters and below battens to draught-proof and weatherproof the roof against driving rain or powder snow that may penetrate the tiles or slates.

Traditional sarkings of reinforced bitumen felt have been largely superseded by lighter, breathable sarkings that can be laid to form an effectively draught-proofed roof but still allow free dispersal of water vapour to avoid roof space condensation; such materials generally avoid the need for eaves, ridge and roof slope ventilators. Where they are laid directly over insulation between rafters, or over a permeable sarking board, tiling battens are raised clear of the sarking by 25 × 50 counter battens nailed down to the tops of the rafters.

Battens

All tiles and slates may be fixed to 50 × 25 mm battens with supports at maximum 600 mm centres. Battens for plain clay tiles may be reduced to 38 × 19 mm when fixed at 450 mm centres.

Matching accessories

Accessories made in materials to match the tiles include the following: Universal angle ridge tiles, mono ridge tiles, specific angle ridge and hip tiles, ornamental ridge tiles, block-end ridge tiles, cloaked verge tiles, ridge ventilation tiles, ridge gas flue tiles, vent tiles for soil pipes and fan ducts.

uPVC/Polypropylene accessories

These include devices for fixing ridge and hip tiles without mortar and for providing under-eaves ventilation and abutment ventilation for lean-to roofs.

Sources: Redland Roofing, Marley Building Materials Ltd, Klober Ltd

Shingles

Shingles are taper sawn from blocks of western red cedar or, less often, oak and sweet chestnut.

No. 1 grade Blue Label is the premium grade for roofs and walls.

Size
The standard size is 400 mm long in varying widths from 75 to 350 mm. The thickness tapers from 3 mm at the head to 10 mm at the butt, or tail, end.

Colour
Reddish-brown, fading to silver-grey when weathered.

Treatment
Shingles are available untreated, tanalized, or with fire retardants. Tanalizing is recommended for external use. Some local authorities may insist on a fire-retardant treatment depending on the nature of the location.

Fancy butt
These are shingles with shaped butt ends such as diamond, half round, arrow, fish scale, hexagonal, octagonal, etc. These are suitable for pitches over 22°.

Accessories
Pre-formed cedar hip and ridge units 450 mm long are available which are normally fixed over 150 mm wide strip of F1 roofing felt.

Pitch
14° minimum pitch
14° to 20° maximum recommended gauge = 95 mm
Over 20° maximum recommended gauge = 125 mm
Vertical walling maximum recommended gauge = 190 mm

Coverage
Shingles are ordered by the bundle. One bundle covers approximately 1.8 m^2 @ 100 mm gauge.

Weight

400 mm long @ 95 mm gauge

untreated	8.09 kg/m^2
tanalized	16.19 kg/m^2
with fire retardant	9.25 kg/m^2

Battens

Shingles are fixed to 38 × 19 mm battens with a 6 mm gap between adjacent shingles using silicon bronze nails – two nails to each shingle. Nails are positioned 19 mm in from side edge and 38 mm above the butt line of the course above.

Underlays are not normally recommended except in cases of severe exposure. For warm roofs, counter battens will be required between the shingle batten and the insulation board.

Flashings

Bituminous paint should be applied to metal flashings to avoid contact between shingles and metal and subsequent staining. As an alternative, GRP valleys and flashings may be more suitable.

Source: John Brash & Co Ltd

Thatch

Water reed
Phragmites communis, grown in British and Continental rivers and marshes. Norfolk reed is the finest thatching material. Water reed thatch is found in East Anglia, the South Coast, S Wales and NE Scotland.

Combed wheat reed
Winter wheat straw, nowadays 'Maris Huntsman', which is passed through a comber. Butt ends are aligned to form face of thatch. Found in the West Country. Sometimes called *Devon Reed*.

Long wheat straw
Threshed wheat straw, wetted and prepared by hand. Ears and butts are mixed up and a greater length of stem is exposed. Found in central, southern and SE regions of England.

Pitch
Recommended pitch is 50°, minimum 45° and maximum 60°.

Weight
Approximately 34 kg/m².

Netting
This is essential to preserve the thatch from bird and rodent damage. 20 or 22 gauge galvanized wire mesh should last 10 to 15 years.

Sedge
Cladium mariscus is a marsh plant with a rush-like leaf. It is still used in the fens and for ridges to Norfolk reed thatch.

Heather
Calluna vulgaris was once in general use in non-corn growing areas such as Dartmoor and the NE and can still occasionally be seen in Scotland.

Thatching data

	Water reed	Combed wheat reed	Long wheat straw
Length	0.9 m–1.8 m	1.2 m	1.2 m
Coat thickness	300 mm	300–400 mm	400 mm
Coverage	80–100 bundles / 9.3 m² (1 bundle = 300 mm Ø)	1 tonne / 32 m²	1 tonne / 36.6 m²
Lifespan	50–70 years	20–40 years	10–20 years
Battens (38 & 25 mm) centres	255 mm	150–230 mm	150 mm

Sources: *Thatch, A Manual for Owners, Surveyors, Architects and Builders*
The Care and Repair of Thatched Roofs, SPAB

Lead

Lead sheet for the building industry may be either *milled lead sheet* to BS 1178: 1982 or *machine cast lead sheet* covered by Agrément Certificates 86/1764 and 91/2662.

Cast lead sheet is also still made by specialist firms using the traditional method of running molten lead over a bed of prepared sand. This is mainly used for replacing old cast lead roofs and ornamental leadwork.

Milled lead sheet is the most commonly available having about 85 per cent of the market. There are no significant differences in the properties, performance or cost between cast and milled lead sheet. Cast lead sheet at first appears slightly darker and less shiny than milled, but is indistinguishable six months after installation.

Thickness
Choice of thickness depends upon use. Additional thickness will cope better with thermal movement, mechanical damage and resist windlift. It will also provide more material for dressing and bossing into shape.

Sizes
Lead sheet is specified by its BS code number or its thickness in millimetres. The range of metric sizes corresponds closely to the former imperial sizes which were expressed in lb/sq.ft. The ends of lead coils may also carry colour markings for easy recognition as shown below.

BS Code no.	Thickness mm	Weight kg/m^2	Colour code	Application
3	1.32	14.99	green	soakers
4	1.80	20.41	blue	soakers, flashings
5	2.24	25.40	red	soakers, flashings, gutters, wall and roof coverings
6	2.65	30.05	black	gutters, wall and roof coverings
7	3.15	35.72	white	gutters, roof coverings
8	3.55	40.26	orange	gutters and flat roofs

Sheet size

Lead sheet may be supplied cut to size or as large sheets 2.4 m wide and up to 12 m long.

For flashings, coils are available in code 3, 4 and 5 lead and in widths from 150 to 600 mm in steps of 50 mm, and 3 m or 6 m in length.

Weight

To determine the weight of a piece of lead, multiply the length × width (m) × thickness (mm) × 11.34 = kgs.

Joints
Maximum spacing

BS Code no.	Flat Roof 0–3°		Pitched Roof 10°–60°		Pitched Roof 60°–80°		Wall Cladding	
	Joints with fall	Joints across fall	Joints with fall	Joints across fall	Joints with fall	Joints across fall	Vertical joints	Horizontal joints
4	500	1500	500	1500	500	1500	500	1500
5	600	2000	600	2000	600	2000	600	2000
6	675	2250	675	2250	675	2250	600	2000
7	675	2500	675	2400	675	2250	650	2250
8	750	3000	750	2500	750	2250	700	2250

Parapet and tapered gutters

BS Code no.	maximum spacing of drips mm	maximum overall girth mm
4	1500	750
5	2000	800
6	2250	850
7	2700	900
8	3000	1000

Flashings

To ensure long life flashings should never exceed 1.0m in length for code 3 lead and 1.5m in length for codes 4 and 5. Flashings should lap a minimum of 100mm horizontally. Vertical laps should be a minimum as shown below.

Roof pitch	Lap mm	Roof pitch	Lap mm
11°	359	40°	115
15°	290	50°	100
20°	220	60°	85
30°	150	90°	75

DPCs

Code 4 lead sheet is suitable for most DPCs. This may be increased to code 5 where a 50mm cavity is exceeded.

Lead DPCs should be covered both sides with bituminous paint to avoid the risk of corrosion from free alkali in fresh Portland cement.

Condensation

In well-heated buildings, warm moist air may filter through the roof structure and condense on the underside of the lead covering, leading in the long term to serious corrosion. Ensure that there is ventilation between the timber decking supporting the lead and any insulation.

Corrosion

Lead may be used in close contact with copper, zinc, iron and aluminium. It may be attacked by organic acids from hardwoods and cedar shingles.

Sources: Lead Sheet Association
Midland Lead Manufacturers Ltd

Copper roofing

Copper is classified as a noble material. It has a long life (75–100 years), is corrosion resistant, and lightweight and workable. It is more resistant to creep on vertical surfaces than lead and can cover flat or curved surfaces.

Copper for roofing, flashings and DPCs should conform to BS 2870: 1980.

Copper strip = 0.15 to 10 mm thickness, of any width and not cut to length. It is usually supplied in 50 kg coils. It is cheaper than sheet.

Copper sheet = 0.15 to 10 mm thick flat material of exact length and over 450 mm wide.

Copper foil = 0.15 mm thick or less.

Normal roofing thickness is 0.6 mm; 0.45 mm is now considered sub-standard. 0.7 mm is used for pre-patinated copper sheet and for sites with exposure to high winds.

Pre-patinated copper was first used in Germany in the late 1980s. 0.7 mm thick copper sheets have a chemically induced copper chloride patina. This produces the blue/green appearance which is more even than the streaky appearance of some naturally induced patinas. The sheet size is limited to 3 m in length so is not suited for longstrip roofing.

Longstrip copper roofing

This method was introduced to the UK from the Continent in 1957. Factory or site formed copper trays are attached to a fully supporting deck with standing seams or roll joints. The copper used has a harder temper and special expansion clips at seams allow longitudinal movement. The main advantage is absence of cross joints on sloping roofs and drips on flat roofs, which saves labour and reduces cost. Suitable for pitches from 6° to 90°.

Bay size = 525 mm centres × 10.0 m. In exposed sites bay widths should be reduced to 375 mm centres.

After 10 m in length, 50 mm high drips should be placed across fall.

Weight
0.6 mm @ 525 mm centres = 5.7 kg/m²

Falls
Minimum fall for any copper roof 1 : 60 (17 mm in 1 m)
Minimum fall for copper gutters   1 : 80 (12 mm in 1 m)

Parapet gutters
Maximum length of any one sheet is 1.8 m. Thereafter 50 mm minimum deep drips should be introduced. Continuous dripping of rainwater from tiled or slated roofs may perforate gutter linings. Sacrificial strips should be placed in gutters and replaced when worn.

Step flashings
Maximum 1.8 m long with welted joints. Single step flashings, with each end overlapping 75 mm, may be easier to repair where small areas corrode.

Laying

Lay with underfelt of impregnated flax felt with ventilation to space or voids under decking to avoid condensation. Fixings are copper clips (cleats) secured by copper nails or brass screws to decking. Avoid any use of soft solder to prevent electrolytic action. Use mastic between apron flashings and pipes.

DPCs

Copper is highly suitable for DPCs as it is flexible and not attacked by cement mortar. Joints should overlap 100 mm.

Corrosion

Copper can be corroded by sulphur dioxide from chimneys unless stacks rise well clear of roof. Copper will corrode when in contact with damp wood impregnated with some fire retardants and from the run-off from western red cedar cladding. Ammonia (from cats' urine) may cause cracking. Copper will corrode aluminium, zinc and steel if in direct contact or indirect contact from water run-off. Copper may leave green stains on masonry.

Patina

This takes 5 to 20 years to form, depending on location. It is a thin, insoluble layer of copper salts which protects the underlying material from atmospheric attacks. It is generally green but may look buff or black in soot-laden air.

Traditional copper roofing

There are two traditional methods of copper roofing:

Batten rolls
40 mm high, shaped wooden rolls are laid parallel to bay slope. Bay sheets are turned up sides of roll and covered with copper capping strip. Ridge rolls are 80 mm high. Suitable for flat and pitched roofs.

Bay size = 500 mm centres × 1.8 m.

Standing seams
These are suitable for side joints on roofs which are not subject to foot traffic, and may be used for roofs over 6°. The seams are double welted joints 20–25 mm high.

Bay size = 525 mm centres × 1.8 m.

Cross joints
At right angles to wood rolls or standing seams. They should be *double* lock cross welts. Above 45° pitch, *single* lock cross welts may be used. Stagger cross joints in adjacent bays to avoid too much metal at seams. On flat roofs, drips 65 mm deep should be introduced at maximum 3 m centres (see Falls above).

Maximum sheet sizes
Sheet sizes should not exceed 1.3 m^2, reduced to 1.10 m^2 where 0.45 mm thick sheet is used.

Source: Copper Development Association

Aluminium roofing

Aluminium is strong but lightweight and malleable, has a long life and low maintenance. A high proportion of recycled material is used in its manufacture.

The most readily available recommended roofing grade is 1050A, which is 99.5 per cent pure aluminium, with H2 temper. 0 temper (fully soft) is suitable for flashings or intricate shaping. See CP 143 Part 15 1973 (1986) for application.

Aluminium is normally available in 'mill finish' which weathers to a matt grey, staying light in unpolluted areas but darkening in industrial atmospheres. It can also be supplied with a factory-applied PVF2 paint in a limited range of colours. Avoid dark, heat-absorbing shades.

Thickness
0.8mm is recommended roofing gauge.

Sheet width
450mm standard.

Bay width
Typically 380mm; longstrip typically 525mm; batten roll typically 390mm.

Bay length
Traditional standing seam – 3m maximum rising to 6m for roofs pitched above 10°.
Longstrip – 10m maximum is typical but is available up to 50m.

Weight
0.8mm @ 525mm centres = 2.6kg/m^2.

Falls
Minimum 1 : 60.

Fixings
All aluminium, including adjacent flashings and gutters.

Joints
Traditional standing seam, longstrip standing seam and batten roll.

Corrosion
Aluminium is corroded by contact with brass and copper. Direct contact with and run-off from lead should be protected with a barrier of bituminous paint. Zinc is sacrificial to aluminium which can lead to premature failure of zinc-coated steel fixings. Avoid contact with wood preservatives and acidic timbers by the use of polythene barrier membranes.

Source: Hoogovens Aluminium Building Systems Ltd

Zinc roofing

Zinc is versatile, ductile, economical, has moderate resistance to atmospheric corrosion and is suitable for marine locations.

During the 1960s zinc alloys replaced commercial zinc for roofing. The material is 99.9 per cent pure zinc alloyed with titanium and copper. There are two types, A and B, which should conform to BS EN 988: 1997. For installation see CP 143-5: 1964.

Type A
Fine, even grain structure with good resistance to creep and thermal movement. Primarily used for roofing. Available in sheets and coils.

Recommended roofing thicknesses are 0.65, 0.70 and 0.80 mm.

Typical sheet size: 2438 × 914 mm (8′ × 3′) in thicknesses from 0.50 to 1.0 mm.

Typical coil size: 500, 610, 686, 914 and 1000 mm widths up to 21 m long.

Zinc can also be supplied pre-patinated in 0.70 mm thickness with blue-grey colour.

Type B

Rolled to a soft temper and used mainly for flashings – also for coverings to small balconies, canopies, dormer windows and for DPCs. Available in coils.

Typical coil size: 150, 240, 300, 480 and 600 mm widths by 10 m long.

Bay sizes

From 500 to 900 mm.
Typical longstrip bay: 525 mm centres with standing seam and 540 mm centres with batten roll.
Maximum bay length: 10 m.

Weight

0.7 mm @ 525 mm centres = 5.1 kg/m^2.

Falls

Minimum 3° but ponding may occur so 7° is the minimum recommended pitch, particularly for longer bays.

Side joints

Standing seam and batten roll – similar to copper.

Cross joints

Between 3° and 10° – 75 mm high drips.
Between 10° and 25° – single lock welt with additional soldered undercloak.
Between 25° and 90° – single lock welt with 25 mm undercloak and 30 mm overcloak.

Fixings

Nails   = galvanized steel or SS.
Screws   = galvanized or zinc anodized steel or SS.
Clips   = zinc to match roofing type.
Solder   = 60 : 40 lead/tin alloy.
Liquid flux = Bakers fluid or killed spirits of salt.

Corrosion

Zinc is non-staining and contact is possible with iron, steel, aluminium, lead and stainless steel. Run-off from unprotected iron and steel may cause staining but no harm. Zinc should not be used directly or indirectly from run-off with copper which will cause corrosion. Zinc may be corroded by contact with western red cedar, oak, sweet chestnut, certain fire retardants and soluble salts in walling materials. Titanium zinc has a long life.

Sources: Zinc Development Association
Metra Non-Ferrous Metals Ltd

Stainless steel roofing

Stainless steel is lightweight, can be pre-formed, has a low coefficient of expansion, high tensile strength, can be worked at any time of year, is resistant to corrosion attack by condensation, and has good environmental credentials, being substantially recycled and very long-lasting; it can match and be used alongside lead. Stainless steel for roofing should conform to BS 1449 Part 2: 1983.

There are two grades normally used for roofing:

Type 304: (Austenitic) Suitable for most UK situations but *not* within 15 miles of the sea or in aggressively industrial atmospheres – 0.38 mm thick.

Type 316: (Austenitic Molybdenum) Highest grade which is now the standard grade recommended, suitable for all atmospheres – 0.4 mm thick.

Stainless steel is naturally reflective but low reflectivity is achieved by:

Mechanical rolling   – Rolling sheets under pressure through a set of engraving tools.

Terne coating   – Coated with tin which weathers to form a mid-grey patina similar to lead.

Sheet width

Coils vary; typically 500 mm and 650 mm wide but sometimes still imperial 457 mm (18″) and 508 mm (20″).

Bay width

385 mm and 435 mm centres with standing seams, 425 mm and 450 mm centres with batten rolls.

Bay length

Maximum is normally 9 m but is available up to 15 m. Over 3 m expansion clips must be used.

Weight

0.4 mm @ 435 mm centres = 4 kg/m^2.

Falls

Minimum 5° up to 90°. 9° minimum recommended for exposed sites.

Joints

Traditional standing seam, longstrip standing seam and batten roll.
Cross joints between 5° and 12° should be lap lock welt.
Cross joints between 13° and 20° double lock welt.
Cross joints between 21° and 90° single lock welt.

Fixings

Stainless steel throughout for all clips, nails and screws.

Corrosion

Resistant to most chemicals. Hydrochloric acid, used to clean masonry, will cause corrosion. Contact with copper may cause staining but otherwise no harm. Migrant rust marks can occur from the sparks of carbon steel cutting/grinding machines. It is not attacked by cement alkalis, acids in timber or run-off from lichens.

Source: Lee Steel Strip Ltd

Profiled metal sheet

Profiled metal sheet may be used for both roofing and cladding. Profiling thin metal sheet gives stiffness, providing greater strength. The deeper the profile, the stronger the sheet and greater the span. Bolder profiles cast darker shadows and may therefore be preferred aesthetically. Coated steel is lowest in cost but limited in life to the durability of the finish. Aluminium develops its own protective film but is less resistant to impact. Cladding to lower parts of buildings should be protected by guard rails or other devices. Avoid complex building shapes to simplify detailing. Profiled sheets are quick to erect, dismantle and repair. The most common profile is trapezoidal.

Curved profiled sheet

Radiused corners may be achieved by using crimped profiled sheets. Typical minimum external radius is 370mm. Non-crimped profiled sheets may be pre-formed to a minimum radius of 3m which may be useful for barrel vaulting. Ordinary profiled sheets may be curved slightly on site. As a rule of thumb, the depth of the trough in mm gives the maximum curve in metres. Mitred units are available for both internal and external corners with flashings purpose-made to match.

Thickness
0.5 to 1.5mm.

Sheet width
500 to 1000mm.

Trough depth
20 to 70mm for roofing – depths up to 120mm are normally used for structural decking.

Weight
0.9mm – 3.7kg/m^2.

Falls
1.5° (1 : 40) minimum.

Finishes
Hot dip galvanizing, stove and vitreous enamelling, terne coating, mill finish aluminium, PVC and PVF2 colour coatings, composite bitumen mineral fibres, etc.

Source: Rigidal Systems Ltd

Flat roofs – non-metallic

A flat roof is defined as having a fall not greater than 10° (1 : 6). BS 6229: 2003 *Flat roofs with continuously supported coverings* deals with design principles.

Design considerations
A flat roof must be *structurally rigid*, and have substantial and *continuous support* for the membrane, provision for *movement joints, rainwater* disposal, *thermal* design, *condensation* avoidance, *wind* resistance, consideration for roof *penetrations* and appropriate *protection* of the membrane.

Rainwater
Flat roofs should have a minimum fall of 1 : 80. However, to allow for construction tolerances, a design fall of minimum 1 : 50 is desirable.

The fail-safe drainage of flat roofs is to fall to external gutters; less good is via scuppers in parapet walls to external RWPs.

Where internal RWPs are planned, position them away from parapet edges where debris will collect and it is difficult to make a watertight seal. Ideally they should be sited at points of maximum deflection.

Avoid only one outlet in a contained roof as this may block, causing water to rise above upstands and cause damage from water penetration or from overloading the structure; ideally provide an overflow in a prominent location to signal blockage of outlets.

Where roofs meet walls, upstands must be a minimum of 150 mm high. They should be protected with lead, copper or super purity aluminium flashing tucked 30 mm minimum into the wall.

Condensation
Condensation is the major cause of failure leading to blistering and decay. Moisture-laden rooms below flat roofs should have good ventilation, extra insulation and vapour control layers which can withstand accidental damage during construction.

Avoid thermal bridges which can result in localized condensation.

Wind
All layers must be properly secured to substrate to resist wind uplift.

Penetration
Keep roof penetration to a minimum. Where available, use proprietary components such as flanged roof outlets and sleeves for cables.

Sunlight
Ultra-violet light will damage bituminous felts, asphalts and some single ply materials. They should be protected with a layer of stone chippings bonded in hot bitumen or a cold bitumen solution. Alternatively, mineral reinforced cement tiles or glass reinforced concrete tiles laid in a thick coating of hot bitumen will provide a good surface for pedestrian traffic.

25 mm thick concrete pavings provide a more stable walking surface and should be bedded on proprietary plastic corner supports which have the advantage of making up irregularities of level and the separation of the promenade surface from the membrane with rapid drainage of surface water.

Light coloured top surfaces and reflective paints reflect the sun's energy but provide only limited protection against damage from ultra-violet light.

Vapour control layer

Proprietary felts incorporating aluminium foil when laid fully supported are the best type of vapour control layer. They are essential in cold and warm roofs but are not required in inverted warm roofs. Over profiled metal decking, two layers bonded together may be required because of lack of continuous support.

Mastic asphalt

Asphalt is a blend of fine and coarse aggregates bonded with bitumen. The ingredients are heated and blended in batches and either delivered hot in bulk or cast into blocks for re-heating on site.

Roofing grade asphalts are described in BS 6925: 1988. For specification and application of asphalt roofing see CP 144: Part 4: 1970.

Recent developments include the addition of polymers which claim to make the material more flexible. These are not yet covered by a British Standard.

Asphalt is laid over a *separating layer* of inodorous black felt to BS 747: 1994 type 4A(i), and laid in two layers of a combined thickness of 20 mm. Application in two layers allows the joints to be staggered. The final surface is trowelled to produce a bitumen rich layer which is then dressed with fine sand to mask surface crazing in cold weather. This should then be protected with chippings or paving. See **Sunlight** above.

Bituminous felt

Formerly roofing felts were made of rag, asbestos or glass fibre cores coated with bitumen. Over the last 15 years or so, most felts have been made with cores of polyester fleece which give increased stress resistance. BS 747: 1994 has been amended to include this type. See CP 144 Part 3 for specification and application.

Newer felts are often made with polymer modified bitumen producing greater flexibility and better performance.

Roofing felts are applied in two or more layers, bonded in hot bitumen, and bonded by gas torch or by means of a self-adhesive layer incorporated onto one side of the felt.

First layer felts, often perforated, bind directly to the substrate.

Intermediate felts are smooth faced for full bonding.

Top layer felts may have the top surface prepared for site-applied protection such as chippings.

Cap sheet felts, designed to be left exposed without further protection, incorporate a surface coating of mineral chippings or metal foil.

Single ply membranes

Developed in Europe and the USA, these are generally available in the UK, commonly referred to as EPDM and TPO membranes (as yet not covered by a British Standard though both BBA and BRE certification is available on some products), and are made of plastics, synthetic rubber-based materials and some modified bitumen materials.

There are thermoset and thermoplastic type plastics:

Thermoset includes all synthetic rubbers. These have fixed molecular structures which cannot be reshaped by heat or solvents and are joined by adhesives.

Thermoplastic materials are those whose molecular structure is not permanently set and welds may be formed by heat or solvents. Welding is more satisfactory than glueing but requires greater skill.

Sheets may be attached mechanically to the substrate with screw fasteners and disc washers set in seams or by welding membrane to disc washers fixed to substrate, or by adhesive. On inverted warm roofs, the membrane is loose laid and ballasted. The main advantage of sheets is that they are flexible and have a very long life.

Some single ply materials may not be used in conjunction with expanded polystyrene insulation.

Source: *Flat Roofing – A Guide to Good Practice*

Glass

Glass used in buildings is composed of silica (sand) 70 per cent, soda 14 per cent, lime 10 per cent and various other oxides. These are added to recycled glass and heated in a furnace to around 1550°C, refined, then cooled before floating the molten liquid onto molten tin to form a perfectly flat surface. This is then cooled from 620°C to 250°C in the annealing chamber before the continuous cold glass ribbon is cut into sheets measuring 6000 × 3210 mm. This material is then used to make a variety of glass sheets with thicknesses from 2 mm to 25 mm and many different properties and coatings, which can be used as follows.

Environmental control

Solar control

The increased use of glass in architecture today makes it imperative to consider the comfort of a building's occupants. Solar control glass can be an attractive feature of a building whilst at the same time reducing the demand on air conditioning systems, reducing running costs of the building and saving energy.

In hot climates, solar control glass can be used to minimize solar heat gain and help control glare.

In temperate regions, it can be used to balance solar control with high levels of natural light.

Solar control glass can be specified for any situation where excessive solar heat gain is likely to be an issue, from large conservatories to glass walkways, and building façades to atria.

The Pilkington range of solar control glass offers a range of performance options to suit most building applications.

All products are available in toughened or laminated form for safety and security requirements and can be combined with other benefits such as noise control.

Thermal insulation

With increasing environmental awareness, more emphasis is now being placed on ways to save energy in any building, domestic or commercial. In recent years, new regulations have been introduced specifying minimum requirements for energy efficiency. Glass can play an important role in this. Heat loss is normally measured by the thermal transmittance or U-value, usually expressed in W/m^2K. In its most basic terms, the lower the U-value, the greater the thermal insulation. Insulating glass units incorporating low-emissivity glass can significantly improve the thermal insulation values.

Insulating glass units

An insulating glass unit (IGU), commonly known as a sealed unit, is the defining component in modern windows, doors and conservatories. It allows a building to resist the entry of wind and rain and also assists in the conservation of fuel and energy, which is one of the requirements of today's exacting standards. It also plays a part in the reduction of noise from outside sources.

Each IGU is manufactured to the very high standards required by BS EN 1279, and when installed and correctly maintained should last 15–20 years or more; well in excess of any guarantee.

The harmonized standard, BS EN 1279 has been recently introduced, and all manufacturers of IGUs in Europe must either comply with its requirements or demonstrate that their standard of manufacture and test is comparable or better than the BS EN 1279 standard.

Environmental control glass properties

Examples of double-glazed units with 6mm K Glass inner pane and 16mm 90% argon-filled cavity.

		Maximum* unit sizes annealed/ toughened mm	Light transmit- tance	Light reflec- tance	Solar radiant heat % transmit- tance	Shading coeffi- cient	U-value W/m²**
	6mm clear float	3000 × 1600	0.73	0.17	0.69	0.79	1.5
	6mm toughened	4500 × 2500					

Examples of double-glazed units with 6mm Pilkington Optifloat clear inner pane, 16mm 90% argon-filled cavity and an outer pane of solar control glass

Solar control glass	Optifloat 6mm Bronze	3000 × 1600 4500 × 2500	0. 44	0.08	0.38	0.55	2.6
	Eclipse Advantage 6mm clear	3000 × 1600 4500 × 2400	0.60	0.29	0.47	0.63	1.6
	Suncool OW 6mm 66/33	3000 × 1600 4200 × 2400	0.67	0.17	0.34	0.43	1.1
	Suncool OW 6mm 70/40 neutral	3000 × 1600 4200 × 2400	0.71	0.10	0.4	0.51	1.1
	Activ Suncool 6mm 70/40	3000 × 1600 4200 × 2400	0.66	0.15	0.35	0.46	1.1

Examples of double-glazed units with 6mm Pilkington Optitherm SN inner pane coating to the inside (cavity) face of the inner pane and 16mm argon-filled cavity***

Thermal Insulation	Pilkington Optifloat 4mm clear	3000 × 1600 4200 × 2400	0.79	0.12	0.59	0.79	1.2
	Optiwhite 6mm	2200 × 3600 2000 × 3600	0.81	0.12	0.63	0.85	1.2

* Maximum sizes are for guidance only and are **not** recommended glazing sizes. Upper figure is for annealed glass, lower figure for toughened glass.

** U-value for air-filled cavity approx 15 per cent higher. Where cavity width is limited, Krypton filling gives a lower U-value than Argon but is not readily available and is more expensive. Warm edge spacer bars instead of aluminium will also reduce the U-value.

*** U-value for K Glass inner pane approx. 15 per cent higher.

See www.pilkington.com for updates.

Acoustic

Pilkington **Optiphon™** glass gives sound control in situations where there is excess noise from roads, rail, air traffic and other sources. Using a PVB (polyvinyl butyral) specific interlayer, Pilkington **Optilam™** is a high quality acoustic laminated glass that offers excellent noise reduction.

Pilkington **Optilam™** is produced by combining two or more sheets of glass with PVB interlayers, and it is this lamination that enables it to offer impact protection and safety. By varying the number of layers and thickness of the glass, it can offer wide-ranging benefits and be used in various applications.

Fire

A range of fire-resistant glass types is available offering increasing levels of protection, which is measured in defined time periods (30, 60, 90, 120 and 180 minutes) and in terms of 'integrity and insulation' or 'integrity only' as designated by the European Standards.

It should be noted that fire-resistant glass must always be specified as part of a tested and approved glazing system, and installation should be carried out by specialists in order to ensure that the expected fire performance is achieved should it be called upon. Areas of glazing are limited by the Building Regulations Part B.

Pilkington Pyrostop™ A clear multi-laminated fire-resistant glass that both retains its integrity and insulates against all heat transfer from fire.
30–60 minutes' insulation, 60 minutes' integrity, thicknesses from 15–51 mm.

Pilkington Pyrodur™ Clear integrity fire barrier – plus protection against radiant heat.
Less than 30 minutes' insulation, 30–60 minutes' integrity, thicknesses 10–13 mm.

Pilkington Pyrodur™ Plus Clear, integrity only, fire-resistant glass with a narrow profile and impact resistance ideal for fire doors and partitioning.

Less than 30 minutes' insulation, 30–60 minutes' integrity, 7mm thickness.

Pilkington Pyroshield™ 2 is a monolithic wired glass, in clear or textured form. It offers reliable, integrity only, fire-resistant glazing in a wide range of applications, including doors, screens and overhead glazing. It can also be used in a variety of internal and external applications for vision or privacy purposes. Offers 30 minutes' integrity.

Safety and Security

From security to fire resistance, safety glass can be used to protect a building's occupants in many ways, while also allowing the creation of bold and attractive designs. The main categories in which glass can be used for protection are outlined here.

Safety glass

Requirement N1 of the Building Regulations concerns glazing in critical locations. In such places glass should either: (1) break safely, (2) be robust, i.e. adequately thick, or (3) be permanently protected. See p. 218.

Glass which is deemed to break safely must conform to BS 6206:1981. Manifestations may need to be incorporated in the glazing or applied afterwards to satisfy the Buildings Regulations Part M.

Toughened and laminated glass can meet these requirements.

Toughened glass

Toughened glass is normal annealed glass subjected to heating and rapid cooling. This produces high compression in the surface and compensating tension in the core. It is about 4–5 times stronger than annealed glass and is highly resistant to thermal shock. When it breaks it shatters into relatively harmless pieces. It *cannot* be cut, drilled or edge-worked after toughening. Any such work must be done prior to toughening. The 'strain' pattern of toughening, i.e. horizontal bands about 275 mm apart, may be noticed in bright sunlight. Can be made to incorporate designs for decoration or obscuration.

Thicknesses	4–19 mm
Maximum sizes	2550 × 1550 mm; 2720 × 1270 mm
Minimum size	305 × 200 mm

Laminated glass

Laminated glass is made from two or more panes of various glasses with interlayers of polyvinyl butyral bonded between each pane. Normal thickness is 3 ply, i.e. two panes of glass and one interlayer. On impact the glass adheres to interlayers.

Unlike toughened glass it can be cut, drilled and edge-worked after manufacture. Screen printed designs can be incorporated during manufacture.

Anti-Bandit glasses have thicker interlayers and are designed to resist manual attack.

Bullet-resistant glasses are made from thicknesses from 20 mm up. They are designed to meet specific bullets from 9 mm automatics up to 5.56 mm military rifles or solid slug shotguns. They can also provide protection against bomb blast.

Thicknesses	from 4.4 mm to 45 mm
Maximum size	3200 × 2000 mm depending on glass used

Glass beams, posts and balustrades can be formed from laminated sheets.

Structural

Structural glazing enables the creation of a complete glass envelope for buildings with frameless façades on any plane.

Support structures, located internally or externally, can use glass mullions, a conventional steel construction or the

Pilkington **Planar™** Tension Structure design to be as subtle or dominant as appropriate.

Pilkington Profilit™ is an alkaline cast glass in U-shaped form. The profiled glass with its installation system offers many interesting and varied architectural solutions. Its main application is in exterior glazing where it is suitable for large glass façades.

Self Cleaning

An applied coating uses the forces of nature to help keep the glass free from organic dirt, providing not only the practical benefit of less cleaning, but also clearer, better-looking windows. The performance of the coating varies according to orientation and pitch.

Decorative

A variety of textured, satin, reflective, etched, screen printed, coloured, stained and handmade glasses are available.

Source: Pilkington Group Ltd www.pilkington.com

Glass blocks

Glass blocks are now no longer made in the UK but are imported from Germany and Italy. Metric and imperial sizes are made, imperial being used not only for new work but also for renovation and the US market.

Metric sizes	115 × 115 × 80 mm; 190 × 190 × 80 and 100 mm; 240 × 240 × 80 mm; 240 × 115 × 80 mm; 300 × 300 × 100 mm.
Imperial sizes	6″ × 6″ × 3$^1/_8$″ and 4″; 8″ × 8″ × 3$^1/_8$″ and 4″; 8″ × 4″ × 3$^1/_8$″ and 4″; 8″ × 6″ × 3$^1/_8$″.
Colours	Clear as standard; bronze, azure, cobalt, blue, turquoise, pink, green, grey.
Patterns	Waves, chequers, ribs, sand blasted, etc.
Specials	Fixed louvre ventilator (190 mm^2), corner blocks, bullet resistant, end blocks with one side mitred for unframed edges to free-standing panels.
Radii	Minimum internal radii for curved walls for block widths as follows: 115 mm = 650 mm; 6″ (146 mm) = 1200 mm; 190 mm = 1800 mm; 240 mm = 3700 mm
Weight	80 mm thick = 100 kg/m^2; 100 mm thick = 125 kg/m^2.
U-values	80 mm thick = 2.9 W/m^{2}K; 100 mm thick = 2.5 W/m^{2}K.
Light transmission	Clear blocks = 80%; bronze = 60% approx.
Fire rating	Class O – fixing systems for both half-hour and one-hour fire rating
Sound insulation	37–42 db over 100–3150 Hz.

Structure   Glass blocks are self-supporting but not load bearing.

Mortar jointed panels should not exceed 5 m long × 3.5 m high (3 m for fire-resisting panels) in any direction, nor be greater than 17.5 m².

Fixing   Glass blocks are generally fixed on site but can be prefabricated in panels. The normal joint is 10 mm but can be wider to suit dimensional requirements.

Blocks are laid in wet mortar with 6 or 8 mm Ø SS reinforcing bars fixed horizontally or vertically, normally about every other block. Joints are then pointed up.

Silicone sealants are applied at perimeters.

Intumescent mastics are applied to internal and external perimeter joints for fire-resisting panels.

There is also a 'Quiktech' dry fix system using plastic profiles to space and centre the blocks and a special adhesive to bond the system together; 5 mm joints are grouted and perimeter joints filled with a silicone seal.

Pavement lights   100 × 100 square, 117 dia., can be supplied separately or set in concrete ribs for foot or vehicular traffic.

Colours   Clear, sandblasted, blue, amber.

Source: Luxcrete Ltd. www.luxcrete.co.uk
www.glassblocks.co.uk

Timber

Timber sustainability

The world's forests are under threat from illegal logging, clearance for agricultural expansion and poor management. However, timber can be a most energy efficient material. A tree grows to maturity in the space of one human lifetime, whereas stocks of oil, fossil fuels and minerals take millennia to produce and are therefore not *renewable* resources. The growth of trees fixes carbon and actually reduces the amount of CO_2 in the atmosphere. This advantage is only realized in well-managed forests where trees are replaced. Timber has seven times less embodied energy (by weight) than that of steel and 29 times less than aluminium, as it needs no heat for manufacture and extraction is relatively cheap compared with mining. How do architects obtain information from suppliers as to whether timber comes from renewable resources?

The **Forest Stewardship Council** (FSC) was founded in 1993 and is an international non-profit and non-governmental organization. It is an association of environmental and social groups, timber trade organizations and forestry professionals from around the world. Its objectives are to provide independent certifiers of forest products and to provide consumers with reliable information about these materials.

It evaluates, accredits and monitors timber all round the world, whether it is tropical, temperate or boreal (northern). Certification is the process of inspecting forests to check they are being managed according to an agreed set of principles and criteria. These include recognition of indigenous people's rights, long-term economic viability, protection of biodiversity, conservation of ancient natural woodland, responsible management and regular monitoring. Timber from FSC-endorsed forests will be covered by a 'chain-of-custody-certificate'.

Consult the FSC for their lists of suppliers and certified timber and wood products.

Sources: Forest Stewardship Council, Friends of the Earth
Forests Forever, *The Culture of Timber*

Timber nomenclature

'Softwood' and 'Hardwood' are botanical terms and do not necessarily reflect the density of the species. Softwoods are coniferous (cone-bearing) trees of northern climates and are relatively soft with the exception of Pitch Pine and Yew ($670\,kg/m^3$). Hardwoods are deciduous trees and vary enormously in density from Balsa ($110\,kg/m^3$) to Lignum Vitae ($1250\,kg/m^3$).

Moisture

Moisture content of newly-felled trees can be 60 per cent and higher. Air drying will reduce the moisture content to approximately 18 per cent. Further kiln drying can reduce the moisture content to 6 per cent.

Recommended average moisture content for timbers from BS 1186 : Part 1

External joinery		16°
Internal joinery	Buildings with intermittent heating	15°
	Buildings with continuous heating from 12–16°C	12°
	Buildings with continuous heating from 20–24°C	10°

Durability

This relates to fungal decay. It is expressed in the five durability classes described below and numbered in the tables on pp. 284–5 and 286–8. Sapwood of all species is non-durable and should not be used in exposed situations without preservative treatment.

1 = very durable	–	more than 25 years
2 = durable	–	15–25 years
3 = moderately durable	–	10–15 years
4 = non-durable	–	5–10 years
5 = perishable	–	less than 5 years

Classes of timber for joinery

These are effectively appearance classes and make no reference to durability and workability, stability or surface absorbency. The four classes characterize the quality of timber and moisture content after machining, at the time it is supplied to the first purchaser. They describe the presence (or absence) of knots, splits, resin pockets, sapwood, wane, straightness of grain, exposed pith, rot, joints (in long timbers), plugs or filler (of knots).

Class CSH   Clear softwood and hardwood, i.e. free from knots or other surface defects. Difficult to obtain in softwoods with the possible exception of selected Douglas fir, hemlock, parana pine and western red cedar.

Class 1   This is suitable for both softwood and hardwood components, particularly small mouldings such as glazing bars and beads.
Also for joinery which will receive a clear finish.

Class 2   Suitable for general purpose softwood joinery and laminated timber. Commonly used for window casements.

Class 3   As class 2 but with greater latitude in knot size and spacing.

Timber sizes

Softwoods and hardwoods are usually available in sizes as shown in the tables on p. 283 and p. 289.

European softwoods are generally supplied in 1.8m lengths in increments of 300mm up to about 5.7m.

North American softwoods are normally supplied in 1.8m lengths up to 7.2m in 600mm increments. Other lengths to special order up to a maximum of 12.0m.

Hardwoods which are imported in log form may be cut to specified sizes and are available in 19, 25, 32, 38, 50, 63 and 75mm thicknesses; widths from 150mm up and lengths from 1.8m to typically 4.5m and sometimes 6m.

Softwood – standard sawn sizes (mm)

Thickness	25	38	50	75	100	125	150	175	200	225	250	300	
12	•	•	•	•	•		•						
16			•	*	*	*	*						
19	•	•	•	*	*	*	*						
22				*	*	*	*						
25	•	•	•	*	*	*	*	*	*	*	*	*	These
32				*	*	*	*	*	*	*	*	*	sizes
36				*	*	*	*						generally
38			•	•	*	*	*	*	*	*	*		from
44				*	*	*	*	*	*	*	*	*	Europe
47				*	*	*	*	*	*	*	*	*	
50			•	*	*	*	*	*	*	*	*		
63					*	*	*	*	*	*			
75				•	*	*	*	*	*	*	*	*	
100					*		*		*		*	*	These
150						*			*			*	sizes
200									*				generally
250											*		from
300												*	N America

• = sizes that may be available from stock or sawn from larger standard sizes
* = sizes laid down in BS 4471 : 1996

Reduction from sawn sizes by planing

Structural timber	3 mm up to	100 mm
	5 mm over	100 mm
Joinery and cabinet work	7 mm up to	35 mm
	9 mm over	35 mm
	11 mm up to	150 mm
	13 mm over	150 mm.

Softwoods

Species	Place of origin	Appearance	Density kg/m³	Durability class	Veneer	Uses (remarks)
Cedar of Lebanon* *Cedrus Libani*	Europe UK	light brown	580	2	✓	garden furniture, drawer linings (aromatic smell)
Douglas Fir *Pseudotsuga menziesii*	N America UK	light, reddish brown	530	3	✓	plywood, construction (long lengths), joinery, vats
Hemlock, western *Tsuga heterophylla*	N America	pale brown	500	4		construction (large sizes), joinery (uniform colour)
Larch, European *Larix decidua*	Europe	pale, reddish	590	3	✓	boat planking, pit props, transmission poles
Larch, Japanese *Larix kaempferi*	Europe	reddish brown	560	3		stakes, construction
Parana Pine *Araucaria angustifolia*	S America	golden brown and red streaks	550	4	✓	interior joinery, plywood (may distort)
Pine, Corsican *Pinus nigra maritima*	Europe	light yellow-brown	510	4		joinery, construction
Pine, maritime *Pinus pinaster*	Europe	pale brown to yellow	510	3		pallets, packaging
Pine, pitch *Pinus palustris*	South USA	yellow-brown to red-brown	670	3		heavy construction, joinery
Pine, radiata *Pinus radiata*	S Africa Australia	yellow to pale brown	480	4		packaging, furniture
Pine, Scots *Pinus sylvestris*	UK	pale yellow-brown to red-brown	510	4		construction, joinery
Pine, yellow *Pinus strobus*	N America	pale yellow to light brown	420	4		pattern-making, doors, drawing boards
Spruce Canadian *Picea spp*	Canada	white to pale yellow	450	4		construction, joinery

Softwoods – continued

Species	Place of origin	Appearance	Density kg/m³	Durability class	Veneer	Uses (remarks)
Spruce, sitka *Picea sitchensis*	UK	pinkish-brown	450	4		construction, pallets, packaging
Spruce, western white *Picea glauca*	N America	white to pale yellow-brown	450	4		construction (large sizes), joinery
Western Red Cedar *Thuja plicata*	N America	reddish-brown	390	2	✓	exterior cladding, shingles, greenhouses, beehives
Whitewood, European *Picea abies* and *Abies alba*	Europe Scandina via USSR	white to pale yellow-brown	470	4	✓	interior joinery, construction, flooring
Yew *Taxus baccata*	Europe	orange-brown to purple-brown	670	2	✓	furniture, cabinetry, turnery (good colour range)

* = limited availability

Source: Trada Technology Ltd

Hardwoods

Species	Place of origin	Appearance	Density kg/m³	Durability class	Veneer	Uses (remarks)
Afrormosia *Pericopsis elata*	W Africa	light brown, colour variable	710	1	✓	joinery, furniture, cladding
Agba *Gossweilero dendron balsamiferum*	W Africa	yellow-brown	510	2	✓	joinery, trim, cladding (may exude gum)
Ash, European *Fraximus exelsior*	UK Europe	pale white to light brown	710	5	✓	interior joinery (may be bent), sports goods
Balsa* *Ochroma pyramidale*	S America	pinky-white	160	5		insulation, buoyancy aids, architectural models
Beech, European *Fagus sylvatica*	UK Europe	pale pinkish brown	720	5	✓	furniture (bends well), flooring, plywood
Birch, European* *Betula pubescens*	Europe Scandinavia	white to light brown	670	5	✓	plywood, furniture, turnery (bends well)
Cherry, European* *Prunus avium*	Europe	pink-brown	630	3	✓	cabinet making (may warp), furniture
Chestnut, sweet* *Castanea sativa*	Europe	honey-brown	560	2	✓	joinery, fencing (straight grained)
Ebony* *Diospyros* spp	W Africa India	black with grey stripes	1110	1	✓	decorative work, inlaying, turnery (small sizes only)
Elm, European* *Ulmus* spp	Europe UK	reddish-brown	560	4	✓	furniture, coffins, boats (resists splitting)
Gaboon* *Aucoumea klaineana*	W Africa	pink-brown	430	4	✓	plywood, blockboard
Greenheart *Ocotea rodiaei*	Guyana	yellow-olive green to brown	1040	1		heavy marine construction, bridges etc. (very large sizes)

Hardwoods – continued

Species	Place of origin	Appearance	Density kg/m³	Durability class	Veneer	Uses (remarks)
Hickory* *Carya* spp	N America	brown to red-brown	830	4		tool handles, ladder rungs, sports goods (bends well)
Iroko *Chlorophora excelsa*	W Africa	yellow-brown	660	1	✓	joinery, work-tops, construction
Keruing *Dipterocarpus* spp	SE Asia	pink-brown to dark brown	740	3		heavy and general construction, decking, vehicle flooring
Lignum Vitae* *Guaicum* spp	Central America	dark green-brown	1250	1		bushes, bearings, sports goods (small sizes only)
Lime, European* *Tilia* spp	UK Europe	yellow-white to pale brown	560	5		carving, turnery, bungs, clogs (fine texture)
Mahogany, African *Khaya* spp	W Africa	reddish-brown	530	3	✓	furniture, cabinetry, joinery
Mahogany, American *Swietenia macrophylla*	Brazil	reddish-brown	560	2	✓	furniture, cabinetry, boats, joinery (stable, easily worked)
Maple, rock *Acer saccharum*	N America	creamy-white	740	4	✓	flooring, furniture, turnery (hardwearing)
Meranti, dark red *Shorea* spp	SE Asia	medium to dark red-brown	710	3	✓	joinery, plywood (uniform grain)
Oak, American red *Quercus* spp	N America	yellow-brown with red tinge	790	4	✓	furniture, interior joinery (bends well)
Oak, European *Quercus robur*	UK Europe	yellow to warm brown	690	2	✓	construction, joinery, flooring, cooperage, fencing (bends well)

Hardwoods – continued

Species	Place of origin	Appearance	Density kg/m^3	Durability class	Veneer	Uses (remarks)
Obeche *Triplochiton scleroxylon*	W Africa	white to pale yellow	390	4	✓	interior joinery, furniture, plywood (very stable)
Plane, European* *Platanus hybrida*	Europe	mottled red-brown	640	5	✓	decorative work, turnery, inlays
Ramin *Gonystylus* spp	SE Asia	white to pale yellow	670	4	✓	mouldings, furniture, louvre doors (easily machined)
Rosewood* *Dalbergia* spp	S America India	purplish-brown with black streaks	870	1	✓	interior joinery, cabinetry, turnery, veneers
Sapele *Entandophragma cylindricum*	W Africa	red-brown with stripe figure	640	3	✓	interior joinery, door veneers, flooring
Sycamore* *Acer pseudoplatanus*	Europe UK	white to creamy yellow	630	5	✓	furniture, panelling, kitchen ware (does not taint or stain)
Teak *Tectona grandis*	Burma Thailand	golden brown	660	1	✓	furniture, joinery, boats (chemical and termite resistant)
Utile *Entandophragma utile*	W Africa	reddish-brown	660	2	✓	joinery, furniture, cabinetry
Walnut, European* *Juglans regia*	Europe UK	grey-brown with dark streaks	670	3	✓	furniture, turnery, gun stocks (decorative)

* = limited availability

Hardwood – standard sawn sizes (mm)

Thickness	50	63	75	100	125	150	175	200	225	250	300
19			*	*	*	*	*				
25	*	*	*	*	*	*	*	*	*	*	*
32			*	*	*	*	*	*	*	*	*
38			*	*	*	*	*	*	*	*	*
50				*	*	*	*	*	*	*	*
63						*	*	*	*	*	*
75						*	*	*	*	*	*
100						*	*	*	*	*	*

* = sizes laid down in BS 5450 : 1977.

Reduction from sawn sizes by planing

Structural timber	3 mm up to	100 mm
	5 mm for	101–150 mm
	6 mm for	151–300 mm
Flooring, matchings	5 mm up to	25 mm
	6 mm for	26–50 mm
	7 mm for	51–300 mm
Wood trim	6 mm up to	25 mm
	7 mm for	26–50 mm
	8 mm for	51–100 mm
	9 mm for	101–105 mm
	10 mm for	151–300 mm
Joinery and cabinet work	7 mm up to	25 mm
	9 mm for	26–50 mm
	10 mm for	51–100 mm
	12 mm for	101–150 mm
	14 mm for	151–300 mm

Softwood mouldings

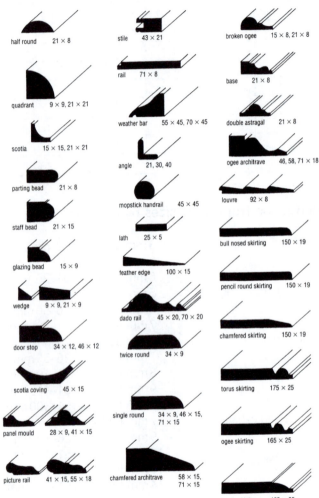

half round   21 × 8

quadrant   9 × 9, 21 × 21

scotia   15 × 15, 21 × 21

parting bead   21 × 8

staff bead   21 × 15

glazing bead   15 × 9

wedge   9 × 9, 21 × 9

door stop   34 × 12, 46 × 12

scotia coving   45 × 15

panel mould   28 × 9, 41 × 15

picture rail   41 × 15, 55 × 18

stile   43 × 21

rail   71 × 8

weather bar   55 × 45, 70 × 45

angle   21, 30, 40

mopstick handrail   45 × 45

lath   25 × 5

feather edge   100 × 15

dado rail   45 × 20, 70 × 20

twice round   34 × 9

single round   34 × 9, 46 × 15, 71 × 15

chamfered architrave   58 × 15, 71 × 15

broken ogee   15 × 8, 21 × 8

base   21 × 8

double astragal   21 × 8

ogee architrave   46, 58, 71 × 18

louvre   92 × 8

bull nosed skirting   150 × 19

pencil round skirting   150 × 19

chamfered skirting   150 × 19

torus skirting   175 × 25

ogee skirting   165 × 25

ovolo skirting   165 × 25

Some sections are available in a range of sizes.
The dimensions given are those most often available.

Hardwood mouldings

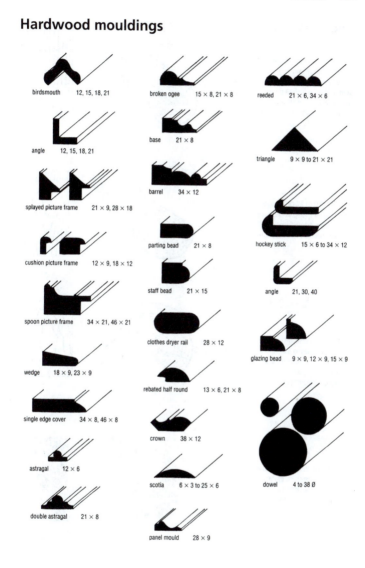

birdsmouth   12, 15, 18, 21

angle   12, 15, 18, 21

splayed picture frame   21 × 9, 28 × 18

cushion picture frame   12 × 9, 18 × 12

spoon picture frame   34 × 21, 46 × 21

wedge   18 × 9, 23 × 9

single edge cover   34 × 8, 46 × 8

astragal   12 × 6

double astragal   21 × 8

broken ogee   15 × 8, 21 × 8

base   21 × 8

barrel   34 × 12

parting bead   21 × 8

staff bead   21 × 15

clothes dryer rail   28 × 12

rebated half round   13 × 6, 21 × 8

crown   38 × 12

scotia   6 × 3 to 25 × 6

panel mould   28 × 9

reeded   21 × 6, 34 × 6

triangle   9 × 9 to 21 × 21

hockey stick   15 × 6 to 34 × 12

angle   21, 30, 40

glazing bead   9 × 9, 12 × 9, 15 × 9

dowel   4 to 38 Ø

Wood veneers

QUARTER CUT veneers are cut at right angles to the growth rings in the logs. The variations in colour brought about by summer/winter growth produce a straight grain effect. This is thought to be an advantage in veneers such as sapele.

CROWN CUT/FLAT CUT veneers are produced by slicing through logs, giving a less straight grained veneer with more figure and in general a more decorative finish.

ROTARY CUT is made by mounting a log on a lathe and rotating it against a sharp fixed knife. The cut follows the annular growth rings producing a bold variegated grain. Rotary cut veneer is exceptionally wide.

BURR/BURL VENEERS are made from the enlarged trunk of certain trees, particularly walnut. The grain is very irregular with the appearance of small knots grouped closely together. Small sections of this veneer are normally joined together to form a larger sheet.

Source: James Latham plc

Wood rotting fungi

Dry rot *Serpula lacrimans*

This is the most damaging of fungi. Mainly attacks softwoods and typically occurs in wood embedded in damp masonry. It needs wood with only 20 per cent moisture content and thrives in dark, humid conditions and so is seldom seen externally. It is able to penetrate bricks and mortar and thus can transport moisture from a damp source to new woodwork.

Fruit body	Tough, fleshy pancake or bracket. Yellow ochre turning to rusty-red with white or grey margins.
Mycelium (fungal roots)	Silky white sheets, cotton wool-like cushions or felted grey skin showing tinges of yellow and lilac. Strands sometimes 6 mm thick, becoming brittle when dry.
Damage	Darkens wood with large cuboidal cracking and deep fissures. Wood lightweight and crumbly. No skin of sound wood. Wood may be warped and give off distinctive musty mushroomy smell.

Wet rots

These can only grow on timber with a 40 to 50 per cent moisture content and tend not to spread much beyond the source of dampness.

Coniophora puteana (cellar fungus)

A brown rot occurring in softwoods and hardwoods. Most common cause of decay in woodwork soaked by leaking water.

Fruit body	Rare in buildings. Thin greenish olive-brown plate. Spores on minute pimples.
Mycelium	Only present in conditions of high humidity. Slender thread-like yellowish becoming deep brown or black.
Damage	Darkens wood, small cuboidal cracks, often below sound veneer.

Fibroporia vaillantii (mine fungus)
A brown rot which attacks softwood, particularly in high temperature areas.

Fruit body	Irregular, white, cream to yellow lumpy sheets or plates with numerous minute pores.
Mycelium	White or cream sheets of fern-like growths.
Damage	Resembles dry rot in cuboidal pieces but wood lighter in colour and cracks less deep.

Phellinus contiguus
A white rot which attacks softwoods and hardwoods and is frequently found on external joinery.

Fruit body	Only found occasionally. Tough, elongated, ochre to dark brown, covered in minute pores.
Mycelium	Tawny brown tufts may be found in crevices.
Damage	Wood bleaches and develops stringy fibrous appearance.
	Does not crumble.

Donkioporia expansa
A white rot which attacks hardwood, particularly oak, and may spread to adjacent softwoods. Often found at beam ends bedded in damp walls and associated with death watch beetle.

Fruit body	Thick, hard, dull fawn or biscuit coloured plate or bracket. Long pores, often in several layers.
Mycelium	White to biscuit felted growth, often shaped to contours in wood. Can exude yellow-brown liquid.
Damage	Wood becomes bleached and is reduced to consistency of whitish lint which will crush but does not crumble.

Asterostroma

A white rot usually found in softwood joinery such as skirting boards.

Fruit body	Thin, sheet-like, without pores rather like mycelium.
Mycelium	White, cream or buff sheets with strands which can cross long distances over masonry.
Damage	Wood is bleached and becomes stringy and fibrous.
	No cuboidal cracking and does not crumble.

Treatment

Timber suffering from fungal or woodworm damage should only be treated if really necessary. Very often the damage is old, as when the sapwood has been destroyed but the remaining heartwood is sufficient for structural stability.

Many defects can be cured by eliminating the source of the damp and improving ventilation. The use of unjustified treatment is contrary to the Control of Substances Hazardous to Health (COSHH) Regulations and is not acceptable.

The person or company applying the treatment could be liable to prosecution.

However, when there is no alternative to chemical treatment, the following action should be undertaken:

Identify fungus. Rapidly dry out any moisture sources and improve ventilation.

Remove all affected timber (about 400 mm from visible signs for dry rot) and ideally burn on site.

Avoid distributing spores when handling.

Treat all remaining timbers with approved fungicide. Replace with pre-treated timber.

Woodworm

Wood boring insects do not depend on damp and humid conditions, although certain species prefer timber which has been decayed by fungi.

The life cycle of a woodworm is egg, larva, pupa and adult. First signs of attack are the exit holes made by the adults who emerge to mate and usually die after reproduction.

The following insects can all cause serious damage and the death watch and longhorn beetles can cause structural damage. Other beetles only feed on damp wood rotted by fungi and, since they cannot attack sound dry wood, remedial action to control wood rot will limit further infestation.

Common furniture beetle (*Anobium punctatum*)
Attacks both softwoods and European hardwoods and also plywood made with natural glues. It is the most widespread beetle and only affects sapwood if wood rot is present. Commonly found in older furniture, structural timbers, under stairs, cupboards and areas affected by damp.

Beetle 2–6 mm long, exit hole 1–2 mm, adults emerge May–September.

Wood boring weevils
(*Pentarthrum huttonii* and *Euophryum confine*)
Attacks decayed hard and softwoods in damp situations, typically poorly ventilated cellars and wood in contact with wet floors and walls.

Beetle 3–5 mm long, exit hole 1.0 mm with surface channels, adults emerge at any time.

Powder post beetle (*Lyctus brunneus*)
Attacks tropical and European hardwoods, not found in softwoods. Veneers, plywood and blockboard are all susceptible.

Beetle 4–7 mm long, exit hole 1–2 mm.

Death watch beetle (*Xestobium rufovillosum*)

Attacks sapwood and heartwood of partially decayed hardwoods and occasionally adjacent softwoods. Often found in old churches with oak and elm structures. Typically found in areas prone to dampness such as wall plates, ends of joists, lintels and timbers built into masonry.

Beetle 6–8 mm long, exit hole 3 mm, adults emerge March–June.

Longhorn beetle (*Hylotrupes bajulus*)

Attacks softwood, particularly in roof timbers. May be overlooked in early stages as there are few exit holes. Scraping noises audible on hot days with large infestations. Prevalent only in Surrey and SW London. Outbreaks should be reported to BRE Timber & Protection Division.

Beetle 10–20 mm long, exit hole 6–10 mm oval, adults emerge July–September.

Treatment

Fresh exit holes and bore dust on or below timbers are signs of active infestation, although vibrations may dislodge old bore dust. Chemical treatment however may not be necessary. See paragraph on Treatment on p. 295.

Identify beetle and treat timbers with appropriate insecticidal spray, emulsion or paste to destroy adults and unhatched eggs on the surface of the wood and larvae before they develop into pupae. Solvent-based products penetrate timber very effectively but have health and safety problems associated with them. Some water-based products claim to be as effective but more environmentally friendly; of these, boron-based products are likely to be least toxic in the environment at large.

If associated with fungal decay, treat as for wood rot and use a dual-purpose remedy (i.e. anti-rot and beetle). Do not use dual-purpose products where woodworm is present in timbers which are dry and expected to remain so.

Source: *Recognising Wood Rot and Insect Damage in Buildings*

Wood boring beetles

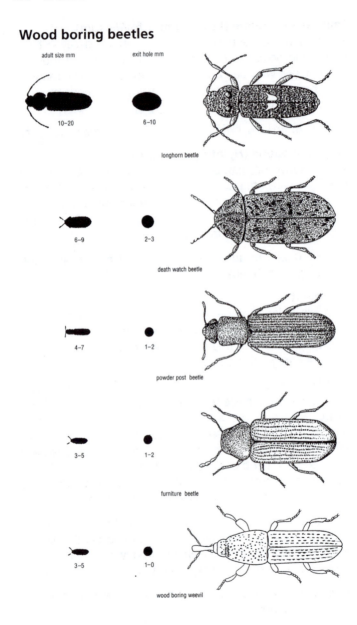

adult size mm

exit hole mm

10–20

6–10

longhorn beetle

6–9

2–3

death watch beetle

4–7

1–2

powder post beetle

3–5

1–2

furniture beetle

3–5

1–0

wood boring weevil

Building boards

Chipboard

Particle board with a variety of woodchips bonded with resin adhesives.

No chipboard is completely moisture resistant and should not be used externally.

Six classes identified in BS 5669 Part 2: 1989

C1	= general purpose use	C3	=	moisture resistant
C1A	= slightly better quality for furniture	C4	=	moisture resistant flooring quality
C2	= flooring quality	C5	=	moisture resistant structural quality

Sheets can be supplied wood veneer and melamine faced; with low formaldehyde rating, or bonded to polystyrene for insulated flooring.

Thicknesses   12, 15, 18, 22, 25, 28, 30 and 38 mm.
Sheet sizes   1220 × 2440 mm, 1830 × 2440 mm,
1220 × 2745 mm, 1830 × 3050 mm,
1220 × 3050 mm, 1830 × 3660 mm
also
600 × 2440 mm for 18 and 22 mm flooring

Wood veneer and melamine faced shelves
Thickness   15 mm
Widths   152 (6″), 229 (9″), 305 (12″), 381 (15″), 457 (18″), 533 (21″), 610 (24″), 686 (27″), 762 (30″); 914 mm (36″)
Lengths   1830 (6′) and 2440 mm (8′)

Source: Norbord Ltd

Blockboard

Composite board with one or two veneers applied to solid core of timber blocks 7–30 mm wide, also available with decorative wood or laminate veneers, commonly 18 mm thick.

Thicknesses 13, 16, 18, 22, 25, 32, 38 and 45 mm
Sheet sizes   1220 × 2440 mm; 1525 × 3050 and 3660 mm;
1830 × 5200 mm

Source: James Latham plc

Hardboard

Thin, dense boards with one very smooth face and mesh textured reverse. Grainless, knotless, and will not easily split or splinter. It can be bent, is easy to machine, has high internal bond strength for glueing and good dimensional stability. Two types available:

Standard hardboard = general internal linings and door facings

Oil tempered hardboard = structural purposes (higher strength and moisture resistance), flooring overlays

Thicknesses 3.2, 4.8 and 6.0 mm
Sheet sizes   1220 × 2440 and 3050 mm

Also available:
Perforated hardboard with
4.8 mm Ø holes @ 19 mm centres × 3.2 mm thick and
7.0 mm Ø holes @ 25 mm centres × 6.0 mm thick

Hardboard with painted finishes.

Source: Masonite CP Ltd

Laminboard

A composite board with veneers applied to a core of narrow timber strips (as opposed to wider blocks in blockboard). It is heavier, flatter and more expensive than blockboard but is less likely to warp.

Thicknesses 13, 16, 19, 22, 25, 32, 38 and 44 mm
Sheet sizes   1220 × 2440 mm, 1525 × 3050 and 3660 mm.

MDF (Medium Density Fibreboard)

Homogenous board of softwood fibres bonded with synthetic resins producing a very dense, fine textured uniform material which can be machined to great accuracy. Normal grades are not moisture resistant but moisture resistant grades are available. Low and zero formaldehyde (Medite, etc.), flame-retardant and integrally coloured boards are also available.

Thicknesses 6, 9, 12, 15, 18, 22, 25 and 30 mm (smaller and larger thicknesses also made by a few manu- facturers).
Sheet sizes   1220 × 2440 mm 1525 × 2440 mm 1830 × 2440 mm
1220 × 2745 mm 1525 × 2745 mm 1830 × 3660 mm
1220 × 3050 mm 1525 × 3050 mm

Medium hardboard

A board with a density between that of wood fibre insulation board and standard hardboard. It has good thermal and insu- lation properties with a fine finish. Can be cold and steam bent. Moisture resistant and flame-retardant grades available. Used for noticeboards, ceilings, wall linings, shop fittings, display work and pin boards.

Thicknesses 6.4, 9.5 and 12.7 mm
Sheet size   1220 × 2440 mm

Source: Medite Europe Ltd

OSB (Oriented Strand Board)

Made from softwood strands, approximately 75 mm long, placed in layers in different directions, bonded and compressed together with exterior grade water-resistant resins. A 'green' product made from thinnings from managed plantations. Process utilizes 95 per cent of the wood, discarded bark being used for fuel or horticulture. Cheaper than plywood, strong in both directions, with a uniform and decorative appearance.

Two grades available, one suitable for formwork, site hoardings and crating, the other for sheathing, flooring and decorative panels.

Thicknesses	6, 8, 9, 11, 15, 18, 22 and 25 mm
Sheet sizes	1200 × 2400 mm; 1220 × 2440 mm; 590 × 2400 mm and 2440 mm for 9 mm thick t & g flooring

Source: Norbord Ltd

Timber cladding

Timber boards, tongued and grooved on opposite sides. Joints can be plain butt joints as for floorboards or moulded with 'V' or quirk (rounded) shoulders for wall cladding.

Typical sizes of cladding

Nominal size mm	Laid width mm	Finished thickness mm
12.5 × 100	80	10
19 × 75	55	15
19 × 100	80	15
19 × 150	130	15
25 × 75	55	20
25 × 100	80	20
25 × 150	130	20

Plywood

Made from softwood and hardwood veneers placed at right angles, or sometimes 45°, to one another. The veneers are strong in the direction of the grain, weak in the other. Thus structural plywoods have odd numbers of layers so that the grain to the outside faces lies in the same direction. Adhesives used are described as WBP (weather- and boilproof) for external or arduous conditions. BR (boil resistant), MR (moisture resistant) and INT (interior) are progressively less resistant. Since many hardwood plywoods are sourced from unstainable forestry, it is advisable to specify softwood ply in preference.

Plywoods are graded according to species and country of origin and are effectively as follows:

Veneer with minimal imperfections as peeled.
Veneer with imperfections plugged or filled.
Veneer with imperfections which have not been repaired.

Thicknesses	0.8, 1.0, 1.2, 1.5 mm (aircraft specification); 2, 2.5, 3, 4, 5, 6, 6.5, 9, 12, 15, 18, 21, 24 and 27 mm
Sheet sizes	1220 × 1220 mm 1525 × 610 mm (t & g)
	1220 × 2440 mm 1525 × 1525 mm
	1220 × 3050 mm 1525 × 2440 mm
	1220 × 3660 mm 1525 × 3050 mm
	1270 × 1270 mm 1525 × 3660 mm

Source: James Latham plc

Impregnated fibreboards

Typically bitumen impregnated woodfibre used for external, permeable but weather-resistant sheathing to timber and steel framing, as well as for expansion joint filler strips in concrete and masonry. Typical sizes 1200 × 2400 in 6 mm, 9 mm and 12 mm thicknesses. Fibreboard sheathing without bitumen also available with greater permeability but less weather resistance.

Insulating fibre boards

Low density wood fibre boards for internal and external vapour permeable insulation to framed and masonry buildings, available with rebated or tongued and grooved joints, typically in thicknesses from 20 to 140 mm.

Strawboards

Low density permeable boards for roofing, ceilings, partitioning, door cores, etc; these boards are fire resistant as well as acoustically and thermally insulating; thicknesses 50 mm and above; sizes 1200 × 2400 and to order.

Flaxboards

Particle boards made of compressed flax shive (70%), sawdust and resin, typically lighter than chipboards; used for similar purposes such as door cores, panelling, furniture, worktops, etc., available in larger sizes up to 6 m in length × 1200 widths, and from 12 to 60 mm thick.

Plasterboard

Boards with a core of aerated gypsum plaster bonded between two sheets of strong paper which should comply with BS 1230 Part 1 : 1985.

There are different grades for dry lining and wet plaster. Dry lining boards have tapered edges to allow for jointing tapes.

Boards are available backed with foil, polystyrene, polyurethane foam and phenolic foam. Others have more moisture-resistant and fire-resistant cores.

Thicknesses	9.5, 12.5, 15 and 19 mm (25–50 mm for boards backed with insulation)	
Sheet sizes	400 × 1200 mm	600 × 1800 mm
		600 × 2400 mm
	900 × 1200 mm	1200 × 2400 mm
	900 × 1800 mm	1200 × 2700 mm
	900 × 2400 mm	1200 × 3000 mm

Source: British Gypsum

Calcium silicate board

Asbestos-free board mainly used for structural fire protection. Cellulose fibres dispersed in water are mixed with lime, cement, silica and fire protective fillers to form a slurry. Water is then removed from the slurry under vacuum to form boards which are transferred to high pressure steam autoclaves for curing. Denser boards are hydraulically compressed before curing. Boards can be easily cut to size and drilled for screw fixing. 9 mm and 12 mm thick boards are available with rebated edges for seamless flush jointing. Boards may be decorated or left untreated.

Thicknesses	6, 9, 12, 15, 20, 22, 25, 30, 35, 40, 45, 50, 55 and 60 mm
Sheet sizes	1220, 1830, 2440, 3050 mm long × 610 and 1220 mm wide
Fire Classification	Class 0 for surface spread of flame
Fire Protection	From 60 to 240 minutes depending on product

Source: Promat

Cement particle boards

These are made of Portland cement and wood particles; they are heavy, robust and fire and water resistant. Typical sizes: 1200 × 2400; various thicknesses from 12 mm upwards.

Gypsum fibreboards

These are made of gypsum combined with cellulose fibre, producing a stronger and more impact version of plasterboard without paper facings. Typical sizes: 1200 × 600 mm, 1200 × 1200 mm, 2400–3000 × 1200; thicknesses: 10 mm, 12.5 mm, 15 mm, 18 mm, square or taper-edged.

Plastics

Plastics – commonly used in building

Plastics are organic substances mainly derived from by-products of coal–gas manufacture and refining of mineral oil. These are manipulated to form long-chain molecules on which the plasticity and rigidity of the material of the products made from them depend. They are made up of three main groups:

- **thermoplastics**, such as polythene, vinyls and nylon, where the structure is not permanently set and which can therefore be joined by heat or solvents.
- **thermosetting plastics**, such as phenol formaldehyde, melamine and fibreglass, which have fixed molecular structures that cannot be re-shaped by heat or solvents and are joined by adhesives.
- **elastomers**, such as natural rubber, neoprene and butyl rubber, which have polymers in which the helical molecular chains are free to straighten when the material is stretched and recover when the load is released.

Plastics – industrial techniques

glass-reinforced plastic (GRP) Synthetic resin reinforced with glass fibre, used for rooflights, wall panels, etc.

injection moulding Similar to die casting for moulding thermoplastics. Plastic is melted and then forced under pressure into a cooled moulding chamber.

plastic laminate Decorative laminate made up of paper or fabric impregnated with melamine or phenolic resins and bonded together under pressure to form a hard-wearing, scratch-resistant finish used primarily for work surfaces.

solvent welding A permanent joint made between thermoplastics by smearing both sides with an appropriate solvent before joining together.

vacuum forming Making components by evacuating the space between the sheet material and the die so that forming is affected by atmospheric pressure.

Plastics – abbreviations in general use

Abbreviation	Plastic	Uses
ABS	Acrylonitrile butadiene styrene	cold water pipes
CPE	Chlorinated polyethylene	water tanks
CPVC	Chlorinated polyvinyl chloride	hot water and waste pipes
EPDM	Ethylene propylene di-monomer	gaskets, single ply roofing
EPS	Expanded polystyrene	plastic foam for insulation
ETFE	Ethyl tetra fluoro ethylene	Film for foil roof cushions
EVA	Ethylene vinyl acetate	weather protective films
GRP	Glass-reinforced polyester (fibreglass)	cladding, panels, mouldings
HDPE	High density polyethylene	flooring, piping
HIPS	High impact polystyrene	ceilings, mirrors
LDPE	Low density polyethylene	bins, pipes, fittings
MF	Melamine-formaldehyde	laminated plastics, adhesives
PA	Polyamide (nylon)	electrical fittings, washers, ropes
PB	Polybutylene	pipe fittings
PC	Polycarbonate	anti-vandal glazing
PE	Polyethylene	electrical insulation, flooring, piping
PF	Phenol-formaldehyde (Bakelite)	electrical fittings, door furniture
PMMA	Polymethyl methacrylate (Perspex)	sanitary ware, transparent sheet
PP	Polypropylene	electrical insulation, piping
PS	Polystyrene	insulation, suspended ceilings
PTFE	Polytetrafluoroethylene	pipe jointing, sealing tape
PU	Polyurethane	insulation, paints, coatings
PVA	Polyvinyl acetate (latex emulsion)	emulsion paint, bonding agents
PVC	Polyvinyl chloride	floor and wall coverings
PVB	Polyvinyl butyral	laminated glass
PVF	Polyvinyl fluoride	protective films
UF	Urea-formaldehyde	glues, insulation
UP	Unsaturated polyester	paint, powder coatings, bituminous felt
UPVC	Unplasticised polyvinyl chloride	rainwater, soil and waste pipes, roof sheeting

Nails and screws

Nails

panel pin		round wire nail	
hardboad panel pin		purlin nail	
lath nail		lost head nail	
plasterboard nail		cut floorboard brad	
gimp pin for upholstery		cut clasp nail for heavy carpentry	
cut lath nail		double head shutter nail for temporary fixing	
cedar shake nail		masonry nail	
carpet tack		helical threaded nail for corrugated sheet	
sprig for fixing glass to timber frames		annular nail for boats and external joinery	
escutcheon pin		convex head nail for corrugated sheet	
clout nail for roofing, felt and fencing		chisel point nail for fixing pipes to masonry	
large clout nail for roofing felt			
clout head peg for roof tiling			

Wood screws

countersunk

raised head

raised countersunk

dome head

coach screw

cross head

Machine screws and bolts

countersunk

raised countersunk

round

binder pan

pan

cheese

fillister

mushroom

Source: *Handbook of Fixings and Fastenings*

Standard wire gauge (SWG)
in millimetres and inches

SWG	mm	inches	SWG	mm	inches
1	7.62	0.300	16	1.63	0.064
2	7.00	0.276	17	1.42	0.056
3	6.40	0.252	18	1.22	0.048
4	5.89	0.232	19	1.02	0.040
5	5.38	0.212	20	0.914	0.036
6	4.88	0.192	21	0.813	0.032
7	4.47	0.176	22	0.711	0.028
8	4.06	0.160	23	0.610	0.024
9	3.66	0.144	24	0.559	0.022
10	3.25	0.128	25	0.508	0.020
11	2.95	0.116	26	0.457	0.018
12	2.64	0.104	27	0.417	0.016
13	2.34	0.092	28	0.376	0.015
14	2.03	0.080	29	0.345	0.014
15	1.83	0.072	30	0.315	0.012

Colour

The *colour spectrum* is made up of colour refracted from a beam of light, as through a glass prism or as seen in a rainbow. The bands of colour are arranged according to their decreasing wavelength (6.5×10^{-7} for red to 4.2×10^{-7} for violet), and are traditionally divided into seven main colours: red, orange, yellow, green, blue, indigo and violet. When arranged as segments of a circle, this is known as the colour circle. The *primary* colours are red, yellow and blue, as these cannot be mixed from other colours. The *secondary* colours are orange, green and purple, and the *tertiary colours* are produced by adding a primary colour to a secondary colour.

Complementary colours are pairs of colours on opposite sides of the circle, which when mixed together make browns and greys. The term *hue* indicates a specific colour, defined in terms of, say, redness or blueness, but not lightness or darkness. *Tone* is the lightness or darkness of a colour. Adding black, white or grey to a hue reduces its intensity.

Colour systems

British Standards Colour System BS: 4800 1989. Colours are defined by a three-part code consisting of hue, greyness and weight. Hues are divided into 12 equal numbers, from 02 (red/purple) to 24 (purple), with an additional 00 for neutral whites, greys and blacks. The greyness is described by five letters: (A) grey; (B) nearly grey; (C) grey/clear; (D) nearly clear and (E) clear. Weight, a subjective term, describes both lightness and greyness, so each letter is followed by a number from 01 to 58. Thus the colour 'heather' 22 C 37 is made up of:

22 (violet) C (grey/clear) 37 (medium weight)

NCS Natural Colour System. The Natural Colour System (NCS), generally referred to in the UK as *Colour Dimensions*, was developed by the Scandinavian Colour Institute in 1978.

It is a colour language system that can describe any colour by notation, and is based on the assumption that human beings are able to identify six basic colours – white W; black S (note *not* B); yellow Y; red R; blue B and green G. These are arranged in a *colour circle*, with yellow, red, blue and green marking the quadrants. These segments are divided into 10 per cent steps, so that orange can be described as Y 50 R (yellow with 50 per cent red). To describe the shade of a colour there is the NCS *triangle*, where the base of the triangle is a grey scale marked in 10 per cent steps from white W to black S. The apex of the triangle represents the pure colour and is similarly marked in 10 per cent steps. Thus a colour can be described as 1080-Y50R for an orange with 10 per cent blackness, 80 per cent chromatic intensity at yellow with 50 per cent red. This system allows for a much finer subdivision of colours than the BS system.

RAL Colour Collection. This system is used within the building industry for defining colours of coatings such as plastics, metals, glazed bricks and some paints and lacquers. It was established in Germany in 1925 and developed over the years, is now designated RAL 840-HR, and lists 194 colours. Colours are defined by four digits, the first being the colour class: 1 yellow; 2 orange; 3 red; 4 violet; 5 blue; 6 green; 7 grey; 8 brown and 9 black. The next three digits relate only to the sequence in which the colours were filed. An official name is also applied to each standard RAL colour, e.g. RAL 6003 olive green.

RAL Design System. This system has 1688 colours arranged in a colour atlas based on a three-dimensional colour space defined by the co-ordinates of hue, lightness and chroma. The colours are coded with three numbers; thus reddish/yellow is 69.9 7.56 56.5. It is similar to the Natural Colour System except that it is based on the mathematical division of the whole visible wavelength spectrum, which is then divided into mostly 10 per cent steps. The system can be easily used by computer programs to formulate colours.

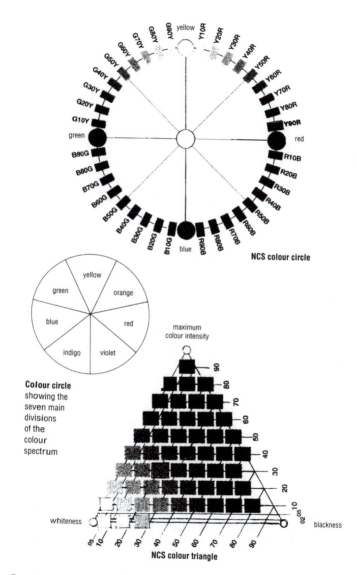

NCS colour circle

Colour circle
showing the
seven main
divisions
of the
colour
spectrum

NCS colour triangle

Source: NCS Colour Centre

Stains

Wood stains are suspensions of pigment in a solvent carrier used both for decorative and protective purposes. Traditional solvents were spirit-based but water-based stains are now widely available and preferred for health and safety reasons.

Interior decorative stains are often simply pigmented, though they can incorporate preservatives and/or insecticides; other pigmented translucent interior finishes include lacquers and oils.

Exterior decorative stains usually include preservatives and need pigment to reduce UV damage and clear stain or oil finishes tend to have shorter lives.

A significant advantage of stain finishes has been their microporosity and non-film structure which minimise water retention, splitting and flaking; semi-transparent and fully opaque coatings with similar properties are available, including some with recommended lives between decorating as long as 10 years.

Successful application of decorative stains requires different techniques from painting: degreasing of some timbers may be required; application is typically by 'laying on' the stain in 1 direction without brushing in, and wiping away unabsorbed surplus: test samples are advisable.

Paints

Paints basically consist of pigments, binder, and a solvent or water. Other ingredients are added for specific uses.

Solvent-based paints and stains are now considered environmentally unsound and are increasingly being supplanted by water-based alternatives. These are less glossy and more water-permeable than oil paints, but are quick-drying, odour-free, and tend not to yellow with age.

Organic paints
It is now possible to use totally solvent-free paints and varnishes containing 0.0 per cent volatile organic compounds

(VOCs). Most paints currently on sale, both gloss and emulsion, contain solvents and VOCs.

VOCs are a major contributor to low-level atmospheric pollution and the use of these compounds leads to global warming. In addition, the use of solvent-based paints is a major cause of 'sick building syndrome', 'Danish painter's syndrome', asthma, allergies, chemical sensitivities and the general flu-like symptoms reported by many people using conventional paints including matt and silk wall paints.

Organic paints are ideal for children's bedrooms, nurseries, kitchens and anywhere in the home, especially for people who are chemically sensitive or suffer from asthma or allergies.

Source: ECOS Organic Paints Ltd

Preparation. Careful preparation is vital if the decorative finish applied is to succeed and be durable. It is important to follow instructions about preparing substrates, atmospheric conditions and drying times between coats. Ensure that the right product is specified for the task, and that primers and subsequent coats are compatible.

Primers offer protection to the substrate from corrosion and deterioration, and give a good base for undercoats.

Undercoats, which are often just thinner versions of the finishing coat, provide a base for the topcoats.

Topcoats provide the durable and decorative surface, and come in gloss, satin, eggshell and matt finishes.

In addition to the paints listed overleaf there are specialist paints such as: *flame-retardant* paints, which emit non-combustible gases when subjected to fire; *intumescent coatings*, which expand to form a layer of insulating foam for structural steel; *multi-colour* paints, which incorporate coloured flecks, or two-part systems which use a special roller for the top coat to reveal partially the darker colour of the first coat; *silicone water-repellent* paints for porous masonry; *bituminous* paints for waterproofing metals and masonry; and *epoxy-ester coatings* to resist abrasion, oil and detergent spills.

Paints – typical products

Primers	Use*	Base*	Description
Zinc phosphate acrylic	M	WB	for all metals inside and out, quick-drying, low odour
Red oxide	M	SB	replaces red lead and calcium plumbate for ferrous metals
Etching	M	SB	factory pre-treatment for new galvanized metal
Mordant solution	M	WB	pre-treatment of galvanized metal
Micaceous iron oxide	M	SB	for marine and industrial steelwork, resists pollution and high humidity
Acrylated rubber	M, Ms	BS	for all metals, plaster and masonry, resists moisture
Wood primer	W	SB	non-lead primer for all woods inside and out
Wood primer/undercoat	W	WB	high opacity, quick-drying primer and undercoat
Aluminium wood primer	W	SB	good for resinous woods and as sealer for creosoted and bituminous surfaces
Alkali-resistant	P	SB	for dry walls under SB finishes, seals stains and fire damage
Plaster sealer	P	WB	for dry porous interior surfaces, e.g. plasterboard
Stabilizing primer	Ms	SB	to seal powdery and chalky surfaces
Undercoats			
Exterior flexible	W	SB	long-lasting, flexible, good opacity for exterior wood
Undercoat	all	SB	for use inside and out under solvent-based finishes
Preservative basecoat	W	SB	for new and bare wood to protect against blue stain and fungal decay
Finishes			
High gloss	all	SB	alkyd high gloss for all surfaces inside and out
Satin, eggshell, flat	W, M, P	SB	alkyd paints in three finishes for interior use
Vinyl emulsion	P	WB	matt, soft sheen and silk finishes for interiors
Masonry – smooth	Ms	WB	contains fungicide, for dry masonry, rendering, concrete, etc.
Masonry – textured	Ms	WB	fine granular finish, for dry masonry, etc
Masonry – all seasons	Ms	SB	flexible, smooth and good for applying in cold conditions
Epoxy floor	Ms, C	WB	two-pack mid-sheen paint for interior masonry and concrete floors
Floor	W, C	WB	quick-drying, for interior concrete and wood floors
Ecolyd gloss	W, M, Ms	SB	high quality, mirror-finish gloss, low solvent content
Protective enamel	M	SB	glossy, protective, quick-drying, for machinery
Exterior UPVC	PVC	WB	for redecoration of weathered UPVC surfaces
Acrylated rubber coating	M, Ms	SB	for steelwork and masonry inside and out, good against condensation
Aluminium	W, M	SB	heat resisting to 260°C, for metals and wood
Timber preservative	W	SB	coloured, water-repellent finish for sawn timber, fences, sheds, etc.
Protective wood stain	W	SB	water-repellent, mould-resistant, light-fast translucent colours
Exterior varnish	W	SB	transparent gloss finish for exterior wood
Interior varnish	W	WB	tough, quick drying, durable clear polyurethane finish
Aquatech basecoat	W	WB	flexible satin finish for bare and new wood
Aquatech woodstain	W	WB	flexible satin coloured finish, resists peeling, blistering
Diamond glaze	W	WB	clear lacquer for interior wood surfaces subject to hard wear

*C = concrete; M = metal; Ms = masonry; P = plaster; SB = solvent based; W = wood;
WB = water based.

Source: ICI Paints

Paint covering capacity

Approximate maximum areas
for smooth surfaces of average porosity

m²/litre

			m²/litre
Preparation	Fungicidal wash		30
	Stabilizing primer		12
	Etching primer		19
	Timber preservative	– solvent based	10
	Timber preservative	– water based	12
Primers	Wood primer	– solvent based	13
	Wood primer	– aluminium	16
	Wood primer	– microporous	15
	Wood primer undercoat	– water based	12
	Metal primer	– solvent based	6
	Metal primer	– water based	15
	Metal primer	– zinc phosphate	6
	Acrylated rubber primer		5
Finishes	Undercoat	– solvent based	16
	Emulsion	– matt	15
	Emulsion	– vinyl silk	15
	Matt finish	– solvent based	16
	Eggshell finish	– solvent based	16
	Eggshell finish	– water based	15
	Microporous gloss	– solvent based	14
	High gloss	– solvent based	17
	Non-drip gloss	– solvent based	13
	Wood stain	– solvent based	25
	Exterior varnish	– solvent based	16
	Interior varnish	– solvent based	16
	Masonry paint	– smooth	10
	Masonry paint	– textured	6
	Acrylated rubber		6

Source: ICI Paints

Wallpaper coverage for walls and ceilings

Approximate number of rolls required

Walls	Measurement around walls (m)	Height of room above skirting (m)						
		2.3	2.4	2.6	2.7	2.9	3.1	3.2
	9.0	4	5	5	5	6	6	6
	10.4	5	5	5	5	6	6	6
	11.6	5	6	6	6	7	7	8
	12.8	6	6	7	7	7	8	8
	14.0	6	7	7	7	8	8	8
	15.2	7	7	8	8	9	9	10
	16.5	7	8	9	9	9	10	10
	17.8	8	8	9	9	10	10	11
	19.0	8	9	10	10	10	11	12
	20.0	9	9	10	10	11	12	13
	21.3	9	10	11	11	12	12	13
	22.6	10	10	12	12	12	13	14
	23.8	10	11	12	12	13	14	15
	25.0	11	11	13	13	14	14	16
	26.0	12	12	14	14	14	15	16
	27.4	12	13	14	14	15	16	17
	28.7	13	13	15	15	15	16	18
	30.0	13	14	15	15	16	17	19

Ceilings	Measurement around room (m)	no. rolls
	12.0	2
	15.0	3
	18.0	4
	20.0	5
	21.0	6
	24.0	7
	25.0	8
	27.0	9
	28.0	10
	30.0	11
	30.5	12

Notes:
Standard wallpaper roll is 530 mm wide × 10.06 m long (21″ × 33′0″)
One roll will cover approximately 5 m² (54 ft²) including waste

Addresses/Sources

RIBA companies

Royal Institute of British Architects
66 Portland Place, London W1B 1AD
email: admin@inst.riba.org
www.architecture.com

tel: 020 7580 5533
fax: 020 7255 1541

RIBA Enterprises Ltd, Manufacturer Network
15 Bonhill Street, London EC2P 2EA
email: info@ribaenterprises.com
www.ribaenterprises.com

tel: 020 7496 8300
fax: 020 7374 8200

RIBA Publishing
15 Bonhill Street, London EC2P 2EA
email: enquiry@ribapublishing.com
www.ribapublishing.com

tel: 020 7496 8300
fax: 020 7496 8500

NBS Services
The Old Post Office, St Nicholas Street,
Newcastle upon Tyne NE1 1RH
email: info@theNBS.com
www.thenbs.com

tel: 0845 456 9594
fax: 0191 232 5714

IHS (Formerly Technical Indexes Ltd)
Willoughby Road, Bracknell, RG12 8FB
email: marketing@techindex.co.uk
www.uk.ihs.com

tel: +44(0) 1344 328 000
fax: +44(0) 1344 328 008

RIBA Bookshops
email: sales@ribabookshops.com
website: www.ribabookshops.com

London, Central	66 Portland Place W1B 1AD	tel: 020 7256 7222
London, Chelsea	Design Centre Chelsea Harbour SW10 0XF	tel: 020 7351 6854
Belfast	2 Mount Charles BT7 1NZ	tel: 028 9032 3760
Birmingham	Margaret Street B3 3SP	tel: 0121 233 2321
Liverpool	82 Wood Street L1 4DQ	tel: 0151 707 4380
Manchester	113–115 Portland Street M1 6DW	tel: 0161 236 7691

Associations, Institutes and other information sources

ACPO Secured by Design
1st Floor, 10 Victoria Street
London SW1H 0NN
www.securedbydesign.com

tel: 020 7084 8962
fax: 020 7084 8951/01

Ancient Monuments Society
St Ann's Vestry Hall, 2 Church Entry,
London EC4V 5HB
www.ancientmonumentssociety.org.uk

tel: 020 7236 3934
fax: 020 7329 3677

Architects Registration Board (ARB)
8 Weymouth Street, London W1W 5BU
email: info@arb.org.uk www.arb.org.uk

tel: 020 7580 5861
fax: 020 7436 5269

Architectural Association (AA)
36 Bedford Square, London WC1B 3ES
email: info@aaschool.ac.uk
www.aaschool.ac.uk

tel: 020 7887 4000
fax: 020 7414 0782

Arts Council of England
14 Great Peter Street, London SW1P 3NQ
email: enquiries@artscouncil.org.uk
www.artscouncil.org.uk

tel: 0845 300 6200
fax: 0161 934 4426

Barbour Product Search
Hinderton Point, Lloyd Drive
Cheshire Oaks, Cheshire CH65 9HQ
email: editor@barbourproductsearch.ifo
www.barbourproductsearch.info

tel: 01344 899 300
fax: 01344 899 332

Brick Development Association (BDA)
The Building Centre, 26 Store Street,
London WC1E 7BT
email: brick@brick.org.uk www.brick.org.uk

tel: 020 7323 7030
fax: 020 7580 3795

British Board of Agrément (BBA)
PO Box 195, Bucknalls Lane, Garston,
Herts WD25 9BA
email: contact@bba.star.co.uk www.bbacerts.co.uk

tel: 01923 665 300
fax: 01923 665 301

British Constructional Steelwork Association Ltd (BCSA)
4 Whitehall Court, London SW1A 2ES
email: postroom@steelconstruction.org
www.steelconstruction.org

tel: 020 7839 8566
fax: 020 7976 1634

British Fenestration Rating Council
54 Ayres Street, London SE1 1EU
www.bfrc.org

tel: 020 7403 9200

British Standards Institution (BSI)
389 Chiswick High Road, London W4 4AL
email: cservices@bsigroup.com
www.bsigroup.com

tel: 020 8996 9001
fax: 020 8996 7001

Building Centre
The Building Centre, Store Street, London WC1E 7BT
email: reception@buildingcentre.co.uk
www.buildingcentre.co.uk

tel: 020 7692 4000
fax: 020 7580 9641

Building Centre Bookshop
The Building Centre, Store Street, London WC1E 7BT
email: info@bcbookshop.co.uk
www.buildingcentre.co.uk

tel: 020 7692 4040
fax: 020 7636 3628

Building Research Establishment (BRE)
Bucknalls Lane, Garston, Watford WD25 9XX
email: enquiries@bre.co.uk www.bre.co.uk

tel: 01923 664 000
fax: 01923 664 010

Cadw – Welsh historic monuments
Welsh Assembly Government, Plas Carew, Unit 5/7
Cefn Coed, Parc Nantgarw, Cardiff CF15 7QQ
email: Cadw@Wales.gsi.gov.uk
www.cadw.wales.gov.uk

tel: 01443 336 000
fax: 01443 336 001

Centre for Accessible Environments
70 South Lambeth Road, London SW8 1RL
email: info@cae.org.uk www.cae.org.uk

tel: 020 7840 0125
fax: 020 7840 5811

Centre for Alternative Technology (CAT)
Machynlleth, Powys SY20 9AZ
email: info@cat.org.uk www.cat.org.uk

tel: 01654 705 950
fax: 01654 702 782

Chartered Institute of Architectural Technologists
397 City Road, London EC1V 1NH
email: info@ciat.org.uk www.ciat.org.uk

tel: 020 7278 2206
fax: 020 7837 3194

Chartered Institute of Building (CIOB)
Englemere, Kings Ride, Ascot SL5 7TB
email: reception@ciob.org.uk www.ciob.org.uk

tel: 01344 630 700
fax: 01344 630 777

Chartered Institution of Building Services Engineers (CIBSE)
222 Balham High Road,
London SW12 9BS
email: info@cibse.org www.cibse.org

tel: 020 8675 5211
fax: 020 8675 5449

Civic Trust
Winchester House, 259–269 Old Marylebone Road,
London NW1 5RA
email: civicsocieties@civictrust.org.uk
www.civictrust.org.uk

tel: 020 7170 4299
fax: 020 7170 4298

Commission for Architecture & the Built Environment (CABE)
1 Kemble Street, London WC2B 4AN
email: info@cabe.org.uk www.cabe.org.uk

tel: 020 7070 6700
fax: 020 7070 6777

The Concrete Society
Riverside House, 4 Meadows Business Park,
Station Approach, Blackwater, Camberley,
Surrey GU17 9AB
email: etrout@concreteinfo.org www.concrete.org.uk

tel: 01276 607 140
fax: 01276 607 141

Construction Industry Council (CIC)
26 Store Street, London WC1E 7BT
email: info@cic.org.uk www.cic.org.uk

tel: 020 7399 7400
fax: 020 7399 7425

Copper Development Association
5 Grovelands Business Centre, Boundary Way,
Hemel Hempstead HP2 7TE
email: mail@copperdev.co.uk www.copperinfo.co.uk

tel: 01442 275 705
fax: 01442 275 716

Countryside Council for Wales
Maes y Ffynnon, Penrhosgarnedd, Bangor,
Gwynedd LL57 2DW
email: Enquiries@ccw.gov.uk www.ccw.gov.uk

tel: 0845 1306 229
fax: 01248 355 782

Department for Culture, Media and Sport (DCMS)
2–4, Cockspur Street, London SW1Y 5DH
email: enquiries@culture.gov.uk www.culture.gov.uk

tel: 020 7211 6000
fax: 020 7211 6171

Department for Environment Food & Rural Affairs
Nobel House, 17 Smith Square, London SW1P 3JR
email: helpline@defra.gsi.gov.uk www.defra.gov.uk

tel: 08459 335 577
fax: 020 7238 2188

Department for Transport
Great Minster House, 76 Marsham Street,
London SW1P 4DR
www.dft.gov.uk

tel: 0300 330 3000
fax: 020 7944 9643

Disabled Living Foundation
380–384 Harrow Road, London W9 2HU
email: info@dlf.org.uk www.dlf.org.uk

tel: 020 7289 6111
fax: 020 7266 2922

English Heritage
1 Waterhouse Square, 138–142 Holborn,
London EC1N 2ST
email: customers@english-heritage.org.uk
www.english-heritage.org.uk

tel: 020 7973 3000
fax: 020 7973 3001

English Nature
Northminster House, Peterborough PE1 1UA
email: enquiries@english-nature.org.uk
www.english-nature.org.uk

tel: 01733 455 000
fax: 01733 455 103

Environment Agency
National Customer Contact Centre, PO Box 544,
Rotherham S60 1BY
email: enquiries@environment-agency.gov.uk
www.environment-agency.gov.uk

tel: 08708 506 506
fax: 01454 624 409

Environment & Heritage Service Northern Ireland
5–33 Hill Street Belfast BT1 2LA
email: nieainfo@doeni.gov.uk
www.ni-environment.gov.uk

tel: 0845 302 0008
fax: 028 9054 3111

Federation of Master Builders
Gordon Fisher House, 14–15 Great James Street,
London WC1N 3DP
email: central@fmb.org.uk www.fmb.org.uk

tel: 020 7242 7583
fax: 020 7404 0296

Forest Stewardship Council (FSC)
11–13 Great Oak Street, Llanidloes,
Powys SY18 6BU
email: info@fsc-uk.org www.fsc-uk.org

tel: 01686 413 916
fax: 01686 412 176

Friends of the Earth Ltd
26–28 Underwood Street, London N1 7JQ
email: info@foe.co.uk www.foe.co.uk

tel: 020 7490 1555
fax: 020 7490 0881

Glass and Glazing Federation (GGF)
54 Ayres Street, London SE1 1EU
email: info@ggf.org.uk www.ggf.org.uk

tel: 020 7939 9100
fax: 020 7357 7458

Guild of Architectural Ironmongers
8 Stepney Green, London E1 3JU
email: info@gai.org.uk www.gai.org.uk

tel: 020 7790 3431
fax: 020 7790 8517

Health and Safety Executive (HSE)
Rose Court, 2 Southwark Bridge, London SE1 9HS
email: hse.infoline@connaught.plc.uk
www.hse.gov.uk

tel: 0845 345 0055
fax: 020 7556 2109

Heating & Ventilating Contractors' Association (HVCA)
ESCA House, 34 Palace Court, London W2 4JG
email: contact@hvca.org.uk www.hvca.org.uk

tel: 020 7313 4900
fax: 020 7727 9268

Historic Scotland
Longmore House, Salisbury Place, Edinburgh EH9 1SH
www.historic-scotland.gov.uk

tel: 0131 668 8600
fax: 0131 668 8669

Institute of Engineering and Technology (IET)
Michael Faraday House, Stevenage, Herts SG1 2AY
email: postmaster@theiet.org
www.theiet.org

tel: 01438 313 311
fax: 01438 765 526

Institution of Civil Engineers (ICE)
One Great George Street, London SW1P 3AA
www.ice.org.uk

tel: 020 7222 7722
fax: 020 7222 7500

Institution of Mechanical Engineers
1 Birdcage Walk, London SW1H 9JJ
email: enquiries@imeche.org
www.imeche.org.uk

tel: 020 7222 7899
fax: 020 7222 4557

Institution of Structural Engineers (ISE)
11 Upper Belgrave Street, London SW1X 8BH
email: mail@istructe.org.uk www.istructe.org

tel: 020 7235 4535
fax: 020 7235 4294

International Lead Association (ILA)
17a Welbeck Way, London W1G 9YJ
email: enq@ila-lead.org www.ldaint.org

tel: 020 7499 8422
fax: 020 7493 1555

Landscape Institute
33 Great Portland Street, London W1W 8QG
email: mail@landscapeinstitute.org
www.landscapeinstitute.org

tel: 020 7299 4500
fax: 020 7299 4501

Lead Sheet Association
Unit 10 Archers Park, Branbridges Road,
East Peckham, Tonbridge, Kent TN12 5HP
email: leadsa@globalnet.co.uk
www.leadsheetassociation.org.uk

tel: 01622 872 432
fax: 01622 871 649

Lighting Industry Federation (LIF)
3 Albert Embankment, London SE1 7SL
email: info@lif.co.uk www.lif.co.uk

tel: 0207 793 3020
fax: 020 8529 6909

National Building Specification Ltd (NBS)
The Old Post Office, St Nicholas Street,
Newcastle upon Tyne NE1 1RH
email: info@theNBS.com www.thenbs.com

tel: 0191 244 5500
fax: 0191 232 5714

National Trust
PO Box 39, Warrington WA5 7WD
email: enquiries@nationaltrust.org.uk
www.nationaltrust.org.uk

tel: 0844 800 1895
fax: 0844 800 4642

Ordnance Survey
Romsey Road, Southampton SO16 4GU
email: customerservices@ordnancesurvey.co.uk
www.ordnancesurvey.co.uk

tel: 0845 605 0505
fax: 0238 079 2615

Planning Appeals Commission (N. Ireland)
Park House, 87–91 Great Victoria Street,
Belfast BT2 7AG
email: info@pacni.gov.uk www.pacni.gov.uk

tel: 028 9024 4710
fax: 028 9031 2536

Planning Inspectorate (England)
Temple Quay House, 2 The Square, Temple Quay,
Bristol BS1 6PN
email: enquiries@planning-inspectorate.gsi.gov.uk
www.planning-inspectorate.gov.uk

tel: 0117 372 6372
fax: 0117 987 8139

Planning Inspectorate (Wales)
Crown Buildings, Cathays Park, Cardiff CF10 3NQ
email: wales@planning-inspectorate.gsi.gov.uk
www.planning-inspectorate.gov.uk

tel: 029 2082 3866
fax: 029 2082 5150

Royal Incorporation of Architects in Scotland (RIAS)
15 Rutland Square, Edinburgh EH1 2BE
email: info@rias.org.uk www.rias.org.uk

tel: 0131 229 7545
fax: 0131 228 2188

Royal Institute of British Architects
66 Portland Place, London W1B 1AD
email: admin@inst.riba.org
www.architecture.com

tel: 020 7580 5533
fax: 020 7255 1541

Royal Institution of Chartered Surveyors (RICS)
Parliament Square, London SW1P 3AD
email: contactrics@rics.org www.rics.org

tel: 0870 333 1600
fax: 020 7334 3811

Royal Town Planning Institute (RTPI)
41 Botolph Lane, London EC3R 8DL
email: online@rtpi.org.uk www.rtpi.org.uk

tel: 020 7929 9494
fax: 020 7929 9490

Scottish Civic Trust
The Tobacco Merchant's House, 42 Miller Street,
Glasgow G1 1DT
email: sct@scottishcivictrust.org.uk
www.scottishcivictrust.org.uk

tel: 0141 221 1466
fax: 0141 248 6952

Scottish Natural Heritage
Great Glen House, Leachkin Road, Inverness IV3 8NW
email: enquiries@snh.gov.uk www.snh.gov.uk

tel: 01463 725 000
fax: 01463 725 067

Society for the Protection of Ancient Buildings (SPAB)
37 Spital Square, London E1 6DY
email: info@spab.org.uk www.spab.org.uk

tel: 020 7377 1644
fax: 020 7247 5296

The Stationery Office (TSO)
St Crispins, Duke Street, Norwich NR3 1PD
www.tso.co.uk

tel: 01603 622211

The Stationery Office Bookshops
16 Arthur Street, Belfast BT1 4GD

tel: 028 9023 8451
fax: 028 9023 5401

26 Rutland Square, Edinburgh, EH1 28W
email: esupport@tso.co.uk www.tsoshop.co.uk

tel: 0131 659 7020
fax: 0131 659 7040

Stone Federation Great Britain
Channel Business Centre, Ingles Manor,
Castle Hill Avenue, Folkestone, Kent CT20 2RD
email: enquiries@stonefederationgb.org.uk
www.stone-federationgb.org.uk

tel: 01303 856123
fax: 01303 856 117

Timber Trade Federation
The Building Centre, 26 Store Street,
London WC1E 7BT
www.ttf.co.uk

tel: 020 3205 0067
fax: 020 7291 5379

Timber Research and Development Association (TRADA)
Stocking Lane, Hughenden Valley,
High Wycombe HP14 4ND
email: information@trada.co.uk www.trada.co.uk

tel: 01494 569 600
fax: 01494 565 487

Town and Country Planning Association (TCPA)
17 Carlton House Terrace, London SW1Y 5AS
email: tcpa@tcpa.org.uk www.tcpa.org.uk

tel: 020 7930 8903
fax: 020 7930 3280

Water Regulations Advisory Service (WRAS)
30 Fern Close, Pen-y-fan Industrial Estate,
Oakdale, NP11 3EH
email: info@wras.co.uk www.wras.co.uk

tel: 01495 248 454
fax: 01495 236 289

Water Research Centre plc
Frankland Road, Blagrove, Swindon,
Wiltshire SN5 8YF
email: solutions@wrcplc.co.uk www.wrcplc.co.uk

tel: 01793 865 000
fax: 01793 865 001

Which?
Castlemead, Gascoyne Way, Hertford SG14 1LH
email: which@which.co.uk www.which.co.uk

tel: 01992 822 800
fax: 020 7770 7485

Zinc Information Centre
Wrens Court, 56 Victoria Road,
Sutton Coldfield B72 1SY
email: zincinfocentre@hdg.org.uk
www.zincinfocentre.org

tel: 0121 362 1201
fax: 0121 355 8727

Manufacturers – referred to in the text

ACP (Concrete) Ltd
Risehow Industrial Estate, Flimby,
Maryport CA15 8PD
www.acp-concrete.co.uk

tel: 01900 814 659
fax: 01900 816 200

Applied Energy Products Ltd
Morley Way, Peterborough PE2 9JJ
www.applied-energy.com

tel: 0844 372 7761
fax: 0844 372 7762

Autopa Ltd
Cottage Leap, Rugby,
Warwickshire CV21 3XP
www.autopa.co.uk

tel: 01788 550 556
fax: 01788 550 265

Banham Burglary Prevention
10 Pascal Street, London SW8 4SH
www.banham.co.uk

tel: 0844 482 9122
fax: 020 7498 2461

Brash, John & Co Ltd
The Old Shipyard, Gainsborough DN21 1NG
www.johnbrash.co.uk

tel: 01427 613 858
fax: 01427 810 218

British Gypsum
East Leake, Loughborough LE12 6HX
www.british-gypsum.com

tel: 0844 800 1991
fax: 0844 561 8816

Buckingham Nurseries
Tingewick Road, Buckingham MK18 4AE
www.buckingham-nurseries.co.uk

tel: 01280 822 133
fax: 01280 815 491

Caradon Ideal Ltd
PO Box 103, National Avenue,
Kingston Upon Hull HU5 4JN
www.idealheating.com

tel: 0870 849 8056
fax: 0870 849 8058

Concord Marlin
Havells Sylvania (Concord)
Avis Way, Newhaven BN9 0ED
www.concord-lighting.com

tel: 0870 606 2030
fax: 01273 512 688

Corus Building Systems, Kalzip Division
Haydock Lane, Haydock, St Helens WA11 9TY
www.kalzip.com

tel: 01942 295 500
fax: 01942 295 508

Corus Group
30 Millbank, London SW1P 4WY
www.corusgroup.com

tel: 020 7717 4444
fax: 020 7717 4455

Cox Building Products Ltd
CRH House, Units 1-3 Protheroe Ind Est, Bilport Lane,
Wednesbury WS10 0NT
www.coxbp.com

tel: 0121 530 4230
fax: 0121 530 4231

CSI Security Ltd
Ronald Close, Kempston, Bedford MK42 7SH
www.csisec.com

tel: 01234 840 840
fax: 01234 840 841

Duplus Architectural Systems Ltd
370 Melton Road, Leicester LE4 7SL
www.duplus.co.uk

tel: 0116 261 0710
fax: 0116 261 0539

Ecos Organic Paints
Unit 19, Heysham Business Park, Middleton Road,
Heysham LA3 3PP
www.ecospaints.com

tel: 01524 852 371
fax: 01524 858 978

Envirograf
Intumescent Systems, Envirograf House,   tel: 01304 842 555
Barfrestone, Dover CT15 7JG   fax: 01304 842 666
www.envirograf.com

GE Lighting Europe
Houghton Centre, Salthouse Road,   tel: 0800 169 8290
Brackmills NN4 7EX   fax: 0800 169 8284
www.gelighting.com

Hepworth Building Products
Edlington, Doncaster, South Yorkshire DN12 1BY tel: 01709 856 300
www.hepworthbp.co.uk   fax: 01709 856 301

Ibstock Brick Ltd
Leicester Road, Ibstock LE67 6HS   tel: 01530 261 999
www.ibstock.com   fax: 01530 257 547

ICI Paints Division
Wexham Road, Slough SL2 5DS   tel: 08444 817 817
www.dulux.co.uk   fax: 01753 578 218

Ideal-Standard Ltd
The Bathroom Works, National Avenue,   tel: 01482 346 461
Kingston-upon-Hull HU5 4HS   fax: 01482 445 886
www.ideal-standard.co.uk

I G Lintels Ltd
Avondale Road, Cwmbran, Gwent NP44 1XY   tel: 01633 486 486
www.igltd.co.uk   fax: 01633 486 465

JELD-WEN UK Ltd
Retford Road, Woodhouse Mill, Sheffield S13 9WH tel: 0845 122 2890
www.jeld-wen.co.uk   fax: 0114 229 3260

Klober Ltd
Ingleberry Road, Shepshed,   tel: 01509 500 660
Loughborough LE12 9DE   fax: 01509 600 061
www.klober.co.uk

Lafarge Roofing Ltd
Regent House, Station Approach,   tel: 0870 560 1000
Dorking RH4 1TG   fax: 0870 564 2742
www.lafarge-roofing.co.uk

Latham, James plc
Unit 3, Swallow Park, Finway Road,   tel: 01442 849 100
Hemel Hempstead HP2 7QU   fax: 01442 267 241
www.lathamtimber.co.uk

Luxcrete Ltd
Unit 2, Firbank Industrial Estate, Luton LU1 1TW
www.luxcrete.co.uk

tel: 01582 488 767
fax: 01582 724 607

Marley Eternit Ltd (Roofing)
Lichfield Road, Branston, Burton upon Trent DE14 3HD
www.marleyeternit.co.uk

tel: 01283 722 588
fax: 01283 722 219

Masonite Beams (UK) Ltd
Water Meadow House, Chesham HP5 1LF
www.masonitebeams.co.uk

tel: 0845 602 3574
fax: 01494 771 292

McAlpine Slate, Alfred Ltd
Penrhyn Quarry, Bethesda, Bangor LL57 4YG
www.amslate.com

tel: 01248 600 656
fax: 01248 601 171

Medite Europe Ltd
Coilite Panel Products, Persimmon House,
Anchor Boulevard, Dartford DA2 6QH
www.medite-europe.com

tel: 01322 424 900
fax: 01322 424 920

Metra Non-Ferrous Metals Ltd
Unit N7, RD Park, Essex Road, Hoddesdon EN11 0FB
www.metra-metals.co.uk

tel: 01992 460 455
fax: 01992 451 207

Midland Lead Manufacturers Ltd
Kiln Way, Woodville, Swadlincote DE11 8ED
www.midlandlead.co.uk

tel: 01283 224 555
fax: 01283 550 284

Milbank Floors Ltd
Earls Colne Business Park, Earls Colne,
Colchester, Essex CO6 2NS
www.milbank.co.uk

tel: 01787 223 931
fax: 01787 220 535

Monodraught Ltd
Halifax House, Cressex Business Park,
High Wycombe HP12 3SE
www.monodraught.com

tel: 01494 897 700
fax: 01494 532 465

Naylor Lintels Ltd
Milner Way, Longlands Industrial Estate,
Ossett WF5 9JE
www.naylor.co.uk

tel: 01924 267 286
fax: 01924 265 674

NCS Colour Centre
71 Ancastle Green, Henley-on Thames RG9 1TS
www.ncscolour.co.uk

tel: 01491 411 717
fax: 01491 411 231

Norbord Ltd
Station Road, Cowie, Stirling FK7 7BQ
www.norbord.com

tel: 01786 812 921
fax: 01786 817 143

NorDan (UK) Ltd
Harcourt House, 19 Cavendish Square,
London W1A 2AW
www.nordan.co.uk

tel: 01224 854 600
fax: 01224 891 036

Osram Ltd
Waterside Drive, Langley, Berkshire SL3 6EZ
www.osram.co.uk

tel: 01753 484 100
fax: 01753 484 222

Philips Lighting Ltd
The Philips Centre, Guildford Business Park,
Guildford GU2 8XH www.lighting.philips.co.uk

tel: 0845 601 1283
fax: 01483 575 534

Pilkington Building Products-UK
Prescot Road, St Helens WA10 3TT
www.pilkington.com

tel: 01744 28 882
fax: 01744 692 660

Premdor
Gemini House, Hargreaves Road,
Groundwell Industrial Estate, Swindon SN25 5AJ
www.premdor.co.uk

tel: 0844 209 0008
fax: 01793 708 280

Promat UK Ltd
The Stirling Centre, Eastern Road,
Bracknell RG12 2TD www.promat.co.uk

tel: 01344 381 300
fax: 01344 381 301

Range Cylinders Ltd
Tadman Street, Wakefield WF1 5QU
www.range-cylinders.co.uk

tel: 01924 376 026
fax: 01924 385 015

Rigidal Systems Ltd
Unit 62, Blackpole Trading Estate West,
Worcester WR3 8ZJ
www.rigidal.co.uk

tel: 01905 750 500
fax: 01905 750 555

Ruberoid Building Products, IKO Group
Appley Lane North, Appley Bridge,
Wigan WN6 9AB www.ruberoid.co.uk

tel: 0844 873 1065
fax: 0844 873 1067

Saint-Gobain PAM UK
Lows Lane, Stanton-by-Dale, Ilkeston, Derbyshire
DE7 4QU
www.saint-gobain-pam.co.uk

tel: 0115 930 5000
fax: 0115 932 9513

Stowell Concrete Ltd
Arnolds Way, Yatton, Bristol BS49 4QN
www.stowellconcrete.co.uk

tel: 01934 834 000
fax: 01934 835 474

Sunsquare Ltd
Unit 5A, Barton Road Trading Estate,
Bury St Edmunds, Suffolk IP32 7BE
www.sunsquare.co.uk

tel: 0845 226 3172
fax :0845 226 3173

Tarmac Ltd
Millfields Rd, Ettingshall,
Wolverhampton WV4 6JP
www.tarmac.co.uk

tel: 0800 1 218 218
fax: 01902 491 674

Titan Environmental Ltd
180 Gilford Road, Portadown,
Co. Armagh BT63 5LF
www.titanenv.com

tel: 028 3836 4400
fax: 028 3836 4445

Ubbink (UK) Ltd
Borough Road, Brackley NN13 7TB
www.ubbink.co.uk

tel: 01280 700 211
fax: 01280 705 332

Velux Company Ltd
Woodside Way, Glenrothes, Fife KY7 4ND
www.velux.co.uk

tel: 01592 778 225
fax: 01592 771 839

Vent-Axia Ltd
Fleming Way, Crawley RH10 9YX
www.vent-axia.com

tel: 0844 856 0590
fax: 01293 565 169

Visqueen Building Products
Heanor Gate, Heanor,
Derbyshire DE75 7RG
www.visqueenbuilding.co.uk

tel: 0845 302 4758
fax: 0845 017 8663

Zehnder Ltd
Unit 4 Watchmoor Point, Camberley,
Surrey GU15 3AD
www.zehnder.co.uk

tel: 01252 531 207
fax: 01252 531 201

Bibliography/Sources

Activities and Spaces: Dimensional Data for Housing Design Noble, J. (ed) 1983 The Architectural Press

AJ Handbook of Architectural Ironmongery Underwood, G. and Planck, J. 1977 The Architectural Press

Building Construction McKay, W. B. M. 2005 Donhead Publishing

Building for Energy Efficiency 1997 CIC

The Building Regulations Explained & Illustrated Powell-Smith, V. and Billington, M. J. 1999 Blackwell Science

Building Regulations Approved Documents 2006 RIBA Bookshops or www.thenbs.com

Buckingham Nurseries Hedging Catalogue

The Care and Repair of Thatched Roofs Brockett, P. 1986 SPAB

The Culture of Timber McCartney, K. 1994 University of Portsmouth

Dampness in Buildings Oxley, T. A. and Gobert, E. G. 1994 Butterworth-Heinemann

Designing for Accessibility 2004 Centre for Accessible Environments

Easibrief Haverstock, H. 1998 Miller Freeman

Fireplace Design and Construction Baden-Powell, C. 1984 Longman

Tarmac Flat Roofing – A Guide to Good Practice March, F. 1995 Tarmac Building Products Ltd

The Good Wood Guide Counsell, S. 1996 Friends of the Earth

Green Guide to the Architect's Job Book Halliday, S. 2001 RIBA Publishing

The Green Guide to Housing Specification Anderson, J., Howard, N. 2000 BRE Press

The Green Guide to Specification Anderson, J., Shiers, D., and Sinclair, M. 2002 Blackwell

A Guide to Planning Appeals The Planning Inspectorate May 2005 www.planningportal.gov.uk

Guide 'A' Design Data CIBSE Guide 2006 CIBSE

Hillier Designer's Guide to Landscape Plants 1999 Hillier Romsey

Home Security & Safety Good Housekeeping Guide 1995 Ebury Press

Illustrated Dictionary of Building Brett, P. 1997 Butterworth Heinemann

Listing Buildings – The work of English Heritage 1997 English Heritage

The Macmillan Encyclopaedia Isaacs, A. (ed) 1989 Macmillan

Managing Health and Safety in Construction, (Construction Design and Management) Regulations 2007 Health & Safety Executive

Materials for Architects and Builders Lyons, A. R. 2003 Butterworth Heinemann

Mathematical Models Cundy, H. M. and Rollett, A. P. 1997 Tarquin Publications

Metric Handbook Adler, D. 1999 Architectural Press

Party Wall etc. Act 1996: explanatory booklet 1997 Department of Communities & Local Government

The Penguin Dictionary of Building Maclean, J. H. and Scott, J. S. 1995 Penguin Books

Recognising Wood Rot & Insect Damage in Buildings Bravery, A. F. 2003 BRE

RIBA Product Selector 2006 RIBA Enterprises

The Right Hedge for You (leaflet) 1999 Department of Communities & Local Government

Stone in Building Ashurst, J. and Dimes, F. 1984 Stone Federation

Thatch: A Manual for Owners, Surveyors, Architects and Builders West, R. C. 1987 David & Charles

Tomorrow's World McLaren, D., Bullock, S. and Yousuf, N. 1998 Friends of the Earth

Water Supply (Water Fittings) Regulations 1999 DEFRA

The Which? Book of Plumbing and Central Heating Holloway, D. 2000 Which? Books

Whitaker's Concise Almanack Ward Inna, (ed.) 1996 A & C Black Publishers Ltd

WRAS Water Regulations Guide 1999 Water Regulations Advisory Scheme (WRAS)

Index